Colonial America:

A Compact History

Other books by Allan Keller

Grandma's Cooking
Morgan's Raid
The Spanish-American War: A Compact History
Thunder at Harper's Ferry
Madami (with Anne Putnam)

COLONIAL AMERICA:

A COMPACT HISTORY

by Allan Keller

HAWTHORN BOOKS, INC.
Publishers
NEW YORK

To
my grandchildren,
each facing his own frontier

Foreword

As AMERICA MOVES forward into the 1970s, the problems confronting her grow more difficult to solve, if not insuperable. Science has taught us many things, including how to journey to the moon, but we have found no easy way to eliminate the poverty, pollution, and blight in our cities. The virgin forests that seemed an endless wilderness to our colonial ancestors have been replaced by homes, farms, industrial plants, and millions of miles of paved highways, parking lots, and airport runways. Many streams and lakes from which the Indian and white pioneer drank without fear are today rank and dying, their once teeming life poisoned by sewage and industrial pollution.

Our children must conquer these ills—and others yet to come —or their lives will lack the beauty, the purpose and spiritual satisfaction Americans of earlier times knew and enjoyed. Believing, as Winston Churchill phrased it, that knowledge of the past is the only key to the future, it is this author's hope that our descendants may gain not only knowledge but inspiration from reading how their forebears conquered the problems of an inhospitable environment.

The pioneers of the thirteen colonies were not of one blood. There were English and Scots and Irish, French and Germans, Dutch and Swiss, Italians and Swedes. There were Catholics, Protestants, Jews, Huguenots, Quakers, Anabaptists, Wesleyan Methodists, and a score of other sects. There were beruffled cavaliers and Pilgrims in somber black, backwoodsmen in deerskin and linsey-woolsey, and Walloons in pantaloons and buckled shoes.

There were landed gentlemen, religious refugees, debtors, indentured white servants, and black slaves.

Together they created a great nation. This book is a foreshortened story of what they did and the heritage they left. From it sociologists could construct many theories and preachers find many topics for their sermons. These were Americans who had started out as colonials, who dared the unknown seas and the dangers of the wilderness with a courage that we would do well to emulate.

Many people contributed in one way or another to this story of early America. I am indebted particularly to Wade Doares, librarian of the Arthur Hays Sulzberger Library at the Graduate School of Journalism, Columbia University; Monroe Stearns, old friend and editor; and Mary Wilson, librarian for the Interpublic Group of Companies in New York. Miss Patricia Reilly was both kind and efficient in preparing the finished manuscript and, as always, my wife lent professional guidance and that unquenchable enthusiasm only an author can understand.

A.K.

Darien, Connecticut

Contents

List of Maps

When Fortune means to men most good,
She looks upon them with a threatening eye.

Shakespeare, *King John*

1

Landfall

As ISLANDS GO, San Salvador is far from unique. From the Atlantic, it is a long strip of sand rising to a bluff and high dunes at its northern end. In a world that contains thousands of islands, this one must be counted one of the least exciting. But to Christopher Columbus and his men, hungry for the sight of land on that October day in 1492, it must have possessed a rare beauty. There it was, where the discoverer had expected land to be, but as yet unaware that it was not China or the East Indies.

Beyond San Salvador were other islands and the mainland of a new hemisphere, but no one, least of all Columbus, dreamed of the true importance of this landfall. Looking for the wealth of Asia, they had found a clutch of barren, sandy islands and a continent of forbidding aspect. In their maddest dreams they could not have envisioned what history held in store for this new world upon which they had stumbled.

Columbus surely sensed that new lands would ultimately change the pattern of life back home. But his vision was limited, and he thought in terms of gold and precious gems rather than of the products that man's husbandry and industry would wrest from the new lands. Having shown the way to others, he died a disillusioned man. Had he lived a little longer, he would have witnessed a Europe gone mad with the frenzy of discovery. Every great power sent expeditions across the seas to stake out claims for territory: the New World had to be mapped, explored, and, eventually, colonized, because only in that way could its riches be reaped.

No gold rush, no land speculation, probably no venture in all history produced such fantastic interest as the discovery of America. Europe, beset by internal problems, its treasuries alarmingly depleted from financing wars, suddenly saw in the new continent unlimited resources.

The word spread from royal households to the narrow, crowded streets of Italian, Spanish, and French cities, to remote English villages and German towns. Kings wanted more land and power. The church gloried in the chance for proselyting. Adventurers responded to the call of the unknown. The poor and oppressed hoped that in the New World even they might stand tall. In Portuguese harbors, Swiss mountain valleys, and Dutch ports the knowledge that a new world had been discovered struck a chord that reverberates even into the twentieth century.

In scores of shipyards vessels were readied for Atlantic voyages. Nothing could halt the movement—not the terrors of the stormy Atlantic, not disease, not endless hardship—nothing could dampen the desire to acquire the new lands. In those early years no man could have surmised that on those distant shores would rise colonies that would one day unite to overthrow the mother country and form a new nation more powerful than any that had preceded it.

Other men too had been sailing upon uncharted seas. They had dared to sail far down the coast of Africa, out to the Canaries and Cape Verde Islands, and up around Norway's North Cape to the coast of Russia. A Venetian sailor named John Cabot, who lived in Bristol, England, might have reached the New World before Columbus had the English monarchs been less niggardly. He had made several voyages out into the stormy North Atlantic, convinced, like Columbus, that the world was round and that somewhere out in the vast unknown was a land known as Atlantis. Memory of Viking discoveries in the tenth century lingered in the oral tradition. But Cabot lacked the money to finance another expedition.

News of Columbus's voyages tantalized the merchants of Bristol, and almost overnight they found the funds to fit out two ships, to be commanded by Cabot and his son Sebastian. But there were delays, and the Cabots did not sail until May 1497. During this five-year period Spain, Portugal, and the pope did their best to bar other nations from the New World. Pope Alexander VI, who was a Borgia and no better than he had to be, ran a line down the Atlantic a hundred leagues west of the Azores and ordered that all new lands east of that imaginary barrier belonged to Portugal

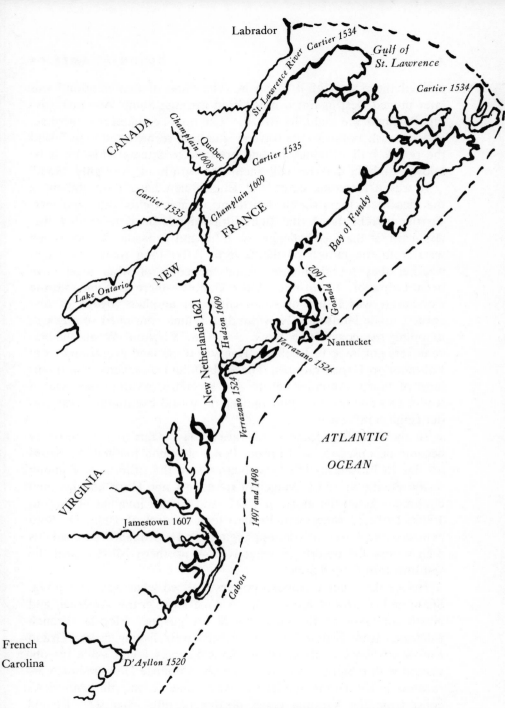

Labrador

St. Lawrence River *Cartier 1534*

Gulf of St. Lawrence

Cartier 1534

CANADA

Champlain 1608

Quebec

Cartier 1535

Champlain 1609

FRANCE

Cartier 1535

Bay of Fundy

Gosnold 1602

NEW

Lake Ontario

New Netherlands 1621

Hudson 1609

Verrazano 1524

Nantucket

Verrazano 1524

ATLANTIC

OCEAN

VIRGINIA

Jamestown 1607

1497 and 1498

Cabots

French
Carolina

D'Ayllon 1520

Discoveries of the English and French

3

and all those west of it to Spain. The "line of demarcation" was later moved west again; it now sliced through South America, giving Portugal the right to Brazil. "Let no one therefore, infringe, or with rash boldness contravene, this our recommendation," said the pope's bull. "Should anyone presume to attempt this, let it be known to him that he will incur the wrath of Almighty God."

It was a fearsome edict, but Englishmen have never taken to the idea that others should tell them of their rights and privileges. To the merchants of that tight little island the pope's edict was less a threat than a challenge, so John and Sebastian Cabot sailed west from the mouth of the Severn. After long weeks of rough weather they found themselves on the coast of what must have been Labrador. Later one of the Cabots—there is some dispute whether it was father or son—sailed on another voyage of discovery, made landfall at Newfoundland, then continued southward, mapping the coast from Nova Scotia to Virginia. When the adventurers got back to England, Henry VII claimed everything from Labrador to Cape Hatteras. The Cabots had discovered the mainland of North America before any Spaniard, so the claim was a sound one and ensured that the region would eventually come under English influence.

In the next few decades the race to lay claim to new territory became an obsession in Europe. Ponce de León planted the Spanish flag in Florida in 1513, Balboa crossed the isthmus of Panama to the Pacific in 1513, Magellan rounded Cape Horn and his men circumnavigated the globe in 1522, and Cortez invaded Mexico in 1519. In rapid succession Pizarro took control of Peru, De Soto explored the lower Mississippi region, and Coronado marched his men across the deserts of what is now northern Mexico and the southwestern United States.

Before the other European powers realized what was happening, Spain had control of most of South America, Central America, and North America as far north as St. Augustine, Florida. French fishermen from Brittany and Normandy were fishing on the Grand Banks off Newfoundland before King Francis I laid aside his obsession with religious wars long enough to finance Giovanni da Verrazano, a Florentine navigator, who sailed along the American coast from the Virginia capes northward into what was deemed the English sphere of influence. In the 1530s Cartier explored the St. Lawrence River and Gulf, which France promptly claimed, thus making inevitable the conflicts between English and French settlers a century later.

Thoughts of colonizing the New World were secondary; the search for gold and precious stones came first. Spain was particularly active in the quest, busily plundering the Incas and Aztecs of their fabulous treasures. If it had not been for the eagerness of the Catholic Church to extend its influence, settlements would not have come until much later. But eventually the need for people to repair ships, to work in the missions, and to handle trade with the natives led to migrations from the Iberian Peninsula to ports in the West Indies, Mexico, and South America.

There was no strong desire to send people to the New World in large numbers; the earliest settlements come about as the result of other forces. Religious pressures in sixteenth-century Europe and the desire for trade sent more settlers to American shores than did the simple urge to populate new outposts. The American schoolboy gathers the impression that Jamestown and Plymouth were the beginnings of colonization, but long before their day attempts to create a new life in the wilderness had been tried and most of them had failed.

In 1562 Huguenots, cruelly persecuted in France, had sailed under Jean Ribaut, of Dieppe, to seek refuge on the Carolina coast. At Charlesfort twenty-six men put up rough cabins and sought to establish a settlement, but the enterprise failed because of hunger and lack of foresight, and Ribaut returned to Europe. Three years later Ribaut sailed from England with seven ships to Fort Caroline, near the St. Johns River in Florida. Hundreds of Huguenot men, women, and children were already on the site—established in 1564 by René de Laudonnière—before the Spanish learned about it. Reaction was swift. Pedro Menéndez de Avilés led a fleet against the little colony, a storm wrecked Ribaut's pitiful ships, and the Spanish force of 2,500 men massacred all but a handful of the defenseless Huguenots. More than nine hundred French settlers were put to the sword. Over the ruins, Menéndez erected a cross bearing the words: "Not as Frenchmen, but as Lutherans and heretics."

Hearing of the massacre, Dominique de Gourgues, a wealthy Huguenot, sold his lands and possessions to outfit a fleet to seek revenge. Reaching the St. Johns River undetected, his force of 150 volunteers overpowered the garrison of a Spanish fort and hanged them all. Above their swaying bodies was a sign de Gourgues had lettered: "Not as Spaniards, but as traitors, robbers, and murderers."

It was one chapter in a long series of crimes committed in the name of Christianity on the shores of the New World.

The long coast of North America, with its many rivers and bays, its richly forested headlands reaching out to sea, and its evidence of great fertility, lured one adventurer after another. At first, none had any success putting down permanent roots.

In 1526 a Spaniard, Lucas Vázquez de Ayllón, had left the West Indies with a fleet carrying nearly six hundred men, women, and children. On the coast of Carolina near the mouth of the Santee River, he lost a ship and built another—the first ship built in the New World. Then he entered Chesapeake Bay and put his company ashore on a sandy peninsula. Almost at once fighting broke out among the settlers, followed by hunger, bad weather, and Indian attacks. Within a few months not one Spaniard was left and this sandy finger of land was deserted—not to be visited again until the English came to found a town they called Jamestown, almost a century later.

The Spanish fared better in Florida. Soldiers and priests went ashore, put up a few buildings, a palisade, and a cross, and named the place after St. Augustine. It was the first successful settlement within the confines of what is now the United States. The year was 1565, seventy-three years after Columbus stepped ashore on San Salvador.

The English explorer Martin Frobisher, who made three Arctic voyages between 1576 and 1578, made a half-hearted attempt to settle the bleak, forbidding coast of Labrador, and Breton fishermen tried the same thing in Newfoundland, but failure was the result in both cases. Then the French settled in various places in Canada, and the English realized that despite the success of their buccaneers and explorers, who had scourged the Spanish Main and captured many a galleon loaded with treasure, not one English colony existed on the North American continent. There were Spaniards to the south and Frenchmen to the north, but in between was a vast territory crying for colonization.

Queen Elizabeth was made of stouter stuff than either Henry VII or Henry VIII, who had failed to follow up Cabot's discoveries with any meaningful attempt to colonize. Elizabeth, motivated in part by her abiding hatred for Catholicism, sent her voyagers far and wide to impede the progress of Catholic France and Spain. One of these, Sir John Hawkins, inadvertently provided great impetus to the idea of settling America. While fighting the Spanish in the Gulf of Mexico, he lost part of his fleet and was compelled to put men ashore in Mexico, promising to return for them later. Three of them, including a redoubtable fellow named David Ingram, having no liking for the prospect of a long wait, struck out to the north. It was the year 1568.

Following the coast, they tramped through swamps of what is now the Gulf coast, across Florida, and up the Atlantic shoreline clear to the St. John River in Canada. Their survival in a strange land, without guides, menaced by hostile savages, with unknown perils at every turn, is one of the marvels of American lore. When they were found by French sailors near the present city of Saint John, New Brunswick, they were treated well and eventually taken back to England.

The stories they told of a rich continent, of fertile lands watered by broad rivers, forest-cloaked mountains, and hundreds of inlets and bays suitable for establishing settlements, spurred Elizabeth and the English traders even more than stories of buried gold in the Spanish territories. Ingram may have added a few fanciful details to make his stories more exciting, but there was no denying the impact when he told of the progress the Spaniards and French had made in colonizing while the English wasted their time fighting them.

It may have been Ingram's tales, or pressure to establish trading posts, but within a short time Sir Humphrey Gilbert had obtained a patent from Queen Elizabeth to plant colonies in heathen lands "not actually possessed by any Christian prince." Gilbert sent John Walker to the Penobscot River, in Maine, but the mission failed when the men in the expedition decided to make a quick profit by selling pelts to France. This misadventure led Gilbert to sail to America. He attempted to settle two places, one in Newfoundland and the other in either Nova Scotia or New Brunswick, but both failed. Gilbert was lost at sea on his way back to England.

The next year, 1584, Walter Raleigh took up the challenge, sending an expedition to the Carolina coast under Philip Amadas and Arthur Barlowe. They landed in Albemarle Sound, induced two Indians to return to England with them, and so pleased the queen that she called the area Virginia (thus making historical reference to her own maidenhood) and knighted Raleigh, naming him governor of the territory.

Despite this surge of interest, there was still no Englishman living in the New World. But one step had been taken that was to prove of inestimable value to those who would one day live in the colonies: Elizabeth granted to Sir Humphrey Gilbert, and later to Raleigh, patents that guaranteed to any of their colonists "all the privileges of free denizens and persons native to England, in such ample manner as if they were born and personally resident in our said realm of England." Nearly two hundred years later this would give the thirteen colonies the justification they needed to repudiate George III.

Sir Walter Raleigh's efforts seemed doomed from the start. The first group of colonists he sent—only a few men—stayed in the vicinity of Cape Hatteras just long enough to become homesick. Sir Francis Drake, fresh from plundering St. Augustine, picked them up and took them home. Drake had barely sailed over the horizon when Sir Richard Grenville arrived at the abandoned settlement with supplies sent out by Raleigh. Grenville left fifteen men on Roanoke Island, with enough provisions for two years, but they were killed by the Indians. Refusing to be discouraged, Raleigh sent a larger group, 150 men and women under John White as acting governor. White laid out a town, planted a few crops, and tried to establish friendly relations with the Indians.

On August 18, 1587, a woman named Dare gave birth to a daughter, whom she called Virginia, in honor of Queen Elizabeth. Word of the birth of the first English child in the New World was carried to England by members of the colony returning for additional supplies. It was the last ever heard of the ill-fated attempt at colonization. When a party sent out two years later landed on Roanoke Island they found no trace of 150 colonists except a word crudely carved on the trunk of a tree. The word was "Croatan." A tribe of Indians by that name lived on the mainland of North Carolina. Had the colony been wiped out by the savages? No one knows. There is a legend that the survivors intermarried with the Indians, and tales tell of "white" Indians found many years later.

Raleigh tried once more, sending a number of colonists to the New England coast under Captain Samuel Mace, but this was surely a travesty on colonization. After sailing into many a pleasant inlet and bay, Mace went home with nothing but a cargo of sassafras, then highly regarded as a cure for many ills.

A new rash of attempts followed but none was successful. Perhaps the most important result was the establishment of a shorter route from England. Captain Bartholomew Gosnold of the *Concord* took a leaf from Verrazano's book and used the Azores as an intermediate port for repairs rather than the West Indies, saving about a week's time in the crossing to North America. When he reached what is now Cape Cod the weather seemed inauspicious to him, so he took his colonists home rather than risk another disaster like Raleigh's lost colony.

Gosnold and the other captains carried many stories of verdant shores and rich opportunity back to England, whetting the appetites of businessmen and adventurers, but the years drifted by and there was still no colony established in the New World. Queen Elizabeth, who had supported so many expeditions with money and enthusiasm, died after forty-five years on the throne, saddened by the knowledge that she still had not one subject living on the far shore of America. Despite the exciting tales of a promising new land, the English seemed to find it a forbidding and unfriendly place.

II

Magnolias Bloom in Virginia

MANY POWERFUL FORCES led to the first successful planting of a colony by the English, not the least of which were the desire for new trade outlets and the necessity of competing with the expansionist policies of France and Spain. The search for new markets had led to the creation of the great trading companies, the Muscovy, Levantine, and East Indian companies. Well-heeled noblemen invested in these enterprises, seeking generous returns, and others used the royal permission to prey upon Spanish shipping, with a percentage of the booty reverting to the Crown.

But it was the common man who gave colonization its greatest impetus. As the upper class amassed new wealth, the lot of the lower classes grew worse. Unemployment and vagrancy became a national disaster, and thousands of penniless men and women roamed the countryside eking out a miserable existence and posing a threat to the established order. Sir Humphrey Gilbert was one of the first to realize that they might have a potential in the New World.

Religious persecution drove many to seek new homes abroad, particularly in Holland, but always in the background was the economic pressure exerted by the unemployed. The Spanish minister to the Court of St. James's sensed this, soon after the establishment of Jamestown. In a report to his government in 1611 he said: "Their principal reason for colonizing these parts is to give an outlet to so many idle, wretched people as they have in England, and thus prevent the dangers that might be feared of them."

Adventurous noblemen, merchants, religious fugitives, and ordinary men of the sea were among the early colonists, but the largest element was made up of penniless, dejected men and women for whom the New World held out the prospect of a better life. So, when entrepreneurs of the aristocracy joined hands with merchant princes to form the Virginia Company to do business there, they knew there would be no shortage of volunteers. If there were any noble motives in their desire to colonize the new land, they were buried deep beneath an urge to make a quick profit.

Because of the hostile Indians on the North American continent, the directors of the Virginia Company used military men to head up their colonizing groups. Captain John Smith had earned his rank as a soldier of fortune, several of the fleet officers had served with Drake or had done their own freebooting on the Spanish Main, and one of the lieutenants had earned his spurs fighting the Spanish in the Low Countries.

If these men looked forward to the adventure with enthusiasm and high hopes, the great majority of those migrating to Virginia faced the future with less assurance. First of all, they had to sign up for seven years' service to reimburse the Virginia Company for their passage. It was a high price to pay for the chance of being drowned at sea, killed by Indians, or dying of plague or hunger. Only insufferable conditions at home could induce them to undertake such risks. The voyage across the Atlantic lasted two or three months, depending on the weather. Life on the little sailing vessels, pounded by gales and rocked by high seas, was sheer hell. Passengers were often shut up in dingy holds to avoid being swept overboard. Food was unspeakably bad, often spoiled, and hygienic conditions were a farce. But in the minds of most of the colonists was the specter of poverty, crime, and lawlessness back home in England.

When the Virginia Company finally gathered enough people to attempt a settlement, winter had come. Nevertheless, on the first day of 1607, amid a howling storm, 105 men—about half of them gentlemen on their uppers and the other half artisans and laborers —sailed for Virginia. Three months later the three ships—the *Susan Constant,* the *Discovery,* and the *Godspeed*—sailed into the Chesapeake and moored off a marshy, low point of land they called Point Comfort. Magnolias, dogwood, and other trees and shrubs were in full bloom, and the colonists thought they had come to a land chosen by God just for their success.

Virginia's springtime glory was deceiving. By the time the expedition had made its way up the river which the leaders named the James and decided to make a start on a tidal spit of land, the heat had become oppressive. Within a few miles there were a dozen better locations for a settlement, but Captain Christopher Newport insisted on this malarial foreshore. An argument followed that lasted for weeks. Finally, on May 13, 1607, tired of living aboard the little ships, the colonists went ashore, named the place Jamestown, and began building what was to become the first permanent English settlement in the New World.

Carpenters nailed a board between two trees for an altar, stretched a piece of sail above it, and the chaplain placed a Bible on the piece of wood. In the first Church of England service in the Western Hemisphere, the sea-weary men thanked God for deliverance from the winter's storms.

Next the colonists opened a strongbox that had been sealed in London before the voyage. It was called the "King's Box," and the documents inside detailed how the colony was to govern itself. A resident council of seven men—Captains John Smith, John Ratcliffe, Newport, and Gosnold; a merchant, Edward Wingfield; and George Kendall and John Martin, gentlemen—was authorized to select a governor. At once an election was held—the first on American soil—and Wingfield won over Captain Smith. It was an augury of political wars to come. Wingfield promptly charged Smith with trying to make himself "king." A jury refused to find the captain guilty and assessed damages against Wingfield. Smith donated the money to the common fund.

Tortured by fevers, weakened by hunger, squabbling incessantly, the men erected crude huts and a palisade. Men who had been clerks, footmen, and perfumers found the work hard, and the absence of women turned the party into a company of bickering, disillusioned men. Wingfield was deposed in favor of Ratcliffe, Gosnold died of what was probably malaria, dysentery broke out from drinking tainted water, and finally Captain Smith was chosen for the post he should have had from the outset.

Smith was by far the most experienced member of the group. He had fought against the infidel Turks, been captured, and suffered the tortures of a galley slave. Escaping, he had made his way through the forests of Transylvania and the petty states of central Europe to Holland. He had learned the arts of war in campaigns against the Spanish and had traveled widely in France and Italy.

Most important of all, he had learned how to command men and win their respect.

Whether any other man in Jamestown could have saved the venture is sheer speculation. Smith did save it, and history acknowledges his role.

Following the James beyond where Richmond now stands, a group of the men set off to find a passage to China. While they were gone Indians attacked the half-completed stockade and killed some of the settlers. Smith sent word to London that at least fifty men had died, mainly of starvation, complaining that they were reduced to eating a handful of corn soaked in water for their main meal.

Just as other Indians would save the Pilgrims in a later attempt to settle America, so did local Indians help the Jamestown colonists. One was a chief named Powhatan, who proved a loyal friend of Smith and his followers. Powhatan supplied the Englishmen with corn, seeds, and venison, and only his intervention kept other tribes from trying to wipe out the colony.

Smith wasted much time seeking a water route to China and the Indies. No one in the colony, indeed no one in England, then suspected that they had landed on a vast land mass half a world away from Asia. They were convinced that just over the mountains was an ocean whose far waters touched the Indies and that there existed in America fabulous cities with great stores of gold and jewels.

Captain Smith explored deep into the Piedmont, undergoing adventures that strain the imagination. His best-remembered tale had to do with a pretty Indian maiden, Pocahontas, daughter of Powhatan, who, Smith claimed, saved his life just as the executioner's ax was about to fall. There is reason to doubt the story in its entirety, but the legend dies hard. If Smith stretched the truth now and again, perhaps he can be forgiven, as his history of the colony, *A True Relation of . . . Virginia,* was the first book written by an Englishman in the New World.

Captain Newport, in the largest of the three ships that had brought the colonists to America, the *Susan Constant,* sailed home to England in the middle of the first summer, carrying with him tons of soil filled with mica-like rocks, which he hoped was gold but which Smith called "yellow dirt." The directors excoriated him for his ignorance and sent him back to Jamestown with orders to return with either a nugget of pure gold, a map of a route to the

Indies, a survivor of Raleigh's Lost Colony, or a cargo worth as much as the cost of outfitting the second expedition.

About a hundred new colonists joined the survivors in Jamestown, but there were still no women. Crops failed, more men died of fever, and for months, according to Smith's journal, only the frequent appearance of Indians laden with venison and wild turkeys sent by the friendly Powhatan saved them from starvation. Smith tried to induce his men to cut wood, to collect pitch and other naval stores always in demand in England, and to build better habitations. Many refused and brought on new troubles for the colony by seeking out Indian women to sleep with, with or without their consent.

This treatment of the Indian women enraged Powhatan and his advisers, who were also worried by mounting evidence that the white men intended to stay in Virginia and would ultimately take away their land. The Indians decided to withhold aid and let the settlers starve. Captain Smith moved swiftly to counter this threat, outwitting the chief with a show of martial force. Then he laid down the law to his followers: "He that will not work shall not eat."

The edict had the desired effect. The men planted new crops, cut down trees, and repaired their shabby dwellings. By the end of the second winter Jamestown was a small hamlet with at least fifty houses strung along several crooked streets and surrounded by a fifteen-foot-high palisade on which guns from the *Godspeed* and *Discovery* were mounted.

But life was still precarious, and the settlers lived each day on the edge of extinction. Swamp fever struck men down in their tracks. Fishing nets rotted, corn was eaten by rats, sailors trafficked with the Indians and drove the barter price of food almost beyond reach of the colonists who had no trinkets with which to buy goods.

Beneath the surface lay a festering sore. The rules governing the settlement provided for communal ownership of land and property, denying the hard-working men any initiative and rewarding the lazy. In London this was finally recognized as one of the basic problems in the new community, and in 1610 the directors altered the charter to permit private ownership of land. Where there had been a general desuetude and lack of interest there now seemed to arise a widespread feeling that the colony could survive.

Ships went back and forth between the mother country and the colony, bringing new settlers—at last, some were women—and taking cedar wood and other products to England. Wood seemed a poor substitute for the gold and gems the Virginia Company had hoped would be found, but it was the start of a growing trade that attracted many investors in London. The company won additional powers from James I, and a grant of all the land two hundred miles north and two hundred miles south of Point Comfort and extending to the farther ocean. This brought in more backers, and soon the richest men in England were waiting for profits from the new colony.

Thomas West, Baron De la Warr, was made governor for life, and more ships loaded with colonists sailed for the New World. Captain Smith left Jamestown for England in late 1609, partly for medical treatment of a gunpowder wound and partly because the new directors wanted more profits than he had managed to supply from his disease- and hunger-ridden settlement.

Almost as if his departure was a signal, events took a turn for the worse. The Indians, learning Smith was gone, attacked and burned the fort. Some of the colonists stole a ship to go off buccaneering and the rest began to starve.

Smith's successor, Sir Thomas Gates, together with Admiral Sir George Somers, left England in a fleet of six or eight ships filled with new settlers. The expedition was blown onto the Bermuda Islands, but repairs were made, and the party reached Virginia the next summer. When they anchored off Jamestown they found only sixty survivors, wretched men and women who had been reduced to eating roots and grasses. Gates and Somers took the colonists aboard their ships and headed for Newfoundland, leaving Jamestown a cluster of deserted log cabins. For an hour it seemed that all the suffering, all the deaths, all of Captain John Smith's devoted leadership had been for naught. Then, as if arranged by a master playwright, over the horizon sailed a new fleet, led by De la Warr, carrying many new colonists, ample food, tools, and supplies for the winter ahead. Jamestown, it seemed, was not doomed to die.

De la Warr improved conditions at once, but illness sent him home and once again the colony fell on evil days. Men played at bowls in the street instead of working, and Indian attacks took many lives. Slatternly women refused to work, and many a settler ate raw fish rather than bother to make a fire. Sir Thomas Dale, appointed high marshal of Virginia, arrived in the nick of time and pulled things together. Gates returned and the two men whipped the colonists into line. Most important, they moved the settlement from the malarial shore of the river and erected a new village in the highlands far upstream. In honor of Prince Henry, they called the little town Henrico. A short time later, with the influx of even more colonists, settlements were started at Bermuda Hundred and other locations.

Among the arrivals on one of the ships that brought new settlers seeking their fortune, and a free parcel of land, was an enterprising young English widower named John Rolfe. Rolfe worked hard, and no one thought he had any interests other than making his fortune until he approached the council and asked for permission to marry Pocahontas, the Indian princess. Sitting soberly in official session, the council decided that Rolfe, "a gentleman of approved behavior and honest carriage," should have his wish. Powhatan, the bride's father, didn't actually object but refused to attend the ceremony, sending an uncle in his stead. The lovers were joined in holy wedlock according to the rites of the Church of England, but not before the lady had her name changed to Rebecca to meet the amenities. Almost overnight the rivalry and tension between whites and Indians were dispelled. After all, that would now mean brother fighting brother.

Poor Pocahontas! Two years later she went to England with her husband and found herself lionized, introduced at court, and feted everywhere. A son was born, and Pocahontas, unable to withstand the rigors of the British climate, died soon after. The boy, Thomas, followed his father to Virginia many years later and there founded one of the finest families in the new land.

John Rolfe's love affair with the pretty Indian girl may be rich in human understanding and a testimony to the brotherhood of man, but his services to the young colony were much more important than his romance with Pocahontas. It was Rolfe who decided that tobacco would grow better if cultivated as a market crop, and not handled carelessly as the Indians grew it. Within a few years it was the colony's greatest asset, providing a steady flow of cash from the motherland.

More settlers arrived from England, plantations were established in many places, and the colony grew so powerful that there was now no question that it would survive. It had been a bitter struggle. The cost in lives was tragic beyond belief. First there were the deaths at sea. Each ship arrived with far fewer souls than had gone on board in England. One, with 185 men and women passengers, reached Jamestown with only 55 persons alive. Yellow fever, smallpox, scurvy, and the plague all took their toll, and hardly a week went by without losses to Indian attacks. Of the original 700 or 800 colonists only 60 were alive three years later.

It must be remembered that Europeans had no experience in establishing colonies. Sending settlers across three thousand miles of ocean was a monumental task, yet there was an almost total lack of planning, and a rather general disinterest at home in the welfare of the people who dared to venture their lives on a foreign shore. The price the settlers paid was enormous, both in suffering and in deaths, but they hung on and multiplied and out of their courage was born the spirit that made America strong.

Although transported far overseas, the people of Virginia were little different from those they left behind. The hostilities with the French on the Continent were reflected on the new continent. Samuel Argall, a sea captain with piratical tendencies and later acting governor of Virginia, launched the first hostile action against the French in the New World. In 1613 he raided a French settlement on Mount Desert Island, off the Maine coast, and the next year sacked Port Royal (now Annapolis Royal) in Nova Scotia, the site of Champlain's most enterprising community. Thus the die was cast for the bitter conflict that would not end until the French forces were finally pushed completely off the continent.

If this truculence bore witness to the ancestral feelings of the English, so did the demands of the Virginians for greater freedom. There was widespread feeling that, having faced the wilderness and conquered it, they had earned the right to a voice in their own government.

On July 30, 1619, the first popular legislative body met in the church at Jamestown. From eleven scattered settlements came twenty-two "burgesses" to enact laws for the better management of the colony. They passed laws against drunkenness, idleness, gambling, and "shameful" dress, levied taxes, and granted ownership rights to wives, "because in a new plantation it is not known whether man or woman be most necessary." It was not a radical gathering; no one spoke of England in unkind tones or of the king in anything but polite terms, but they did want to make simpler their own governance.

The king still had absolute authority in most things, but delegated many powers to the Virginia Company and the royal governors. But now the people of Virginia had met to discuss their own problems, naming representatives and passing laws of their own. The Declaration of Independence would not be written for more than 150 years, but a spark was glowing brightly, a spark that would one day turn into a raging flame.

Wintry Landing at
Plymouth Rock

WITH CONSIDERABLE JUSTICE, it can be said that England's second successful colony, Plymouth, began in an ancient Yorkshire inn beside the royal road leading from London to Scotland. Here William Brewster, between serving food and ale and supplying fresh horses for stagecoaches, risked his life to support the spread of religious freedom.

In the Manor House at Scrooby, which he rented with the profits from his little tavern, Brewster held services for those who believed in a complete separation of church and state. He found ministers to preach the new concept of religion, organized those Puritans who were so eager to worship in their own way that they were willing to leave their homeland, and eventually led them to Holland. There, with other English Separatists, they settled in Leyden, took the name Pilgrims, and dreamed of a day when they could establish their own home far from repression and hatred.

For several years the Pilgrims enjoyed the freedom and enlightenment that marked the Netherlands, but time was running out. The truce between Holland and Spain, mortal enemies for years, was about to end. Brewster and his supporters drew up plans to emigrate to the New World. One of the directors of the Virginia Company lent the Pilgrims enough money, without interest, to charter two ships, the *Speedwell* and the *Mayflower*. After a false start, leading to the abandonment of the former vessel, the *Mayflower* sailed on September 16, 1620, from Plymouth. On board were 101

19

passengers willing to risk everything for their faith and the hope of establishing a new and better world. Storms buffeted the little sailing vessel. One of the main timbers of the frame was twisted out of place, nearly wrecking the ship, but a jackscrew was used to force it back. Open seams were calked, sails were patched, and the voyage continued.

On the day before they landed, the Pilgrims signed a set of laws known as the Mayflower Compact. It was a unique document. For the first time a group of people organized themselves from within, by mutual agreement, rather than accept laws from higher authority. It was effrontery, of course, because James I was supposed to be the seat of all power, but these stout-hearted men covenanted with one another to make their own laws.

In November they made a landfall at the tip of Cape Cod, having been carried far north of their intended destination by the Gulf Stream. The Jamestown colonists had discovered dogwood in bloom. The Pilgrims found a barren shore, little vegetation, and bitter winds blowing down from the northwest. A few days later, on the twenty-first, they crossed the bay and landed on a beach they called New Plymouth. The women and children remained aboard the *Mayflower* until the men could build cabins, a meetinghouse, and a fort. By January the common house was roofed and immediately turned into an infirmary. Scurvy struck down whole families, consumption decimated the little band, and by February, when the *Mayflower* finally set sail for home, nearly half the Pilgrims were dead. Nothing dampened their faith, however; not one survivor elected to return with her.

What remained of the winter was a fearsome time for the hungry, emaciated colonists. They had no hope of help from England or Holland for months to come, a recent plague had wiped out the Indian tribes that normally roamed the Massachusetts coast near Plymouth, and not even a fishing boat from the Grand Banks came by to give them food. But these staunch Puritans did not fight and brawl as the colonists at Jamestown had. They read their Bibles, prayed often and long, and survived. In the spring Indians came by, showed them how to plant corn with a fish in each hill to fertilize the plants, and brought in venison and other game. The women gathered greens with which to counter scurvy.

Governor John Carver died, and William Bradford was named

in his place. The crops flourished, everyone worked diligently, and for a while the Indians remained friendly. When fall came the Pilgrims decided to give thanks for their survival. Bradford sent out five men to shoot wild turkeys, and Indian braves brought in venison, ducks, and geese. The squaws showed Pilgrim housewives how to cook squash, pumpkin, and corn pudding. When, on November 25, 1621, white settlers and red natives sat down to a bountiful feast, Thanksgiving Day was born.

The early years at Plymouth were hard ones. The colonists fought famine, drought, cold, locusts, and snakes. At first it was a communal undertaking, noble in concept but impractical in fact. Healthy men, laboring in the fields, became disgruntled to see the elderly and weak receiving equal shares. Married men disliked the idea of their wives cooking for bachelors. It was an old problem, and one that has recurred many times since. Governor Bradford cured it the only way he knew how: each family was granted its own plot of land and dissension died down.

New groups of settlers came from Leyden and Amsterdam and from England, eager to escape the oppression that was steadily worsening as James I bickered with his enemies. Yet the colony grew slowly, deaths often offsetting the gain in numbers from Europe. The Pilgrims arrived with little but hope and an abiding faith in God. After the communal arrangement had been set aside, everyone willingly helped one another. Women cared for the ill, served as midwives, and gathered clams and mussels. Men fashioned the crude pine boxes in which their friends were laid to rest on Burial Hill, prayed over the open graves, and went back to tilling the fields, building homes, and cutting down the forest for new settlers.

Raw courage and deep faith saw the Pilgrims through those first years. So fervent was their devotion to the church that women rose from their beds within a few days of childbirth and walked through blizzards to the meetinghouse so their offspring could be baptized. According to early historians of the colony, the sacramental bread froze and rattled on the plates at communion and infants shuddered in the cold. Lips blue, hands and feet aching from chilblains, the mothers watched the icy water fall on their babies' brows and sang their hymns of praise to God. Yet beneath the austerity and religious zeal that was almost fanaticism, life in the Plymouth colony was not entirely devoid of pleasure. Love bloomed, families grew, and word went back to Europe that New England, if not a Garden of Eden, was still preferable to Amsterdam or London.

If any one factor is responsible for the survival of the colony, other than the indomitable courage of the members themselves, it was the plague that had wiped out so many Indians shortly before the *Mayflower* landed: unlike Jamestown, Plymouth had no problems with the natives until it was fairly well established.

The Pilgrims had drafted the Mayflower Compact with the sure knowledge that they were affronting royal prerogative. The Church of England held that no marriage was sacred unless a minister officiated. Edward Winslow, destined to be a leading light of the colony, lost his wife during the first winter, and Susanna White, who on the voyage from England had given birth to Peregrine White, the first child of the colony, lost her husband. The Pilgrims said Winslow and Susanna could be married "as were Boaz and Ruth, in the presence of the people," and so they were. William Brewster preached each Sunday—not because he had been ordained, for he hadn't been—but because the people themselves delegated to him the authority to preach. These were rebellious acts that cast long shadows ahead. Democracy was already taking shape on Plymouth Bay.

The success of the Pilgrims in holding their own on a foreign strand led other groups to emulate them. Some were well-intentioned people, others roistering characters having little respect for law, whether the Pilgrims' or the king's. Small settlements were made at Wollaston, and a few Plymouth families crossed the bay to settle at Duxbury. Captain Miles Standish, the colony's stout right arm, made it clear to the Wollaston settlers that Bradford was governor and was to be obeyed, and he assured the Duxbury group that his authority would shield them even on the far side of the bay. The Indians who had fled the plague returned, and petty warfare developed. Standish stepped in, won a few small skirmishes, and averted major trouble.

It was eight years after the Pilgrims landed before a major effort was made to establish a colony elsewhere in the Massachusetts Bay area. John Endecott led a band to what is now Dorchester and sent back word to the Puritans in England that good land was to be had for all.

Meeting at Cambridge, a group calling itself the Massachusetts

Bay Company decided to sponsor a new Puritan migration and elected John Winthrop as governor. They intended to assume full control over their own group, outwitting the new king, Charles I. Winthrop and the other leaders moved with great dispatch and energy. In 1630 the first English Puritans descended on the shore around Boston, Charlestown, Dorchester, and Salem from more than a score of ships. By summer more than a thousand had landed, well equipped with tools and supplies, reserves of food, and the will to make their settlement succeed. It had taken ten years for little Plymouth to reach a population of that size.

These Puritans differed in many ways from the Pilgrims. They were, for the most part, better educated. Many were merchants and had good connections with rich backers in London. But they were no less God-fearing than their predecessors in New England. The Massachusetts Bay Company was a successful welding together of business and clergy, united, in their own words, for "God's glory and the church's good."

What had gone wrong at Plymouth went right at Salem, Boston, and Charlestown. The Massachusetts Bay people set foot on rich soil. Strawberries tinted the hills pink, and cattle brought from England thrived on the thick meadow grass. Bradford, Winslow, Standish, and the other Pilgrims were brave men, but simple and uneducated. Winthrop was a man of considerable intellect, educated at Cambridge, an inspired leader and eminently suited to command.

Winthrop made his home in Boston, which became the capital of seven or eight communities that sprang up on Boston Bay before the year was out. Tents gave way to log cabins, meetinghouses, forts, blacksmith shops, and small stores. Seeds were planted and crops harvested. There was a stability here that was in bold contrast to the shiftlessness at Jamestown and the pathetic, slow progress at Plymouth. Unlike the almost ne'er-do-well character of the early Virginians and the ineffectiveness of the Pilgrims forty miles down the coast, the Massachusetts Bay Colony bustled with religious fervor, business acumen, and the solid qualities needed to establish a new home in the wilderness.

At first, power rested mainly in Winthrop's hands, but the clergy exerted a growing influence. Under the terms of the charter a General Court was set up, consisting of the governor, his assistants, and magistrates elected by the freemen of the colony. Only church members could vote, but as all the early colonists were devout Puritans this caused no trouble at first. Unfortunately, the harmony was short-lived.

Whereas the Pilgrims had been kind-hearted and tolerant, perhaps because of their years in Holland among men of many beliefs, the Massachusetts Bay Puritans became bigoted and intolerant. They had fled England to find religious freedom, but once established in New England they brooked no dissent. When two men conducted a service based on the Book of Common Prayer they were expelled from the colony. Quakers and Anabaptists were hounded and persecuted. The Puritan believed he had a special understanding with God, and any divergence from this covenant was forbidden. There was separation of church and state in name only. Clergymen controlled the General Court.

During this period business thrived. Most of the settlements clung close to the shore, and the men combined many activities. The small shipyards on the waterfront were operated by men who also farmed. Fishing was a main industry off both Cape Cod and Newfoundland, and commerce boomed with the West Indies and England. Before the Boston colony was a year old, a merchant vessel, the *Blessing of the Bay,* had been launched to meet the growing trade of the settlement.

King James II heard that his subjects across the seas were enacting their own laws, electing their own leaders, and behaving with singular independence, but there was not much he could do. The Massachusetts Bay Company had quietly and steadily altered the provisions of their charter and trading agreement until it became a viable set of laws by which the people governed themselves. Bay Colony government was now an admixture of old English common law, biblical admonitions, and Puritanical strictures.

Weakness developed in the colony when clergymen and laymen interpreted God's will in different ways, and two groups suffered in the process: the Indians, and the freethinkers and other dissenters. By some strange rationalization the Puritans excluded the Indians from the brotherhood of man, denying them equality and taking their land without permission or payment. (Mark Twain wrote that the pious fanatics "first fell on their knees, and then on the aborigines.") Whatever amity existed between Indian leaders such as Massasoit, Samoset, and Squanto and the Pilgrims at Plymouth was almost nonexistent in the Bay Colony. The Puritans were quick to suppress those colonists who were disturbed by the growing power of the clergymen. Men such as Roger Williams, Henry Vane, and John Wheelwright, seeking their own form of religious freedom, discovered there was little tolerance in the Bay Colony.

When Williams was chosen minister at Salem, turmoil bubbled to the surface immediately. Stiff-necked and truculent, he preached against the king's right to grant territory in the New World, persuaded Endecott to eliminate the cross from the British royal ensign because it connoted a marriage of church and state, and constantly decried the growing influence of secular power in the church. His sermons on the mistreatment of Indians were bitter and persistent. Most of the congregation, being interested in trade and profits, had salved their consciences on the question by holding that the Indians were savages and heathens and thus entitled to nothing.

Although Governor Winthrop, fundamentally a good and kind man, liked Williams, he saw a threat to the General Court in the preacher's arguments. He prevailed upon Williams to temper his remarks, and then, when the court voted to banish him, paid a clandestine visit to urge him to leave the colony before worse steps were taken. In the winter of 1635 Williams quit Salem in the midst of a severe snowstorm, taking twenty of his disciples with him on an arduous trek south through the wilderness. In the spring he founded Rhode Island, which was to become a haven for people of all creeds.

Anne Hutchinson arrived in the Bay Colony about the same time Williams took up his pulpit at Salem. Brilliant, gifted in debate, but impetuous and hardly discreet, she criticized the clergy for their hypocrisy and quarreled with the Puritans over points of theology. Looking back at it after all these years, it is almost impossible to see where the differences existed, so slight were they. Even Governor Winthrop wrote, "No man could tell, except some few who knew the bottom of the matter, where any difference was." But in the 1630s there was no place in Massachusetts for such free expression of opinions. The General Court ruled that Mrs. Hutchinson was tainted with the same evil that marked Roger Williams and ordered her banished as a heretic.

While these ideological disputes shook the higher levels of the new colony, life itself followed its pattern of labor, hardship, and dreariness.

Whether it was fear of starvation, literal interpretation of their preachers' warnings that laziness was a device Satan employed to ruin the souls of the weak, or a natural industry and eagerness to do well, the colonists devoted most of their waking hours to drudgery. Women in particular counted few happy hours. They had to cook and bake on open hearths, spin, weave the cloth with which to make the family's clothes, tend the kitchen garden, make candles, and perform a dozen other back-breaking chores. Childbearing started with marriage in the late teens and continued until middle life. Smallpox, diphtheria, pneumonia, and "summer complaint," probably caused by tainted food, took a grievous toll of children. Lucky was the mother who saw half her children reach maturity.

The corn-huskings, house-raisings, quilting bees, and other homely entertainments that marked New England a century later were almost unknown in the early days of Massachusetts. There was a little gossip over the back fences for the women, and an occasional glass of cider or ale for the men, but little else. And every Sunday they sat on hard benches in the meetinghouse and heard their preachers warn that sloth and sin and covetousness would be punished by the undying fires of hell, that for every wayward thought, every Godless act, they would suffer the tortures of the damned down through the centuries.

With all the hardships and disputes, there was never any real danger of failure in the Massachusetts Bay Colony. The people were of solid stuff, hard-working and respectable. The religious supervision may have been onerous at times, but it lent invaluable strength to the community. The Puritans were determined to make the enterprise work. Behind their eagerness was a factor that cannot be underestimated: most of them had come from parts of England where landholding was a privilege of the rich, but here in the New World there was land to be had for the asking. The bonded servants who came with the first wave of migration were given their freedom almost at once because there was not enough food or money to support them out of another's earnings. So within a short time everyone stood on an equal footing, and the roots of democracy found nourishment in the rich soil.

Within a few years the Bay Colony had spread up and down the coast and a short distance inland. Boston, Salem, Dorchester, Charlestown, Cambridge, Watertown, Roxbury, Lynn, and Cohasset became the nexus for future growth all through New England. In most ways, these towns were much like those in old England. People lived close together, partly for reasons of defense, but mostly because that was the way it had been at home. A house might be set in a small garden or orchard, but the main acreage under cultivation was at the edge of town and men went out to till the fields, a considerable distance from their homes. Everyone had the right to graze his animals on the common, and few of the early villages lacked this open patch of green pasture, usually right in the center of the community.

Religion may have held the preeminent place in the activities of the Puritan communities, but the settlers did not forget education. Six years after the Massachusetts colony had dug in, a well-to-do man named John Harvard left half his estate to found a college. With alacrity a wooden building was put up, and the educational process began. A few years later Charles II sent a group of commissioners to inspect the institution and they disdainfully reported that it was only "a wooden colledge." Two Dutch visitors, in Boston from New Amsterdam in connection with the growing trade between English and Dutch colonies, were more blunt, saying Harvard smelled "like a tavern." But education was on the way in New England.

Everywhere the early colonists looked, everywhere they went, the land stretched away, richly forested, watered by myriad streams, beckoning to the adventurous. When an Indian chief from the banks of the Connecticut River offered the Pilgrims at Plymouth eighty beaver pelts if some of them would settle on that river they accepted his invitation gladly. By 1633 they had established a small settlement and trading post at Windsor, Connecticut. Others soon sprouted up.

After the first fiascos at Jamestown, which were largely a result of the all-male population, the English made certain that women and children accompanied the settlers. Permanence was a central factor in the success of any colony, and this stability depended on family life. The sense of permanence ultimately gave the English the upper hand in North America. The Spanish and French sent only men abroad. The Spaniards interbred with the natives, establishing a largely different ethnic society. The French sent men who were motivated by two widely different purposes: fur trading and spreading the gospel. The French had tried to establish colonies well before Jamestown. One with convicts as settlers failed on

Sable Island, another barely held a grip on Tadoussac, on the St. Lawrence at the mouth of the Saguenay River, and Champlain helped start another at Port Royal in Nova Scotia—all before the English gained a foothold in Virginia. Champlain founded Quebec City the year after the landing at Jamestown, and two years later there was a French settlement on the Penobscot River in Maine. But these were mainly bachelor colonies, established almost entirely for the purpose of trading with the Indians.

Hand in hand with the *voyageurs* and fur traders went the Recollet fathers, seeking to convert the Indians to Catholicism. Long before the Pilgrims landed on the *Mayflower,* missionaries had explored to the regions near Lake Huron and along the Ottawa River.

The movements of the Spaniards and the French to the south and north of the English colonies would have their repercussions, but the die was cast. The English colonists were putting down roots, setting up stable governments, establishing trade, and luring thousands to the New World. Their colonies would grow strong. They were the seedbeds of a great nation.

IV

The Stuff upon Which
Nations Thrive

FROM BOSTON RADIATED the first movements of settlers that resulted in new colonies, first to the south, into Connecticut and Rhode Island, and soon after, into New Hampshire and Maine to the north. Behind the migrations were many forces: a search for the religious freedom the Puritans denied, a desire to settle the inland wilderness, an eagerness to establish trade with the Indians, and a compulsion to offset French movements down the coast from Port Royal and Acadia.

Although the Massachusetts Bay Colony encouraged expansion, the first step was taken, as already noted, by the Pilgrims of Plymouth. It involved courage and persistence, but the adventure was not without humor. Captain William Holmes and his company of stouthearted Pilgrims sailed from Plymouth, rounded Cape Cod and Nantucket, and made their way up the Connecticut River. To their surprise they found at what is now Hartford a small fort erected by Jan Van Corlear of New Amsterdam. Holmes sailed on a few miles upriver, built a house with a palisade around it, ran up the British flag, and called his settlement Windsor.

Wouter Van Twiller, governor of the New Netherlands, was furious at the news and ordered Van Corlear to clear the invaders out of what he felt was clearly Dutch territory. At this time in American history claims by various powers to land in the New World frequently overlapped, partly because of bad geography and partly because European monarchs had a grandiose way of giving away vast areas they did not own and for which they could not even fix boundaries. So Dutch and English faced one another on the Connecticut, each thinking his cause the just one.

With a few soldiers from Fort Good Hope, his outpost at Hartford, Van Corlear marched up the river to Windsor and demanded that Captain Holmes quit trading with the Indians and leave the area immediately. Holmes placed his men at the loopholes in the palisades and invited the Dutch to try to evict them. Van Corlear looked at the muskets pointed his way, thought things over, and retreated to his fort downstream. If the Dutch ever had had any chance of making good their claim to Connecticut they lost it that day in 1633 when they let Pilgrim muskets overawe them. Not long after, they left the valley entirely.

The Plymouth Company, sitting three thousand miles away in England, had given most of what is now Connecticut "north to Massachusetts Bay and west to the Pacific" to the Earl of Warwick, who had subsequently transferred title to Lord Saye and Sele and Lord Brook. The Dutch claim was based mainly on purchase from the Pequot Indians.

Hearing of the confrontation at Windsor, the leaders in Boston decided to settle things their way. They would send colonists into the area and make the attachment a *fait accompli* before the slow-moving Dutchmen at the mouth of the Hudson could intervene.

Historians have noted many times the strange predilection of mankind for doing things the hard way. So it was in this case. Instead of starting out in the spring, about sixty men from Boston and Dorchester, with their wives and children, set out for the Connecticut River in October of 1635. They took their horses and cattle and tools but not nearly enough food. Their route led through uncharted wilderness, up and down hills, over rivers and swamps where no Englishman had ever trod before. Cold weather came, hampering the slow hegira, but the settlers finally reached Hartford and threw up rough cabins.

Then winter set in. Food ran low, the cattle had no feed and started to die off, and starvation confronted all of them. Many of their number headed for the mouth of the river, found a boat, and returned home, but the others survived, mainly through donations of food from friendly Indians. One might expect that the stories they told would have discouraged their friends, but the Puritans were a dedicated breed. The next spring a new group headed for Hartford, with their preacher, the Reverend Mr. Thomas Hooker, at their side. Their journey was less harrowing, and with their arrival the settlement of the Connecticut River valley became assured.

Expansion from Boston often coincided with new migrations from England. While Hooker's people were establishing Wethersfield and Hartford, a party of Puritans sent out by Oliver Cromwell and John Hampden arrived to take up the claims awarded Lord Saye and Lord Brook. Settling at the mouth of the Connecticut, they called their village Saybrook after their patrons. In time people from Hartford joined them to strengthen the outpost. These colonists picked for their governor a young man named John Winthrop, Jr., son of the Massachusetts Bay leader.

Another settlement completed the process of making the Connecticut area an English colony. It had a strange beginning under the leadership of Theophilus Eaton and John Davenport. These men, coming from England to Boston, decided that the Massachusetts Bay area was far too crowded for their tastes. They gathered a few followers, sailed down to Long Island Sound, and landed at a place that they called New Haven because it would afford them an opportunity to found a new colony more to God's liking.

Although these new settlers in the Connecticut Valley were deeply religious and eager to spread the gospel, they were rudely indifferent to such things as the rights of the Indians. The valley was a rich, fertile paradise, ideal for many crops, but no one thought much about the Pequots when the log houses went up in the clearings. God, the Puritans were sure, would have wanted it that way. The Pequots, not privy to God's feelings, rebelled at the invasion of their hunting grounds. Within a few months outlying homes were burned, settlers killed, children stolen. Thirty whites lost their lives. From Springfield on the north to Saybrook on the south there were the sounds of the war whoop, of muskets booming, of women weeping.

Boston and Plymouth were asked for aid. The first town voted to send 160 men, and little Plymouth ordered forty men under arms. Connecticut settlements mustered ninety men under Captain John Mason, who had fought in the European wars. An advance party from Massachusetts under Captain John Underhill joined Mason's force at Saybrook. While hundreds of Pequots on the shore jeered them as cowards, the colonists sailed eastward to attack the Indians from the rear. Mason led his men ashore near Point Judith, found a war party of Narragansetts and Mohegans waiting to aid him against their long-time enemies, and all marched toward a huge Pequot encampment near what is now Mystic, Connecticut.

Early on the morning of May 24, 1637, with a full moon riding in a cloudless sky, Mason woke his men, waited while prayers were said, and then advanced on the Indian fort. Underhill led his men around to the rear for a concerted attack. When the Indian sentinels awoke, some of the colonists were already inside the palisades. There was a brisk engagement, arrows against bullets, and then the white men put the wigwams to the torch. Onshore winds from the Atlantic sent the flames racing through the fort. When the Englishmen withdrew, nearly six hundred blackened Pequot corpses lay in the embers. Seven Indians were captured, and seven escaped. "In the Span of an Hour," according to an early account, "the whole Business was dispatched."

For the forseeable future, peace was ensured in Connecticut and the way open for new white settlements. The inexorable march against the red man was under way.

While the settlements on the Connecticut were multiplying, Roger Williams, the Salem cleric, was asking embarrassing questions of the Massachusetts Bay elders. He disliked the idea that only church members could serve in government posts. "Do you employ a doctor because he is a good physician? Do you trust your ship to the pilot because he is a member of the church, or because he knows where the rocks are?" he asked.

This was too much for the Puritans, so they banished him and he went off into the wilderness. Governor Bradford of Plymouth offered him shelter, and when it was refused, warned Williams that he was still living on land under Massachusetts Bay suzerainty and had better be on his way. This advice Williams took, going down the Pawtucket River into the land of the Narragansetts. There he founded a new colony on land given him by Canonicus, chief of the Narragansetts. He called it Providence Plantation. The year was 1636.

Providence, under Williams, was possibly the most free governmental entity anywhere in the world. He welcomed dissenters of all persuasions. No matter what opinions he held, a man was welcome. So, in this liberal climate, Mrs. Hutchinson, along with William Coddington and William Gorton, had no opposition in founding Portsmouth two years later.

A fury approaching that of the woman scorned must surely be that of a dissenter whose followers dissent in turn. Mrs. Hutchinson soon found Coddington "erring" in his ideology and ousted him from Portsmouth. The disciple went off and founded Newport. Not long after that the lady with the volatile temper and acidulous tongue quarreled with Gorton and sent him packing. He thereupon founded Warwick.

Despite all the silliness and acerbity in Rhode Island, the colony grew in strength because of its freedom of religious expression, a freedom that was now in its infancy but would someday be every American's constitutional right.

The founding of Connecticut and Rhode Island, although effected by different forces and types of people and for different reasons, followed a rather straightforward pattern. Groups spread out from Massachusetts, settled in various places, and then spread out again. The Puritans who settled New Haven, being fresh from England, still were stiff-necked enough to rule that only church members could have a voice in public affairs. But other Connecticut towns, Hartford, Windsor, Wethersfield, took pride in a government where any man "of good character" could vote. It was the first government in America that could claim to represent all the people.

In contrast to the rather even development of the Connecticut and Rhode Island colonies, those north of Massachusetts grew in fits and starts, with confusion the order of the day.

As early as 1607 the Plymouth Company had sent a group of 120 persons, led by George Popham and Raleigh Gilbert, to settle at the mouth of the Kennebec River in Maine. Popham died during the winter, and about a year later the fierce weather drove the colonists home.

Sir Ferdinando Gorges, a member of the Plymouth Company, was an indefatigable backer of colonization attempts, putting his own wealth into one venture after another. None was truly successful until after the Council for New England, successor to the Plymouth Company, received a grant of land between latitudes 40 degrees and 48 degrees north. Out of this John Mason received in 1622 the land from the Piscataqua south to the Merrimack River, and Gorges took that from the Piscataqua north to the Kennebec.

Gorges called his holding Lygonia, after his mother, Cicely Lygon, but it did not thrive. Mason called his section of the grant New Hampshire and found that there were already a few small villages within its confines. David Thompson had settled Little Harbor, now Rye, as early as 1623, and Dover had been settled in 1630. John Wheelwright, a preacher who was also Anne Hutchinson's brother, helped settle Exeter after he was ordered out of the Bay Colony for heresy. Like Connecticut and Rhode Island, New Hampshire too would exhibit a greater spirit of freedom than existed in the parent colony.

At almost the same time grants were issued to others, and the territories overlapped. Captain Christopher Levett was given a patent for six thousand acres wherever he chose. He sailed up and down the coast, liked the looks of a peninsula on which Portland, Maine, now stands, and claimed it. It was right in the middle of Gorges' grant, but Sir Ferdinando made no fuss about it, eager only to get colonization started. Some of the settlements in "ye Maine land" were made by groups from England, some from Newfoundland, and some from Massachusetts. They were small fishing stations at first but gradually grew as lumbering and shipbuilding lured more colonists.

During the rule of Oliver Cromwell disputes were few, but after the Restoration and the return of the monarchy bitter feuding started again. The king gave grants to Anglican groups, and the Bay Colony, fearing the establishment of a state church in the neighboring colonies, did its best to send Puritans to settle the northern lands, New Hampshire in particular. The clergymen who were running things in Boston were not above using any trick in the bag to gain their ends. After studying their original charter, which made indefinite mention of a northern boundary three miles above the Merrimack, they blatantly suggested that it did not refer to the mouth of the river but to its uppermost reaches in the mountains. Thereupon they laid claim to all of New Hampshire.

Mason's heirs appealed to the king to have his grant validated, and the king did so, making New Hampshire a royal province. The dispute smoldered for years. Massachusetts officials arrested New Hampshire men on the border for nonpayment of taxes, claiming they were living in the Bay Colony. The rivalry continued until 1741, when New Hampshire's southern boundary was settled for all time.

The Boston Puritans had better success in Maine. They took the new colony under their wing to thwart the king's plans to make it a royal province, as he had done with New Hampshire, and in 1677 bought all the claims then outstanding from the heirs of Sir Ferdinando Gorges. It was not until well after the Revolutionary War, in 1820, that Maine broke away and became a state in the new union.

Perhaps the most important thing about the settlement of New Hampshire and Maine was the fact that they provided a northern bastion against French encroachment. Once these areas were settled, it was made clear that the English would not brook any attempt by the French to lay claim to lands between Maine and Florida.

Colonization in New England had gone relatively well. The type of people who migrated to those bleak shores were the stuff upon which new nations thrive. Within two decades after the landing on Plymouth Rock there were 14,000 settlers in Massachusetts, 2,000 in Connecticut, 1,500 in Maine and New Hampshire, and 300 in Rhode Island. The nation to be born from the thirteen colonies was already taking form.

V

A Good Bargain on the Hudson

WHILE THE PILGRIMS were suffering through their third year at Plymouth, the Dutch made their opening bid for a place in the sun on the North American continent. In 1609, Henry Hudson had sailed his ship, the *Half Moon,* into the finest harbor on the continent and several score miles up what he called the North, or Hudson's, River. This harbor, which became New Amsterdam and eventually New York, was claimed for the Netherlands, and within a few years other Dutch explorers had laid claim to the Delaware and the Connecticut as well.

There were delays in taking possession of the territory Hudson had discovered because the Dutch East India Company was using its ships to harass Spanish treasure galleons, and in 1623 another company, the Dutch West India Company, was assigned the task.

The first settlers were not Dutchmen alone. Many were Walloons, Protestants who had fled Catholic oppression in France and along the Rhine and Moselle rivers, and thus they were originally French, Belgian, or German nationals. The Dutch had welcomed them, and by the time the West India Company began soliciting settlers the Walloons were well assimilated.

In the little sailing vessel *New Netherlands* thirty Walloon families headed by Cornelis May made a landfall in 1623 on an island occupied by the Manahatta Indians. Some of the families went ashore on the tip of the island and others scattered, going to the Delaware Bay area, Long Island, and along the Connecticut River. A few went on up the Hudson River to Fort Orange (now Albany), where Dutch fur traders had already established a post.

The Dutch expedition was most fortunate in its timing. As the *New Netherlands* sailed inside Sandy Hook Bay, about fifteen miles south of Manhattan, Captain May saw a French vessel that had also arrived for the purpose of colonizing the mouth of the Hudson. He was not making much headway persuading the French that this was Dutch country when a small armed yacht, the *Mackerel,* flying the flag of Holland, came downstream from Fort Orange. The French quickly decided that they should seek other worlds to conquer.

Within months there were Dutch settlements at Fort Orange and New Amsterdam; Wallabout (a name corrupted from Walloon's Bend), Long Island; Fort Good Hope on the Connecticut; and Timmer's Kill, now Gloucester, New Jersey. Even before Captain May sailed for home, crops were coming through the soil from seeds planted within hours of the first landfall. A few weeks later three other ships, the *Eagle, Love,* and *Orange Tree,* brought more families. It looked as if what we know as New York, New Jersey, and southern Connecticut would constitute a foreign wedge between the English colonies in New England and Virginia.

In the summer of 1626 Peter Minuit, director general and governor of the new colony, arrived on Manhattan Island with his staff and a new group of settlers. On the steps of a stone fort at the tip of the island, Minuit gave needles, red cloth, brass buttons, fish hooks, and other trinkets worth sixty guilders to the sachems of the Manahatta tribe in payment for the island. This gesture, of which so much has been made in word and song, whereby for $24 in English money the Dutch purchased one of the most valuable pieces of real estate on earth, was no happenstance. The Netherlands government had made it clear to all settlers that the natives must be paid for their lands. It turned out to be an excellent insurance policy against war with the Indians, until the Dutch canceled it themselves.

The Dutch colonized their segment of the North American continent for one reason: trade. They were probably the best businessmen of their time. Whereas New England was settled by religious fugitives and Virginia by adventurers seeking gold, New Netherland was settled by a commercial organization, the Dutch West India Company. It had been granted administrative rights to govern the colonists, and its sole purpose was to establish trade with the Indians. Furs were eagerly sought in Europe, and beaver skins even became a form of currency. The industry of the Dutch traders is best revealed by a look at the ship's manifest from the *Arms of*

Amsterdam, a trading vessel that returned to Holland soon after Peter Minuit took office. In the hold of the ship were 7,246 beaver skins, 853 otter pelts, 151 skins of lynx, muskrat, and mink, and stacks of walnut and oak timbers for the shipyards of the mother country.

The Dutch took it more or less for granted that there would be religious freedom and got on with the business of establishing trade. Peter Minuit ruled with absolute power, but not too harshly, as he oversaw the establishment of a colony that might have been one of the most valuable in the New World, had it survived.

Holland, at the time one of the most culturally advanced nations in all Europe, enjoyed freedom of religion and a secure way of life. Not many men wanted to leave such security for a life in the wilderness, and for this reason the surge of colonists to New England was never duplicated in New Netherland.

Gillis Hossett was named governor of the small enclave on the Delaware, which was really only a patroonship. He nailed a shiny piece of tin to a tree, saying it represented the sovereignty of Holland. When an Indian cut it down to make it into jewelry, Hossett killed him. Shortly after, a number of Indians came to the little fort, killed the men there, and then went into the fields and killed the rest of the settlers.

For the Dutch, this was the exception. Throughout most of their tenure in New York they fared well with the Indians. This was due in part to their practice of paying for what they took, whether land or food, but perhaps even more to the fact that Samuel Champlain, meeting the Iroquois for the first time when on his way down the lake to which he gave his name, had shot and killed several braves. The Iroquois never forgave him, sided first with the Dutch and then with the British against the French and their Indian allies, and proved invaluable to them in the wars that bloodied the northern frontier.

In Virginia the cavaliers, as spokesmen for the king, were the governing body of the young colony. In New England the clergymen had the most to say. In New York control was vested primarily in a soulless corporation, the Dutch West India Company, which looked upon New Netherland as a place to make profits. Wealthy burghers in the homeland sat in their countinghouses waiting for income from fur-trading, lumbering, shipping, and warehousing.

Within five or six years New Amsterdam became the busiest

port in the New World. Ships came and went carrying on a tri-angular trade between North America, the West Indies, and Europe. Very soon the Dutch captains realized that by adding a fourth leg, Africa, to their international voyages they might produce even greater profits. They thereupon entered the slave trade, already thriving with the West Indies.

As a means of tempting settlers, the West India Company offered a large tract of land, tax-free for a decade, to any person who could get fifty people to emigrate to the colony. These holdings, called patroonships, were granted with as much carelessness as some of the royal patents made by the English kings. Each patroonship was to extend along the Hudson, Delaware, or Connecticut rivers either for sixteen miles along one bank and as far inland as the owner cared to claim, or eight miles along both banks.

The weak timber in this structure was the status of the settlers themselves. The patroon was a virtual feudal chief, reaping all the profits, holding all rights as landowner and magistrate, and depriving the settlers of an equitable return for their labor. Two decades after most of the land on the eastern shore of the Hudson had been granted to a handful of patroons, only one patroonship could be called successful. This was Vanrensselaerwyck, owned by Killiaen Van Rensselaer, a diamond merchant of Amsterdam. His agents put together a 200,000-acre empire that included much of present-day Albany, Rensselaer, and Columbia counties.

Men named Van Cortlandt, de Peyster, and Van der Donck owned patroonships in what is now the Bronx and Westchester County. Michael de Paauw appropriated all of Staten Island and much of the New Jersey shore facing the island. Samuel Godyn and Samuel Blommaert took a huge acreage on the lower Delaware, near Cape Henlopen. It was within the limits of the present state of Delaware and was the first Dutch settlement in that colony. It was a Dutch ship that delivered the first slaves to Virginia, even before New Amsterdam was settled. By the time Peter Minuit, the best Dutch governor in the New World, had been replaced by the choleric Wouter Van Twiller, Negro slaves were working in the fields of Manhattan Island, on the docks, and in Dutch homes.

New Amsterdam must have been an exciting place in those early days. The Dutch erected stout blockhouses, built homes of brick that had come from Holland as ballast in ships, started flour mills and bolting mills, cooperages and warehouses. Life centered around the area now known as the Battery—Stone Street and the lower extremity of Broadway. A wooden palisade, later strengthened with stones, stretched across Manhattan Island from the Hudson to the East River as a protection against Indians. This barrier gave its name to Wall Street.

After the fort the first structure built was the West India Company's warehouse, a square building of stone. Soon after that a mill went up, with a high loft and a belfry in which bells stolen from Puerto Rico were hung. Before a church was built, the Spanish bells called the citizens to Sabbath services in the mill loft.

Homes, first of wood, then of stone or brick, were strung along narrow streets just as they were in Holland and, with their crow-step or gabled roofs, they resembled those at home. Along the East River were many farms, or "bouweries," all owned by the company at first. After a while the people insisted on more rights for themselves, and Great Burgher Rights and Small Burgher Rights were granted, permitting the chosen few at the top to own large properties and all freemen to own smaller parcels.

With the notable exception of Killiaen Van Rensselaer, far up the Hudson, the patroons failed in the effort to colonize the interior. They were supposed to supply preachers and teachers for their bonded settlers and to till the fields. Instead, most of them trafficked in furs, letting their vast holdings run down. The West India Company had retained for itself a monopoly in the fur business, but the patroons, being miles away from the seat of government, did as they wished. Van Twiller sided with the powerful landowners, even after he left office. At one point the patroons defended their privileges against company agents with *steenstucken,* the Dutch stone guns.

Bad as Van Twiller was, his successor, Wilhelm Kieft, was worse. For ten years he ruled like a despot, imposing laws and taxes, collecting fees right and left and putting them in his own pantaloon pockets. He set aside both company regulations and Dutch laws, opened taverns on nearly every street, started the first brewery in New Jersey, and peddled guns and powder to the Indians. Kieft nearly wrecked the colony and the company's enterprises. Before he was done he had conducted two pointless massacres of Indians, killed many others, and stirred the tribes into open rebellion. Only the intervention of Captain John Underhill from Connecticut and the arrival of a hundred or so troops sent by Governor Peter Stuyvesant of Curaçao prevented the Dutch settlers outside Manhattan Island from being annihilated.

While these events were happening, the West India Company suffered a loss in trade amounting to thousands of guilders, the Swedes had the temerity to establish a colony on the Delaware River on land claimed by the Dutch, and the English settled New Haven.

Yet New Amsterdam itself grew into a small metropolis, churches went up, *dominies* (pastors) were sent to the colony by the Dutch Reformed Church, and, what seemed best of all, Kieft was summoned home and Peter Stuyvesant arrived from Curaçao to replace him.

Alas, Stuyvesant was not the man for the deed. He arrived with pomp and circumstance, strutting on his peg leg with its fancy silver bands, kept the populace standing for hours until he deigned to step forth before them, took the fancy title "director general," and charged the colony for maintaining a sizable standing army of more than one hundred soldiers.

He was a strong leader, true, but a religious bigot and an autocrat. He saw at once that traffic in rum and guns would wreck relations with the Indians, and he forbade both, and he closed the taverns Kieft had peppered through the town, which enraged the burghers. Stuyvesant was a builder. Nothing pleased him more than to see stones and bricks going up, and he increased taxes to pay for repairs to older buildings. Yet he spent nothing to rehabilitate the fort. He broke up some of the patroonships—those wasteful failures at colonization—and made land available to many settlers.

Stubborn and harsh, Stuyvesant halted the illicit fur trade with the New England colonies, which had benefited the English more than the Dutch, and he built Fort Casimir down on the Delaware to show the Swedes that he did not intend to let their colony expand. But none of this made up for his failure to keep defenses in order or for the reduction of privileges and the heavy burden of taxation he imposed on the citizens.

When the burghers got together and drew up a list of remonstrances in 1649, and later when a committee of nineteen delegates met at New Amsterdam to complain of the arbitrary government, they found they had an ally in the Dutch West India Company itself. The company had come to the opinion that the colony was being ruined by poor government, and so it made no protest when the States-General of Holland rebuked Stuyvesant and forced him to show greater leniency in his administration of the colony.

In a letter to a friend in 1650, a lawyer named Adrian Van der Donck revealed some of the decay that had infected the colony:

> The Managers of the Company adopted a wrong course at first, and as we think had more regard for their own interest than for the welfare of the country . . . The Company have sought to stock this land with their own *employes,* which was a great mistake, for when their time was out they returned home, taking nothing with them, except a little in their purses and a bad name for the country, in regard to its means of sustenance and in other respects . . .
>
> The fort under which we shelter ourselves, and from which as it seems all authority proceeds, lies like a mole-heap or a tottering wall, on which there is not one gun carriage or one piece of cannon in a suitable frame or on a good platform . . .
>
> In our opinion this country will never flourish under the government of the Honorable Company, but will pass away and come to an end of itself, unless the Honorable Company be reformed; and therefore it would be more profitable for them, and better for the country, that they should be rid thereof, and their effects transported hence.

Even though the government criticized Stuyvesant and a degree of freedom did result, he denied the delegates the right to assemble. "We derive our authority from God and the Company," he told the burghers, "not from a few ignorant subjects; and we alone can call the inhabitants together."

It was no wonder the colony crumbled. Soldiers spent their time drinking—and so did a goodly number of inhabitants—and only the Almighty knew who was an honest trader carrying goods across the seas and who was a pirate whose cargoes had been stolen rather than bought. Many a buccaneer with a price on his head was welcome in the warehouses and countingrooms scattered along the docks at the tip of Manhattan Island.

The Puritans in Connecticut, eager to enhance the glory of God as well as extend their own frontiers, sent colonists across the water to Long Island, where they built towns that were replicas of those in Massachusetts and Connecticut. The Dutch at the western end of the island looked on with dismay but without the power to interfere.

Final proof of the sad collapse of New Netherland came when an English vessel, seeking to trade up the Hudson, sailed into the harbor. At a conference with Dutch officials the shipmaster said the land was rightly England's. When, a few days later, the English ship sailed boldly past the Dutch line of defenses, not a shot was fired, the soldiers being half drunk.

Despite its weaknesses, the colony had prospered in many ways. It had attracted settlers from England, Scandinavia, Bohemia, Switzerland, and Germany. There were Waldensians, Huguenots, and Mennonites among them, and the English church had almost equal rights with the Dutch Reformed. Most of these immigrants gladly paid homage to Holland, well aware that next to Rhode Island the colony probably enjoyed the purest brand of religious freedom in the New World. The English, however, were opportunists and sensed that Dutch power was crumbling. Those who migrated to Long Island, Westchester, and elsewhere east of the Hudson—which was a no man's land always in dispute as to ownership—openly, if not treacherously, urged Connecticut's officials to "cast the skirts of its government" over their villages.

Stuyvesant cannot be blamed for the collapse of the colony. He was but one factor in the system that was doomed from the outset to fail. Neither can he be excused, however. Despite his military fame and his other claims to high place, he was a religious bigot. He prevented anyone not a member of the Dutch Reformed Church from working or doing business in the colony, kept other unwanted persons out of the area entirely, and oppressed believers in other creeds. He imprisoned Lutherans who refused to have their children baptized in the Dutch church and banished Anglicans and Baptists. For reasons known only to himself, he was harshest of all on the Quakers. The case of Robert Hodgson, a leader of the Friends, is an example of Stuyvesant's cruelty towards these people.

Hodgson had tried to interest residents of Flushing and Wallabout in the Quaker movement. Officials seized him and two followers, both women, one of whom had a babe in arms, and tied them together. They were taken in a cart to a filthy dungeon to await trial. In truth, there was no trial. Stuyvesant's minions found Hodgson guilty and sentenced him to pay a fine of six hundred guilders or to work two years chained with a Negro to a wheelbarrow. When Hodgson refused to do either, he was tied up and whipped, again and again. If it had not been for the intercession of Stuyvesant's sister, who could not countenance such cruelty, he would have died under the lash.

So, in the last years of New Netherland, the religious liberty that had made it a haven for people of different creeds was crushed by a pig-headed bigot.

Stuyvesant showed his dictatorial leanings in other ways, none more flagrant than his appointment of Cornelis Van Tienhoven as *Schout*. In Dutch government of this era a *Schout* was a man who combined the duties of deputy governor, undersecretary of state, sheriff, bailiff, and prosecutor. Van Tienhoven abused these powers; he cheated prisoners, taxed men who should not have been taxed, and was a scoundrel of the first water. In 1649 a remonstrance against him was prepared by the residents of New Netherland for presentation to Stuyvesant. Its characterization of the *Schout* must surely stand as one of the bitterest denunciations of a public official in history: "He is subtle, crafty, intelligent, sharp-witted for evil . . . he is a dissembler, double-faced, a cheat; the whole country proclaims him a knave, a murderer, a traitor—he fleeces the people." The record doesn't show whether this criticism led Van Tienhoven into the paths of righteousness and piety, but Peter Stuyvesant himself remained stubborn and arbitary to the last.

As the end of Dutch rule in the New World approached, the citizens of New Netherland could take solace in the fact that they had opened a vast section to settlement. There were towns all along the Hudson and well out on the Mohawk River. The beginnings of Brooklyn could be seen at Wallabout, Gravesend, Flatbush, and on the heights across the river from downtown New Amsterdam. Northern New Jersey had settlements at Hoboken, Pavonia, Bergen Point, and Hackensack.

What had happened to the colony resulted from its initial concept: A proprietary province, with the Dutch West India Company as proprietor, it suffered from being looked upon as a commercial investment. Any movement toward representative government was fought by the company. Strangely enough, the individual had considerable freedom but almost no privileges of self-government. Nor did he have the spirit to fight for it as those in New England did.

The end came not as a direct result of decay and lack of enterprise, but these made it inevitable. King Charles II, greedy for power and income—the Stuarts were always shy of cash—listened to his advisers as they told about the rich lands held by the Dutch in the New World. On the basis of the discoveries of John and

Sebastian Cabot, Charles claimed the entire North American continent. Stuyvesant had been governor of New Netherland for thirteen years when Charles called in his brother James, the Duke of York, circled the Dutch holdings on a map, and bestowed them on the duke. A fleet of men-of-war under Colonel Richard Nicolls was sent to seize the Dutch province.

Nicolls sailed arrogantly into the harbor, informed the Dutch they were usurping English territory, and offered them equal rights with Englishmen if they surrendered peacefully. Nothing would be changed so far as the average citizen was concerned, except the flag flying over the ramparts. Stuyvesant wanted to fight the accursed interlopers, but his cannon were rusty, his powder old, and most of his soldiers disenchanted with the idea of fighting. There was a passionate scene in the upper rooms of Kieft's old tavern, which served as the city hall, but Stuyvesant could not arouse any enthusiasm for battle. The Dutch burghers thought it better to swear allegiance to another government and get on with the business of doing business.

When Nicolls sent his troops ashore on September 8, 1664, they met no resistance. There was no will to resist. New Amsterdam became New York.

In August 1673 the Dutch recaptured the city and called it New Orange after the prince of Orange, but war overseas led to Holland's defeat and the city passed back into English hands in November 1674. This time it remained English until the patriots took it away in the war of independence.

Any account of the colonization of the New World has to include mention of attempts made by the fifth European power to establish a colony in the Western Hemisphere. Spain and France had been active before the English landed at Roanoke, and the Dutch had followed soon after the Pilgrims arrived at Plymouth. The next nation to try was Sweden, whose king, Gustavus Adolphus, had enlarged his nation's territory by handsome victories in northern Europe. The king formed a company along the lines of the Dutch trading companies and gave it a charter in 1626. There the matter hung for years, during which Gustavus Adolphus died and the country was swept into the Thirty Years War.

When the project was taken up again in 1638, the Swedes found an excellent man to lead its colonists. He was Peter Minuit, the former governor of New Netherland. Minuit was a colorful character. Born in Rhenish Prussia, he had moved to Holland and so impressed the government leaders that they named him to the post in the New World. He was recalled, not because he was a bad governor, but because the West India Company directors wanted bigger profits.

Downhearted, Minuit entered the service of Sweden. In March 1638, with two boatloads of settlers from Sweden and Finland, he landed on the western shore of lower Delaware Bay, close to present-day Wilmington. The Dutch soldiers at Fort Nassau confronted the small Swedish group and forbade them to stay. Minuit outfoxed them by saying he was headed for the West Indies but had come up the bay to get wood and water. By the time the slow-witted Dutchmen realized what was going on, Minuit had put cannon ashore, begun the stone foundations of a fort, and was building cabins. He called his settlement Fort Christina after the queen of Sweden.

All told, there were only half a hundred men and women in the colony, but Minuit paid the Indians well for the land and they remained friends for many years. These Indians must have had a good sense of humor. When the Reverend Mr. Riorus Torkillus, a Lutheran minister, held divine services in the fort the local Indians were invited to attend. An early historian, writing of the Swedish settlement, noted that the Indians "expressed their amazement that one man should detain his tribe with such lengthened harangues without offering to entertain them with brandy."

Support for the colony was slow in coming. The Swedish queen asked for volunteers to go abroad, but few accepted the challenge. Then the governors of Värmland and Älvsborg were instructed to round up married men who had evaded military service or committed some other crime and to send them to the new colony with their wives and families. So that it would not seem too cruel a fate, the soldiers were told they could return after a year or two.

Each year a few ships brought more Swedes and Finns to Fort Christina as the government back home invested heavily in the extension of its empire. Peter Minuit died in 1641 and was buried with the honors due a man who had established two of the thirteen colonies that later became the United States. Few men have had such an opportunity, and few have carried it off as well.

Minuit's second successor was Johan Printz, a Swedish military man of great ability. He built up an army large enough to keep the Dutch at bay for several years and erected outlying forts, one in western New Jersey and one upriver near where Philadelphia now stands. A party of convicts was sent over from Sweden to aid in building fortifications and, unlike those who went to many another foreign land under duress, became good citizens.

A foreboding of trouble came when Peter Stuyvesant, annoyed at the Swedish "invasion" of what he believed was Dutch territory, ordered construction of Fort Casimir at Newcastle, not many miles south of Fort Christina. Yet the two small settlements got along well enough until Printz sailed for home. The commander who took over, Johann Rysingh, immediately sent men to seize the Dutch fort.

This was too much for the Dutch government to swallow. Word went to Stuyvesant in New Amsterdam to recapture the fort and make good Holland's claim to all of the land nearby. While the peg-legged governor prepared for action, a group of Connecticut colonists from New Haven, seeking to establish a new home on the Delaware, were driven off by the Swedish militia, and another group of Englishmen, under Sir Edward Plowden, sailed into the bay but were quickly convinced that here was no place for an English colony.

The end of New Sweden came in 1655. Stuyvesant, at the head of a force of seven hundred Dutch soldiers, easily recaptured Fort Casimir and then seized Fort Christina without bloodshed. There were almost as many Dutchmen in Stuyvesant's army as there were Swedes and Finns in all of North America.

Whatever personal gratification Stuyvesant acquired by his easy victory was offset by its expense. He should have been at home in New Amsterdam building up the fortifications there and training his men to oppose the might of England. The New Sweden expedition drained the resources of New Netherland, and Colonel Nicolls had little trouble capturing the colony.

A new flag went up on the battlements at Fort Christina, but there was little else to show a change in ownership. Some Swedes went home, others drifted into Maryland, but most elected to remain. It was all a headache for the Dutch West India Company. Seeking to cut its losses, it sold the colony to the city of Amsterdam, retaining the land on both sides of the fort. The burgomasters of Amsterdam renamed the fort New Amstel and inveigled William Beekman, of New Amsterdam, into serving as governor. Illness, hatred between Swedes and Dutchmen, a poor harvest, and a general malaise weakened the little settlement. About this time—the year was 1659—the Puritan newcomers in Maryland decided it would be a good chance to annex all the land on the west shore of the Delaware, which seemed to them to lie within the confines of Lord Baltimore's original Maryland charter.

Led by Colonel Nathaniel Utie, a delegation of rather down-at-the-heels Marylanders appeared outside the walls of Fort Christina, or as the Dutch called it, New Amstel, and demanded its surrender. Beekman knew he had less than a dozen men under arms, but he was no coward and he must have had a tongue of silver. He chatted with the party of Marylanders, behaved as if he had unnumbered legions behind him, and finally talked Utie into leaving empty-handed. A shaky peace followed, and as the Maryland proprietors showed little interest in the area, New Amstel fell on dull days until the English finally ran the Dutchmen off the mainland of North America.

When, several decades later, William Penn established his colony on the Delaware, he discovered more than a thousand colonists scattered along the west bank of the river, more than half of them Swedes and Finns. Industrious, honest, and deeply religious, they found a brighter future as members of Penn's successful colony.

VI

"Here Wants Nothing But People"

DURING THE YEARS when New England, New York, and Virginia were developing into deeply rooted, flourishing colonies, the land between the latter two provinces developed almost by sufferance, almost as an afterthought. Nowhere was this more true than in New Jersey.

From the earliest days of exploration seafarers had shown little interest in this region bordered by the Atlantic Ocean and the Hudson and Delaware rivers. Attention was always focused elsewhere. To the north, Manhattan Island and its surrounding waters made that area such a wonderful harbor that the New Jersey coast played second fiddle. To the south the early settlements arose in Delaware, across from the New Jersey littoral on the eastern shore of Delaware Bay. To the colonists of Virginia and New York, the area between the two rivers was a bothersome barrier. It wasn't until land travel became more important that this corridor territory really came into its own.

Michael de Paauw, as noted before, grabbed a large slice of New Jersey when forming his patroonship based on Staten Island. He started a small outpost called Pavonia, a Latinized version of his last name, which means "peacock." The French later called it the Commune de Paauw, which deteriorated into the present name, Communipaw. Another settlement by the Dutch was made across the Hudson from New Amsterdam at a place the Indians knew well because the ledges of soft rock there provided the base for their hand-tooled pipes. They called it Hobocan, after the name of their stone tobacco pipes. Today's geographies list it as Hoboken. Little by little the Dutch spread out until they had farms or small villages where Bayonne, Jersey City, and Hackensack are now. For years they went no farther because the mosquitoes in the salt marshes beyond the southernmost reach of the Palisades were too formidable an obstacle.

There was also some small activity down at the southern end of the region. Captain Cornelis May, who had founded New Amsterdam on Manhattan Island, also laid claim to most of southern New Jersey. He gave his name to Cape May at the northern entrance to Delaware Bay, and to Cape Cornelis, guarding the southern entrance, which later became Cape Henlopen. Samuel Godyn and Samuel Blommaert, the land-hungry patroons who staked a claim to most of the territory where New Sweden was established, also laid claim to much of the land near Cape May.

When Governor Nicolls seized New Netherland from the Dutch in 1664 he found these scattered settlements on the shoreline of New Jersey but little development elsewhere. The Indians and the mosquitoes had done an excellent job of keeping settlers out of the interior.

The Duke of York, to whom Charles II had granted the land the Dutch had colonized, was also the Duke of Albany. Colonel Nicolls honored his sponsor by naming one part of the area New York. What we know as New Jersey he called Albania, in another gesture honoring the king's brother.

Nicolls did his best to rule well. Although his main concern was with New York, he set out to develop Albania and sent agents throughout New York City, the Hudson Valley, Long Island, and even into Connecticut, offering land to settlers. Then he laid out new towns. Dutch farmers whose soil had disappointed them, Puritan dissenters from New England, and Connecticut whalers and fishermen listened to the siren call and moved to New Jersey. Soon there was a village, made up mostly of New Englanders but with a sprinkling of other groups, approximately where Elizabethport stands today. They bought the land from the Indians and set up a government much like those in Connecticut. Nicolls supported and encouraged them.

But neither Nicolls nor the settlers realized what a scoundrel the Duke of York was. The governor was astounded to learn that all the nice things he had done for the king's brother, naming the colo-

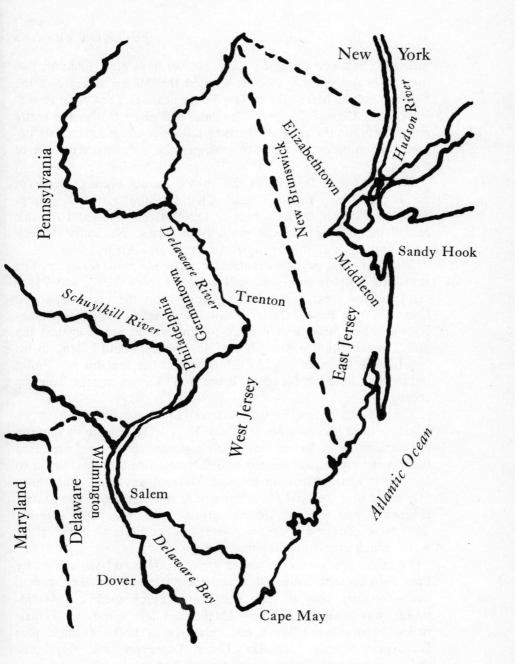

Middle Colonies

nies after him and the like, might as well have gone undone: two months before Colonel Nicolls wrested the colony away from the Dutch the duke had sold the New Jersey grant to Lord John Berkeley and Sir George Carteret. The duke had given title to the entire region between the ocean and the Delaware south of latitude 41 degrees, 40 minutes, to the two noblemen for a "competent sum of money."

Carteret was a favorite of the duke's, having been governor of the Isle of Jersey in the English Channel—the last royal stronghold to surrender to the forces of Oliver Cromwell—and for this reason the duke called the grant New Jersey. Naturally, Nicolls knew nothing of all this when he named the area Albania.

The two royal proprietors decided to divide New Jersey. A line stretching roughly from where New Jersey, New York, and Pennsylvania now meet to Little Egg Harbor on the coast separated East and West Jersey. Carteret took the eastern section and Berkeley the other. Nicolls went back to England to argue against the grant, but the king was stubborn: New Jersey would belong to his two friends. Carteret stayed on in England but sent his son Philip out to New Jersey in his place. It was good fortune for the fledgling colony.

Legend has it that Philip Carteret landed on the shore of his colony with a hoe over his shoulder. He seemed sincere in wanting the settlements to thrive, invited all residents to stay on, promised them a representative, elected assembly and freedom of religion so long as it was a Christian religion. He said any man could have fifty acres in a freehold for a one-penny rent per acre. The Dutch, Huguenot, and Walloon settlers agreed to the terms with alacrity. The New England Puritans were less enthusiastic, but there wasn't much they could do but accept.

In swift sequence other towns grew up. Newark was settled by Puritans who took issue with Connecticut's liberalism; they wanted the vote given only to men who were church members. Woodbridge was built up by New Englanders less arbitrary in their beliefs, and other villages had mixtures of both of these plus Huguenots, French Catholics, Dutch Lutherans, and Anglicans. Quakers, despised almost everywhere in Europe and in the American colonies, laid out the town of Shrewsbury—probably the first town in the world where they had the upper hand. The stiff-necked Puritans would have sent the Quakers packing, but Philip Carteret was not a man to forget his promise of toleration toward all Christians.

Carteret had a son, James, who was everything the father wasn't; in short, he was a scoundrel. While the governor was away from Elizabeth Town on business, James stopped by on his way to take up proprietary duties in the Carolinas and played the role of governor for a while. He sided with noisy residents who had refused to pay their penny-an-acre rent, disrupted the colony, and forced his father to go into hiding for a time. Finally the king and the assembly cracked down, and James took a ship for Carolina. It led to one of the oddest historical events in the history of Dutch colonialism in America.

James Carteret's ship had barely reached deep water when it was captured by a large Dutch war fleet. One of his companions, ingratiating himself with the Dutch, revealed that the English defenses in all New York were barely worthy of the name. The Dutch squadron, with young Captain Carteret's friend going along as hostage and observer, sailed into New York harbor and took both New York and New Jersey away from the English—but only for a short time.

Old John Berkeley had stayed in England when his partner's son left for New Jersey. As reports of disunity, tax strikes, and other troubles in East Jersey drifted back he grew less and less eager to go across the ocean to rule his own province. In 1674 the Society of Friends, as the Quakers usually referred to themselves, bought Berkeley's title to West Jersey for £1,000. John Fenwick organized a small expedition to the banks of the Delaware and called the site Salem. Later Burlington was established as the capital, and other small settlements sprang up between the two towns.

Notwithstanding friction with the king and all the disputes over religion and voting rights, both East and West Jersey thrived. Fishing, agriculture, lumbering, and iron mining brought substantial wealth to the colony. Within a few decades hides and meat from New Jersey were going to Barbados and Europe, its tobacco was a prime provider of credit in England, and its salt fish was being sold in many foreign ports. Between the Quakers and Governor Carteret, relations with the Indians had been handled so fairly and humanely that there was little difficulty. The Indian wars that tortured New England, New York, and Virginia left the two Jerseys unscathed.

When the Dutch were kicked out of New York the second time the Duke of York sent over Major Edmund Andros as royal governor. Andros was typical of the very worst sort of English military man who puts aside his sword to pick up pen and scepter. He was stubborn, arrogant, and greedy for both personal wealth and power. The two Jersey provinces soon discovered that they were not beyond Andros' reach. The New York governor won permission from the duke to intervene in New Jersey affairs, both commercial and governmental. The people of East Jersey rallied behind Carteret, but this did not deter Andros. He sent a party of soldiers to Elizabeth Town under cover of night; the governor was routed out of bed in his nightclothes and taken by boat to New York. With insufficient covering he was exposed to the weather and his health permanently damaged.

Andros had his eye on the commerce of New Jersey as well as the prestige that would go with ruling it. He faked charges against Carteret and sat as special judge himself, but the jury would not find for him. Carteret went home to recover, and Andros appealed to the king. By now it was but a tempest in a teapot. While the bickering had gone on, old Sir George Carteret had sold East Jersey for £3,400 to an organization made up mainly of Quakers and Presbyterians. Then he died, at peace with his world.

A number of the directors and officials of the group that purchased East Jersey were Scots Presbyterians. They of course sought to make a handsome profit out of the thriving industry and commerce of the region, but they were also determined to make the colony a place of refuge for fugitives from religious persecution.

The Presbyterians thought Elizabeth Town a little too close to New York and Andros for a capital. A site at the mouth of the Raritan River, just opposite the lower tip of Staten Island, seemed to offer added distance as well as a good location for shipping, so a new capital, Perth Amboy, was established there. In no time at all residents were proudly boasting that as many as forty vessels could be seen loading and unloading cargo at one time.

Gaven Laurie was named deputy governor. His chief pleasure seemed to lie in luring more settlers to his paradise of East Jersey. From these words in a letter he sent back to Scotland there is no mistaking the governor's pride in the new capital:

Now is the time to send over people for settling here . . . Here wants nothing but people. There is not a poor body in all the province, nor that wants; Here is abundance of provision Pork and Beef at 2d. per pound. Fish and Fowl plenty. Oysters I think would serve all England. Sider good and plenty for ld. per Quart. Good Venison, plenty brought us (by Indians) at 18d. the quarter, eggs at 3d. the dozen, all things very plenty. Land very good as ever I saw. Wines (grape and berry vines) walnuts, peaches, Strawberries, and many other things plenty in the woods. Nor is this all. We have good brick earth and stone for building at Amboy and elsewhere.

The Quakers in West Jersey were blessed with a constitution of sorts called the Fundamental Laws. Under these edicts it was provided that the assembly was to be chosen "not by the confused way of cries and voices, but by the ballot box." Any man in the colony could be elected for membership, no man could be imprisoned for debt, and every person was guaranteed freedom from oppression and slavery.

When Queen Anne mounted the throne in 1702, the two Jerseys were combined into a single royal colony with a governing council. Considering the commercial rivalry, it worked well, with the council meeting alternately in Burlington and Perth Amboy or Elizabeth Town.

The queen appointed a royal governor, Lord Cornbury, who thought New Jersey could help him line his purse. Making a deal with the Royal African Company, he imported a large number of slaves. The Quakers and Presbyterians remonstrated manfully— but when profits are at stake good intentions often go out the window. Most of the well-to-do families soon had Negro servants, and some farms used them in the fields. The high-sounding Fundamental Laws which had forbidden human oppression gathered dust on the shelves.

As the years went by the province thrived, despite royal concern that a spirit of insubordination was spreading daily. Jerseymen found ways to avoid direct confrontation with the royal governor, and life was not too unpleasant. In 1740 various churches founded the College of New Jersey, now Princeton University, as a place to educate young men for the ministry.

Of the many governors who ruled New Jersey at this time none worked harder or more earnestly than Benjamin Franklin's son, William, who gathered about him devoted and able administrators. Unfortunately, he was a Tory and when the final rupture with the mother country came, he turned his back on the patriots, and on his father, one of the greatest of them all.

VII

Lord Baltimore's Pleasant Land

EVEN TO THIS day a resident of Maryland thinks fondly of Lord Baltimore, the colony's founder, and of the *Ark* and the *Dove,* the two ships that brought the first settlers, but very few remember, if they ever knew, that it was loyalty to a lovesick prince that brought such great rewards on the Chesapeake.

A year or so before Charles I ascended the throne he went to Spain, hoping to marry the daughter of that country's rulers. With him went a young man named George Calvert, who did his best to arrange the union. Politics wrecked the plans and Charles went home, but when he became king he remembered his old ally in romance.

In 1623 Calvert was given all of Newfoundland as a reward for his loyalty and, to gild the lily, two years later he was given the title Lord Baltimore. Upon receiving the Newfoundland grant, Lord Baltimore had tried to establish a colony which he called Avalon, but the poor soil, bitter winds, and cold winters brought it to naught. In 1632 the king gave him another piece of North America, in a milder latitude. It was bounded by the Potomac River on the south and the 40th parallel on the north. Within its confines lay the present states of Maryland and Delaware, a southern portion of Pennsylvania, and much of West Virginia.

Although Maryland was set up primarily as a refuge for English Catholics who were being harried by the Anglican lord bishops, it began its existence under extremely favorable conditions. Lord Baltimore's charter was one of the most generous documents ever granted a colonizer. It gave him the power to create courts, set up trade anywhere, appoint judges, coin his own money, and veto any laws enacted by the freemen in their assembly. All he had to do for this was to give the king two Indian arrows every year and a fifth of all gold and silver found in the colony. (It was a bad bargain for the House of Stuart, as no precious metals were found.) The king agreed not to levy any taxes, and Lord Baltimore decreed that although he himself was a Catholic, any Christian would be welcome in Maryland. It was an act of understanding and nobility.

Lord Baltimore did not survive the year. Had he lived longer, he would have been grievously hurt to see the Puritans he welcomed bite the hand that helped them. At his death his son Cecilius Calvert took over the colony. For four of the next five generations the charter remained the law of the land—in fact until the colony became a state—and it was only the last Baltimore heir who ruled unwisely.

On March 25, 1634, the *Ark,* a stout ship of 350 tons, and the *Dove,* a little cockleshell of only 50 tons burden, made landfall on the shore of Chesapeake Bay on a peninsula extending southward between the bay and the Potomac River. Naming their settlement St. Mary's, and paying the Indians in cloth and hatchets for the land they took, the three hundred or so colonists went briskly to work planting crops.

Calvert's adventurers and freemen established an assembly, whose first act was to pass a law guaranteeing religious liberty. To prove that they meant what they said, they invited the oppressed Puritans of Virginia to move to Maryland. These people settled a town called Providence, on the site of present-day Annapolis.

The royal grants usually gave the various colonies all the land to the Pacific Ocean. They were so broad that there was enough land for everyone, yet no one was satisfied. Friction and border wars existed for decades, even after the colonies had united into a new nation.

So it was in Maryland. Years before the *Ark* and the *Dove* arrived in American waters Virginians had sailed far up the Chesapeake Bay and settled small towns. By 1631 William Claiborne had bought and populated islands near present-day Baltimore and Easton. When Lord Baltimore's colonists arrived at St. Mary's, Claiborne refused to recognize the new charter. Suddenly Virginia and Maryland found themselves at war. Before long, boats were firing at each other, men were being captured and imprisoned, a few were hanged, and at one time the governor of Maryland himself was held hostage by Claiborne's men.

Much of the dissension leading to the Claiborne rebellion reflected the bitterness existing in England between supporters of Oliver Cromwell and Charles II. Finally Parliament decided in favor of Maryland.

If human avarice and hatred had not stood in the wings, the drama of Maryland's growth would have been nearly idyllic. The Jesuit missionaries who had come over with the first settlers influenced both white and red men into living amicably. When Indian wars swept the northern colonies, Maryland remained unharmed. Maryland's soil was rich and its weather equable, and crops flourished from the outset. Tobacco became a money crop that gave the growers credit abroad and considerable affluence at home. The Calverts were a unique family, kind-hearted, believers in an advanced form of equality, considering the era, and more than willing to allow the colonists to enact their own laws. They were lord proprietors, but probably the most fair-minded of all those who guided the early days of any American province.

But the religious question, so bitter in England, gnawed at the colony's vitals. When Cromwell seized power at home the Englishmen in Maryland found themselves with a small civil war on their hands. The fine words of the charter and the religious-freedom law enacted by the assembly were forgotten under the impact of bigotry and Puritanism. A Puritan sea captain, Richard Ingle, triggered a new conflict when he publicly excoriated the king. Calvert's bailiffs seized him and charged him with treason, but later decided it would be better to let him go. It was a mistake. With the aid of the troublesome Claiborne, Captain Ingle led his men ashore, captured St. Mary's, sent the Jesuit missionaries back to England in chains, and forced Calvert and his followers to flee to Virginia. For two years Ingle and Claiborne plundered the colony, while a Puritan element, setting up a government at Providence, handed power to a "Governor" William Fuller. Virginia's leaders found it expedient to fish in the troubled waters of Chesapeake Bay, backing Fuller and arming a small Puritan force.

Lord Baltimore heard of this in England and sent his brother, Philip Calvert, to Maryland in an effort to restore order. The rightful governor, William Stone, at the head of 130 men, marched to overthrow the Puritans at Providence but was ambushed by a force twice as large. The black-and-gold banner of Baltimore went down, Stone was shot four or five times, and when his men came under enfilading fire from two armed merchant ships, the Battle of the Severn was over. A third of Stone's men were dead.

For a time Catholics were deprived of almost every right, often expelled from the colony, and held in contempt by those very persons to whom the first Lord Baltimore had guaranteed equality and protection. Strangely enough, all the Calverts were nearly always championed by the Stuart kings, and it was this that led to ultimate victory for them. Faced with animosity, religious intolerance, even armed rebellion, the Calverts still managed to keep the colony together, helping to heal ideological wounds and building up its strength.

Settlements spread up the peninsula at first, across to the eastern shores and then up the Potomac River. The first Lords Baltimore dreamed of a colonial peerage and, in fact, had been given the right to grant titles and honors, but an aristocracy was somehow unseemly in the new land. Aside from a score or so of "gentlemen adventurers," the earliest colonizers had been several hundred freemen and indentured servants. These last had to agree to work out their passage by laboring for three to five years for those who had put up the money. But once they had freed themselves all they had to do was to shoulder a gun, load a horse with a few tools, and head into the wilderness to make a new life for themselves. An ex-servant with ambition and courage could gain title to fifty acres of rich Maryland land and establish himself as an important member of the community almost overnight. Peers would hardly have been welcome in this land of self-made men.

During the early years the settlers raised only what they needed to survive, but soon they realized that their neighbors, the Virginians, were thriving by raising tobacco. This crop then became a major force in Maryland's economy, remaining so even in the face of European struggles, when many ports were closed to colonial vessels and the plague swept England.

In New England, parts of New Netherland, and Virginia the settlers were never entirely free of concern about the Indians. Even before the bitter conflicts between the French and English and their Indian allies broke out, any isolated settlement lived under constant threat of attack. Yet this was not true during the first decades of colonization of Maryland. Local tribes remained peaceful. Most of them owed a casual allegiance to a fierce tribe known as the Susquehannocks, whose main villages were on the river now

known as the Susquehanna. Whatever it was the Chesapeake Bay
Indians told their brethren to the north, it had a good effect. Perhaps the incident described by a Jesuit, Father White, who landed
with the earliest settlers, proved a restraining force. The chief of
the Patuxent Indians was deeply impressed when guns on board
the English ships were fired. Urging his compatriots not to break
the peace, he said, "When we shoot, our bowstrings give a twang
that's heard but a little way off, but do you not hear what cracks
their bowstrings give?"

Lord Baltimore's colony prospered in spite of its internal differences. Crops turned out well, farm stock multiplied, and fishing
was excellent. The Marylanders had been in the New World but a
short time before they discovered that the eastern shore of the
bay abounded in food. Few areas on the Atlantic seaboard could
equal the district in its plenitude of shellfish, oysters, terrapin,
and untold varieties of ducks.

Lack of currency was a perennial headache in the colony, but
Maryland was better off than its neighbors. Lord Baltimore authorized the coining of shillings, sixpence, and groats, which were
backed by tobacco. Because of the widespread local acceptance of
the currency, many economic worries were averted (although tobacco itself had to serve for many years as the medium of exchange
in international trade).

All in all, Maryland could face the future with considerable assurance of survival. It suffered from the greediness of Charles II,
who tried to forbid local manufacturing and who cavalierly sliced
off that part of Baltimore's lands we now call Delaware and gave it
to his brother the Duke of York. Then, on Virginia's insistence,
a further royal adjustment was made which gave the older colony
rich acreage in both tidewater and upland sections of the original
Maryland patent.

Before history had finished with the colony, it had been squeezed
between the Potomac and a surveyor's line marking the boundary
with William Penn's holdings. Nevertheless, its inhabitants could
boast that of all the colonies established on the North American
coast it was second only to Pennsylvania in providing for the welfare and happiness of the common man.

VIII

Strange Partnership: The Carolinas

THE SETTLEMENT OF North Carolina was begun when Virginians found their boundary with the Carolinas too confining and chose to disregard it. Old records do not agree on the precise date when this spreading out over an imaginary line put Virginians beyond the limits of their own colony. It is likely that within two generations of the founding of Jamestown some ambitious families looked toward the south, circumvented the Great Dismal Swamp, and settled on Carolina soil. Edenton records claim that its first inhabitants arrived in 1658. Other documents indicate that even before this date small clusters of homes went up on the banks of the Chowan River near where it empties into Albemarle Sound. This was the first concerted effort to establish homes in the region where Raleigh's "Lost Colony" had disappeared so long before. The waters of the Chowan empty into the sound, and the waters of the sound find their way into the Atlantic almost exactly where Raleigh's efforts had failed.

As in so many areas where new frontiers called to the ambitious and energetic, this area attracted scoundrels and criminals, and debtors seeking refuge from the bailiffs of Virginia's tidewater villages. But the good outnumbered the bad. Many were seeking the freedom that had proved so elusive in other colonies. The history of early America is studded with breakaway attempts to establish new churches. Just as Roger Williams and Anne Hutchinson quarreled with the Puritans in New England, so did ministers in Virginia differ with the Church of England.

Roger Greene, a tidewater Virginia preacher, obtained a grant
from the Virginia assembly—which was giving away something it
did not own—for a thousand acres on the Chowan River. Taking a
hundred settlers with him, he established a village, but it did not
take root and there are no records to speak of. Soon after, a Quaker,
George Durant, essayed the same task and succeeded at a town
called Durant's Neck.

From the 1660s on there was a sporadic movement into the Albemarle Sound country by ministers with small congregations,
traders, farmers, and fishermen. Once a considerable number of
settlers had established themselves, word spread rapidly and colonists from even more distant areas decided to seek their fortune
here. A group of plantation owners arrived from the West Indies,
soon followed by a number of shipbuilders from Bermuda, who
settled on the sound near the Outer Banks, built their little log huts,
and cut down great pine trees to erect their launching ways.

At first the settlers looked more to Virginia for protection than
to England. Each village set up a local government to meet its own
problems, and life was too rigorous for the villagers to worry about
events in the mother country. Thus they were undoubtedly shocked
to learn that in 1660 Cromwell's Commonwealth had fallen and that
Charles II, with the monarchy restored, had made a gift of all the
land between Virginia and the Spanish settlements in Florida to
eight of his friends, including the Earl of Clarendon; the Duke of
Albemarle, who had been General George Monk and a prime architect of the royalist victory; and the Earl of Shaftesbury, Anthony
Ashley-Cooper.

A hundred years earlier the Huguenots had tried to settle at Port
Royal, naming their colony Carolina in honor of the French king,
Charles. When the English lords received their vast grant they also
chose the name Carolina, honoring their own Charles. Their first
step was to seek colonists. They welcomed settlers from many lands,
promising them not only free land but an opportunity to choose a
representative assembly to aid a proprietary council in governing
the territory.

As royal proprietors went, these men were not too bad, although a
more disparate group of individuals could hardly be found. The
Duke of Albemarle had fought for Cromwell with the Roundheads
and later had fought with the royalist Cavaliers. It was he who
devised the scarlet uniforms made famous by English soldiers

around the globe, never dreaming the redcoats would one day be anathema in his own province.

Another proprietor was Sir William Berkeley, who had been governor of Virginia until chased out by the colonists, and then restored to office. His fellow proprietors gave Berkeley the task of establishing the new government. He carried it out by naming William Drummond of Virginia as his representative. It was a fortunate choice for the settlers. Drummond, a Scot devoted to the rights of the common man, soon saw to it that laws were enacted to ensure freedom of conscience. Tax remissions helped the poor to obtain farms which they could claim after two years of "respectable residence."

There never was a period when Albemarle County could boast of wealth, at least not in colonial days. Hard times cast their shadow over the territory, largely because of apathy and greed.

In 1660 England adopted the notorious Navigation Acts, aimed at protecting home trade from any possible competition in the colonies. Anything produced in the overseas provinces had to be sold to British merchants, who set the prices and handled the distribution. The settlers were caught in a vise: they had to sell their tobacco and other crops for low prices and buy manufactured goods from England at outrageously high prices. The people in Albemarle were in financial straits even before they had planted their second season's crop of tobacco.

Human folly played its role when Virginians used the Chowan River and other tributaries of the Albemarle Sound for disposal of refuse and sewage. Parasites from this effluvia infected most of the families, leaving many lethargic and ill and thus adding to the grinding poverty induced by England's exploitative trade laws. William Byrd, a Virginia planter and diarist, traveled through this backwoods section early in its existence. His description of the rustic settlers reveals something of the depths to which poverty and disease had dragged them:

> The men, for their parts, just like the Indians, impose all the work upon the poor women. They make their wives rise out of their beds early in the morning, at the same time that they lie and snore until the sun has risen one-third of its course, and dispersed all the unwholesome damps. Then after stretching and yawning for half an hour, they light their pipes, and under the protection of a cloud of smoke, venture out into the open air.

Lord Shaftesbury is quoted in old documents as warning his agents in America not to lure too many poor people to Carolina—a switch from the earlier pleas for colonists. What was wanted, said the snobbish proprietor, were families of standing who could hire hands and import slaves, that is, families who could establish a landed gentry. Preserve this lovely land, Shaftesbury wrote, for the "better folk."

There were not too many of these better folk to be found. George Fox, the Quaker preacher, traversed the sand hills and pine forests of North Carolina on a tour of the colonies and left a description of hardships endured by residents and travelers alike. He told of the difficulty walking around the snake-infested bogs of the Great Dismal Swamp, of having to sleep many a night in the open to the accompaniment of cries from bobcats. But Fox found the settlers themselves to be honest, friendly people, willing to share their all. This "all" might be nothing but a rough pallet by the hearth to sleep upon and cornbread and water to eat, but it was given happily. Other travelers went home calling Albemarle "Rogue's Harbor" and a land of treacherous men, but Fox's most harrowing adventure was a near capsizing of his canoe when visiting the governor, Samuel Stephens.

Back in England the proprietors made plans for developing the entire territory as a unit, despite its considerable size. Among these plans was a constitution drafted at the behest of Shaftesbury by John Locke, a very peculiar gentleman who was a physician, a philosopher, and also Shaftesbury's private secretary. As with so many events of long ago, there is no documentation to prove that this "Fundamental Constitution" actually existed. Some writers say Locke did draw it up, others doubt it. But there must have been some fire under all the smoke, for there was much talk about it in the colony, as though somewhere in England there was in fact such a document.

The "Fundamental Constitution" was said to be a remnant of the feudal era. Under its terms, real or imagined, four groups of men —called proprietors, landgraves, caziques, and lords of manors— would retain all rights and privileges. The common man was to be a "leet man," which was not much better than a serf. The year 1667 is the one most often given for the writing of this strange document. Perhaps it is wiser to eschew debate over its authenticity and to remember that by 1670 there was an assembly in session in the colony, with power to appoint officials, establish courts of law, and maintain military forces necessary for the defense of the settlers.

That same year two ships entered a fine harbor down the coast and the passengers settled on a point of land where two rivers meet before emptying into the Atlantic. The rivers, quite understandably, were christened the Ashley and the Cooper, after Shaftesbury's family name. The settlement was given the name Charles Town (later Charleston). Residents of the area thus opened up came mainly from England, with a sprinkling from the West Indies. Their interests differed from those of the people in Albemarle County, partly because of origin, but mainly because the land, climate, and character of this tidewater area bore few resemblances to that of the sandy, pine-covered county to the north.

One after another, men carrying the title of governor or deputy proprietor arrived in Albemarle, sent there to collect taxes and to represent the king. They were incompetents, rascals, or drunkards for the most part. Virtual anarchy became the way of life around Albemarle and Pamlico sounds. The erstwhile Virginians wanted nothing to do with officials, whose sole interest, they believed, was in bleeding them of their earnings. Nor did they want any traffic with the planters, who soon established a more profitable life on the plantations back of Charleston.

One of the officials was Thomas Miller, a customs officer. Whatever malefactions he planned came to naught, however, because local characters, finding him intoxicated most of the time, assumed his privileges and pocketed the monies that should have gone to the Crown. Another unscrupulous overlord was James Carteret, son of the esteemed proprietor of East Jersey. Having abused his father and dealt traitorously with the Dutch admiral who recaptured New York, young Carteret arrived at Albemarle looking to feather his nest, but the corruption there was too much even for him. He resigned after two years, leaving the colony in worse shape than before he took over.

It must not be assumed that all the Carolina settlers were rogues and tax evaders, although there were enough of these to spare. Most of the people were imbued with an independent spirit and a distaste for bungling government imposed by selfish men. A rebellious feeling was coming to the surface—a feeling that would ultimately lead to the struggle for independence.

Despite Shaftesbury's avowed dislike for Catholics, no restrictions were raised against them, or any other sect. As a result settlers came in from many places. Some arrived from England, some from the islands of the Caribbean, and some, disenchanted with conditions in older colonies, sought a new life in this young one. One ship, the *Phoenix,* carried scores of families—among them Swiss, Scots, French, Irish, and English—from New York to settle the town of Jamestown. These were industrious people, but despite their back-breaking labor, the soil yielded meager crops.

To the south, at Charleston, another labor force came into being when in 1672 a ship loaded with African slaves sailed into port. From that day slave labor was used to work the large plantations and a much different society emerged from that in the northern part of Carolina.

For the first forty or fifty years of its existence, the Albemarle and Pamlico regions of Carolina must surely have been the poorest in all the English colonies. Farmers raised enough for their own sustenance but little more. They added to their fare by hunting the abundant game, and they did a little trapping and trading with the Indians for pelts, which provided them with ready cash. Tobacco was grown by most families, but because of the English tax of a penny a pound most settlers tried to sell their crop in Virginia or to sea captains who carried on illicit trade between the colonies and the West Indies. A few customs officials permitted the settlers to pay their taxes in tobacco, furs, and corn, using it to pay officials in kind, but others demanded taxes be paid in currency. This was a ridiculous order, as there were neither coins nor paper money, the proprietors having failed to send any out to the new colony.

While near anarchy reigned along the tidal flats near the Atlantic, another migration of settlers brought new blood into the uplands known as the Piedmont. These people were, in the main, Germans, Scots, and Irish from the north of Ireland. This migration was an unusual one; it was made on foot and had little to do with any fresh influx from Europe.

It is hard to believe that back in the seventeenth and early eighteenth centuries people were already finding the settlements along the sea too crowded for their liking. But the Scottish and Irish yeomen in particular wanted more space in which to farm and hunt. Some had forged their way into Indian country west of New York, New Jersey, and Maryland. Then, hearing that the plateaus of

Carolina would yield better crops, they started working their way south through the Shenandoah Valley, the western reaches of the James, and into the sand-hill country of northern Carolina.

These were self-reliant, independent men and women. They had no affection for aristocracy and little more for the landed gentry who were raising cotton, indigo, and wine grapes down on the tidewater. They lived on amicable terms with the Indians when they could. When they couldn't, they relied upon their uncanny marksmanship with the long rifle.

Restless, convinced from their own interpretation of the Bible that they had every right to slay the heathen and take his property, they moved almost at will through the wilderness. The Ulster Scots were particularly fearless and took with them a weapon that was to win the frontier for the whites and later win them independence: the long-barreled rifle. This gun, heavy and awkward by today's standards, was a precision weapon. With practice, a man could shoot the head off a turkey or "bark" a squirrel so as not to spoil the meat for the table. This accuracy enabled the settlers to survive even when outnumbered by Indians. The gun was designed and improved over the years by German gunsmiths in Pennsylvania, but it first made a name for itself in the hands of the Irish, Scottish, and Yankee frontiersmen.

Confusion, knavery, tax evasion, oppression of the poor—all these existed in northern Carolina during its early decades. With the arrogance and disregard of the proprietors and the greed and inefficiency of their agents, it could hardly have been otherwise.

There is no need to name all the men who were sworn to govern the people and lead them toward the prosperous society mentioned in almost every charter or constitution. But a few stand out. Thomas Eastchurch spent two years of his governorship on the island of Nevis in the West Indies, courting a Creole beauty with whom he had fallen in love on an earlier voyage. There was no particular evil in his nature, just a complete indifference about his duties. The men England chose to hold office in the colonies seemed, in the main, to be totally irresponsible. While a few were blatantly corrupt, most of them were simply arrogant, incompetent, amoral men who had no realization that they were playing a major role in one of the great social adventures of all time.

John Culpepper was of another stripe. He preached sedition, favored the common man, and was admired for upholding popular liberties. He nearly was undone by the drunken former governor, Miller, but Shaftesbury, risen to great power as lord chancellor, sided with Culpepper against the man who had looted the royal treasury of much of its rightful revenue.

Seth Sothel, en route to govern the Albemarle counties, was captured by Barbary pirates and held in a dungeon for two years. It must have been an embittering experience. For five years he ruled with an iron hand. He squeezed every penny he could get from the inhabitants, throwing debtors into jail, stealing land, and robbing anyone luckless enough to fall into his clutches. For a time the settlers endured his rapacity. Then they rose in wrath and said they would send him back to England. Sothel must have known what fate awaited him there, for, bawling like a baby, he pleaded to be tried by the provincial courts. He was tried, found guilty on all counts, and exiled from the colony.

While the northern region was being torn asunder by all this turmoil and dissension, the plantations around Charleston fared much better. A constitution gave the people the right not only to elect members of a house of representatives but also to nominate half of the council members. This was not a full loaf by any means, because so many powers were held by the governors, but it was better than no loaf.

Much of the trouble in the lowlands was generated by the people themselves. An influx of additional settlers had arrived from Antigua, Nevis, and Barbados—Carolina Englishmen who had migrated to the islands and then found themselves unhappy about the frequent hurricanes. Seeking better weather, they moved again to Charleston. In the West Indies they had to become accustomed to using Negro slaves, and while some slaves were already on the American mainland, more field hands were needed to cultivate rice, a new crop that had recently been introduced from Madagascar. Looking for cheap labor, some of the plantation owners tried to force Indians to till the soil but the natives refused. Occasional skirmishes between greedy white men and Indians smart enough to realize what serfdom could mean kept the lowlands in a state of unease.

In the end, however, it was the very nature of the soil and climate around Charleston that led to the difficulties that were ultimately to result in civil war. The planters found that almost any crop would grow, and grow well. As one historian said, lower

Carolina was a vast botanical garden. Indigo and rice grew abundantly in the marshy land along the coast. Later, cotton took a preeminent position as the major crop. Unfortunately, before technology altered everything, these crops required a large supply of cheap labor. As the Indians refused such degradation, more and more blacks from Africa's west coast were brought into the colony. It was a temporary solution to a pressing problem, and no one then sensed that it would create a much more serious problem in the future.

As the people in Albemarle and Pamlico became more militantly independent and as settlers in the low country became more prosperous, they pressured the proprietors into permitting greater home rule. At the same time the various names for the two sections of the colony were changed once and for all. The proprietors selected the obvious: from about the last decade of the seventeenth century they became known as North Carolina and South Carolina, and in 1729 the division was made official.

New Jersey had started its colonial existence as two separate entities. Under the stress of political necessity and religious influence, it became one colony. Carolina started out as one province, but the differences in soil and climate, plus the different origins of the settlers themselves, produced a disunity that could end only in one way: the colony split up and became two.

Just a few years before the division became official the white men of both sections showed how hopeless was the cause of the Indian in his own domain. It wasn't the first time that natives had learned how futile it was to stand in the way of European expansion, but it was the most dramatic. The stage was set along the shores of Pamlico Sound when French Huguenots, Swiss Protestants, and German Palatines settled near the mouth of the Neuse River. Establishing the village of New Bern, they soon discovered that they had chosen for their new home an area long held sacred as a hunting preserve by the Tuscarora Indians. Baron de Graffenreid, leader of the Germans, and John Lawson, a Scottish surveyor, tried to work out a solution, but the Indians saw no need for compromise: it was their land and they wanted it left a virgin wilderness. In 1711 the tribe seized Lawson and burned him at the stake. Later they held the baron captive for more than a month while a war party attacked New Bern and murdered hundreds of colonists.

The scattered residents of North Carolina could hardly hope to seek vengeance alone. Virginia's assembly turned its back on their plea for help, voting not to send troops, but South Carolina responded valiantly. Colonel John Barnwell, with a small force of militiamen and hundreds of Indian allies, marched swiftly northward to punish the Tuscaroras. The Indians in Barnwell's party were Creeks, Catawbas, Yamasees, and Muskogees—all bitter enemies of the Tuscaroras.

Fighting their way for 250 miles through a winter storm of unusual severity, Barnwell and his men fell upon the Tuscaroras upriver from the gutted settlement of New Bern, defeating them with horrible losses. The chief signed a peace treaty to save the remnants of his band.

If the militia had been alone the war might have ended there, but their Indian allies had tasted victory and wanted more. They attacked several Tuscarora villages on the way south, putting them all to the torch. Rising to this challenge, the Tuscaroras began a guerrilla war that cost the lives of scores of white settlers. Other colonists fled to Virginia for safety. In the midst of their travail an epidemic of yellow fever swept through the colony, killing the governor and hundreds of others. It seemed doubtful that the upper reaches of the colony could survive this double tragedy, but again South Carolinians came to the rescue.

Colonel James Moore, with fifty white soldiers and a thousand Indians, invaded the Tuscarora strongholds, captured six hundred braves, many of whom were sold in the Charleston slave market, and forced the remainder to flee. Months later, after a tragic march through the Appalachian Mountains clear to western New York, the survivors of the once powerful Tuscarora tribe found refuge on Lake Oneida. The Five Nations of the Iroquois met in the longhouse of the Onondagas, debated the issue for days, and finally invited the Tuscarora refugees to join them. So the Five Nations became the Six Nations, and irony piled on irony when the Iroquois Confederacy chose to side with the English in the long wars with the French.

Hardly had the North Carolinians recovered from the twin blows of Indian uprising and yellow fever than they became the victims of pirates and buccaneers, who found the many inlets behind the Outer Banks a fine place to hide after their forays. Although some of the Albemarle Sound people found it profitable to traffic with the freebooters, most of them were robbed and forced to supply the pirate ships.

Onto this scene came Charles Eden, appointed governor by the remaining proprietors. Eden was the best man ever to hold that post under royal assignment. He set up office in the little hamlet of Edenton, which took its name from his, although it boasted only fifty cabins and no place of worship. Eden cooperated with the royal navy, seeking to wipe out the buccaneers. So effective was the effort that Blackbeard himself, most notorious of the pirates, sailed in to call on the governor and ask for a pardon from the new king, George I. Blackbeard, whose real name was either Teach or Drummond, depending upon which records are believed, lived in Edenton for a time with his fourteenth wife—the very model of a good citizen. But once a buccaneer always a buccaneer. Either tiring of his latest light-o'-love or finding the respectable life distasteful, he prepared his ship for sea again.

Governor Eden was no fool. He sent a courier to Governor Alexander Spotswood of Virginia asking for help, and two royal navy armed sloops under a Lieutenant Maynard sailed into Pamlico Sound just as Blackbeard started raising canvas. There was a bloody fight, and when it ended Maynard sailed back to Virginia with Blackbeard's head swinging from the bowsprit. Many a colonist, particularly the traders and shipowners, breathed a sigh of relief.

When Eden died, North Carolina fell on evil days again. George I, being both greedy and overbearing, bought back the rights to the colony from the proprietors, paying them about £50,000. All but George Carteret, still at Albemarle, were happy to get this cash, as earnings from the settlers had been meager or wanting entirely. Carteret took a slice of territory in the far south as his quit-claim, and North Carolina became a Crown colony. But its troubles were far from over.

IX

Carolina Routs Its Enemies

FAR ACROSS THE Atlantic, the lord proprietors of the Carolinas decided that more control was needed to keep their colonies from total fragmentation. In 1679, to further this end, they ordered that Charleston be made the capital of the southern province.

Surveyors went to work to fashion a settlement worthy of its position, laying out streets that were broader than those in most colonial towns. Property rights were adjusted so that a planter with a large plantation in the back country was entitled to a town holding in proportion to his agricultural establishment. It was a case of the rich getting richer, but no one raised strenuous objection.

New appeals for colonists went out and lured many French Huguenots who had found themselves unwelcome in the French Catholic colonies in Canada. Anywhere the Huguenots went, that place benefited by their industry and loyalty to their new home. Attempts were made to produce the commodities with which they were familiar—oil, wine, and silk—but within a few years they found it more profitable to turn to raising indigo, rice, and cotton.

A succession of governors, most of them inefficient or venal, discovered that their regulations were flouted by settlers, that the New World was engendering a strong spirit of liberty. Joseph West was the best of the early governors, but even he permitted the colonists to oppress the Indians. White men cheated the natives in every trading venture, stole and abused their women, and sold untold numbers of men into slavery in the West Indies, where most of them died before acclimating themselves.

By now Negro slaves from Africa were arriving by the boatload, some seized directly on the Gulf of Guinea and others supplied by the slavers of Barbados. When West was removed because of his disregard for the rights of Indians, worse men followed on his heels until Joseph Archdale, one of the proprietors, who was a Quaker, arrived to restore order. He and his nephew Joseph Blake, who followed him, exerted a beneficial influence on the colony, increasing the revenues sent back to the proprietors, instituting reforms, and improving the conditions under which the Indians lived. These two Quakers showed what fair-minded, honest men in high office could do to better the lot of virtually all those in the colony. Standing debts were checked to see if they were fair and legal, grievances were heard openly, and a new council was selected by the people voted into office.

Although devoted to nonviolence themselves, these men of the Quaker faith realized the menace implicit in the Spanish colony in Florida and built up South Carolina's defenses. As one historian noted, Archdale "exempted those of his own faith from military service, provided they could show that they objected to it from conviction, and not from cowardice." The danger from the Spaniards was not exaggerated. Soldiers from Florida intruded openly into the territory claimed by the English, seized vessels sailing from southern ports, and bribed the Indians to attack outlying settlements. In 1680 a Spanish force drove a group of Scots Presbyterians out of Port Royal.

The Carolinians decided that if England would not supply troops or a fleet to protect them, they would take on the task themselves. When the War of the Spanish Succession broke out in 1701, they decided the time had come. Colonel James Moore, whose swift intervention later drove the Tuscaroras out of North Carolina, led five hundred white men and a large number of Indian allies into Florida and captured the area around St. Augustine. Without siege guns, and open to attack from the sea, he was unable to capture the fort itself, however, even after three months.

Several years later Moore headed another force, which laid waste a large area west of St. Augustine. This was too much for the Spaniards. Two years later a fleet of ten men-of-war, some Spanish and some French from Martinique, with eight hundred troops on board, sailed into Charleston Harbor and launched a combined land and sea assault. There were hardly that many able-bodied men

in the town, as a tragic outbreak of yellow fever was raging in the
lowlands, but Sir Nathaniel Johnstone mustered what militiamen
and volunteers he could find and whipped the enemy decisively.

Governor Blake was also responsible for reducing another problem: the pirates who made the Carolina coast a refuge after their
forays at sea. For decades the buccaneers had made themselves at
home on the streets of Charleston, often robbing legitimate business houses and forcing shipbuilders to repair their ships. It wasn't
all one-sided, as there was a sizable element among the merchants
who found it to their advantage to deal in the goods brought in by
the freebooters.

All this was distasteful to Blake's Quaker sensibilities. It also
ran against the grain of many of the Presbyterians, Huguenots, and
other God-fearing settlers in the colony. Blake moved quickly, held
trials, and hanged some of the worst of the pirates on the parade
ground overlooking the channel to the sea. Their comrades decided
other ports were healthier, and Charleston entered a more peaceful
era.

People whose rulers leave them to their own resources in a time
of peril cannot be expected to maintain allegiance to those rulers.
The Carolinians, both north and south, realized that they had a
strength of their own, that if they could govern themselves when
the enemy threatened their outposts, they could govern themselves
in the everyday affairs of life. This was no spirit of truculence, nor
was it yet a full-blown desire for independence. It was simply a sign
that the people wanted to manage their own destinies.

The Scots-Irish and Germans who lived in the Piedmont were a
yeasty people, and felt little kinship with the traders and plantation owners in the tidewater region, and even less with a monarch
thousands of miles away. The French Huguenots, on the other hand,
found easy acceptance in South Carolina society, and contributed
great strength to the communities where they settled. They were
artisans, builders, blacksmiths, leather workers, weavers, shipwrights, wheelwrights, druggists, and coopers. By the second and
third generations many of them were among the most prominent
members of the colony.

Another group of Frenchmen did not fare so well. These were
the Acadians, driven out of Nova Scotia by the English, who feared
their proximity to the New England colonies. The English troops
dumped six thousand Acadians at various port cities along the

coast of North America. Of these more than a thousand were put off at Charleston, without homes, without jobs, and with little hope. They were Catholics, and hated for it by the Carolinians. Some stayed on as indentured servants, but most found it advisable to drift away. Many found their way into the Spanish colonies in Florida, and others headed westward to where the French were building up their line of outposts along the Mississippi.

In 1707 the Act of Union united Scotland and England, and many a Scot left his homeland rather than pay homage to an English king. Most of them migrated to the American colonies and, filtering rather swiftly through the seacoast towns, settled on the frontier. The Ulster Scot from Northern Ireland was more restless, less easy to deal with, and less gifted in the arts of trade and commerce than his mainland counterpart. The Scots who migrated from Scotland admired learning and culture and provided the new country with many of its teachers and not a few of its preachers. A few of the latter stayed on in the seaports and quickly became known for their acumen in the handling of international trade.

As Charleston grew into a thriving port and the plantations expanded upriver, the South Carolinians began to extend their trade westward, seeking furs for the European markets. Incredible distances were covered by traders working out of Charleston and Port Royal. Their trails led them up beyond the Piedmont, into the rugged ranges of the Smoky Mountains, and down the other side of the Appalachian massif clear to Indian towns on the lower Mississippi.

Some of these routes were more than a thousand miles long, yet so valuable was the traffic in pelts that hundreds of men made the trek. At first the Indians were friendly. The Yamasees, in particular, befriended the whites, and it was this tribe, more than any other, that had driven the Tuscaroras out of the Carolinas. But even their patience wore thin as the whites took advantage of them in trade and settled on more of their land. In the winter of 1714–15 the Yamasee chiefs and their Indian neighbors discussed war.

In the early spring of 1715 native runners hurried over the trails carrying their "bloody stick," symbolizing an uprising, and calling upon the other tribes to join in wiping out the whites. Most of the Creeks, some Cherokees, and other scattered tribes, reaching from the Outer Banks of North Carolina to the frontier with Florida, voted in their councils to ally themselves with the Yamasees.

As South Carolinians went to their Good Friday services in village and frontier settlements, the Indians swooped down upon them from the forests. Three villages were the main targets, and when the massacres were over, more than two hundred whites had perished. It was only the beginning.

Down from the mountains, out of the cypress swamps and savannahs poured the aroused Indians, until at least ten thousand were on the warpath. Colonists were killed in their sleep and in the fields. Those who could escape fled to the larger towns, and for a time even the capital was not sure it could defend itself.

As terror stalked the frontier and the lowland plantation country, Governor Charles Craven sent to the other colonies for aid. Slaves were armed, often against their owners' better judgment, but the crisis was so terrifying that old rules were forgotten. New York sent money and guns and ammunition. Virginia sent a company of militia, and from the sparsely colonized reaches of North Carolina came long-legged, keen-eyed riflemen who were experienced Indian fighters.

An encircling movement drove the Indians toward Port Royal, and in a fierce battle outside of town they were beaten badly. The survivors were driven clear to the border of Florida, where they found refuge with the Spaniards.

One can only imagine the rancor with which the colonists reacted when they learned that the proprietors—although they had not lifted a hand or sent a shilling to help fight the Indians—intended to claim all the Indian lands taken over by South Carolinians. These Yamasee preserves seemed only fair payment for the bloodshed and terror caused by the uprising, and the colonists could see no reason why the lands should revert to the absentee proprietors.

As their ire rose over what they considered unmitigated greed, new pirate attacks on shipping—even a threat on Charleston itself—led to a fresh mustering of troops. Some buccaneers demanded ransom for crews of captured ships. It was paid, but Captain William Rhett—that name would echo on the silver screen more than two centuries later, as Rhett Butler in *Gone with the Wind*—went after the pirates with a company of militia. The infamous Stede Bonnett and his lieutenants were captured and hanged at Execution Dock.

This proprietary, one-way government—with the profits going

to London but no help coming to South Carolina—could hardly survive in the face of the colonists' anger. In 1719 the local parliament petitioned the governor to cease representing the proprietors and rule for the king alone. When he refused, the colonists named that old war horse, Colonel Moore, as governor in his stead, and an emissary was sent to London to offer allegiance to George I. The king saw how things were, rescinded the proprietors' charter, and sent over a new governor. South Carolina, like her sister to the north, became a royal colony.

It is interesting to note just what the colony was like at the time. It spread over an area that ran from Cape Fear to beyond present-day Savannah, Georgia, and although it was supposed to extend to the Pacific, it was, in fact, hemmed in by the Appalachian Mountains and, beyond that barrier, by the French forts on the Mississippi. Within its vast boundaries lived fewer than seven thousand white and more than ten thousand blacks in addition to the Indian population.

There were only a few schools and very few churches. The plantation owners saw no great need for either, and the inland residents could not afford many. There were more dissidents than there were Anglicans, more non-churchgoers than loyal members. Most important of all, however, was the existence of a strong yearning for self-government. It was foolish for the Hanoverian Georges to say that the spirit of independence had been spread by New England traders and merchants. It had not: it was the inevitable result of leaving a resourceful people to their own devices.

A Good Man Comes
to Pennsylvania

IT IS NO easy matter to keep diaries when dodging Indian arrows or grubbing for food, and so the exact story of the first European settlements in what is now Pennsylvania is cloudy and indistinct. Musty records hint that the Dutch built a log fort called Beversrede at the confluence of the Delaware and Schuylkill rivers, where Philadelphia was founded later. Some reports indicate that Johan Printz, the governor of New Sweden, tore the fortification down to prevent trade between Dutch and Indians. There is also reason to believe that the Dutch erected a fur-trading post at the falls of the Delaware even farther north.

More explicit is the evidence that the Swedes and Finns had an outpost called Upland on the site of present-day Chester. English Quakers from New England and from the homeland also settled along the river, not seeming to care whether the territory was claimed by the Dutch or the Swedes.

Then, early in July 1681, three ships loaded with Quakers from the old country landed below the mouth of the Schuylkill—the first colonists organized by William Penn. Led by Captain William Markham, this vanguard found, not a virgin wilderness, but a river valley where perhaps two thousand Finns, Swedes, Dutch, and English settlers dwelled on isolated farms or in hamlets with names like New Gottenberg, Printzhof, Fackenland, Fort Korsholm, and Printz's Mill.

Sir William Penn, admiral of the English fleet, had lent Charles

II £16,000, and the monarch, always shy of cash, solved the problem of repayment by offering the admiral's son forty thousand square miles on the west bank of the Delaware extending roughly between the fortieth and forty-third parallels.

Broadsides went up all over England inviting men, particularly Quakers, to become colonists. For only forty shillings they could have a hundred acres of land in the new province. Applicants appeared from everywhere, the first ones sailing with Markham in the spring of 1681. In the years since Jamestown and Plymouth, the English had learned a great deal about colonization, so affairs on the Delaware went smoothly.

The remnants of the earlier settlements gladly joined Penn's people, and many of them espoused the Quaker form of worship. Markham selected the patch of land between the Delaware and the Schuylkill as the site of the capital and named it Philadelphia. Penn had chosen this name—meaning the City of Brotherly Love —in anticipation of the philosophy he hoped would govern his province.

Word of the grant reached the current Lord Baltimore in Maryland. He at once objected, holding that his own grant included some of the land the king had given to Penn. Both proprietors took their claims to the king, who found in Penn's favor. Actually Penn's cause was the more just. Most of the land had been taken from the Dutch and was an extension of New York. More important, none of the Lords Baltimore had done anything to support their claim—if the one fruitless visit by the delegation led by Colonel Utie to Fort Christina (later New Amstel) is exempted.

With the border dispute settled, Penn himself sailed to the New World. He liked what he saw at Philadelphia. Markham, following instructions, had laid out the town with broad streets crossing at right angles. Unlike the crooked, twisting, narrow streets of Jamestown, Salem, Providence, and New York, the new city on the Delaware had a tidy appearance and suggested the way to future urban planning. Penn always claimed that he had made the plans after studying the layout of ancient Babylon.

While work at Philadelphia progressed, Penn lived in Chester, working on the form of government he would propose to offer his people. The constitution he finally made public was surely the most carefully thought out in the New World. It was liberal without divesting Penn of his own great power. It provided for a council elected by the people, which, with Penn, would propose all laws and enforce them, establish courts, schools, and reformatories, build roads, and arrange for necessary financing. A general assembly, also elected by the people, would have the right to pass or veto such laws, but not to suggest any of its own. It was unwieldy, but it worked for many years.

Schools were opened within a few years, at which, unlike those in the other colonies, girls were educated as well as boys. Quaker meetinghouses went up, together with churches of other denominations. Mennonites from the Rhineland found the colony to their liking, and hundreds settled at Germantown, welcomed by the English Friends.

Only Rhode Island could claim greater religious freedom than Pennsylvania. In the latter colony no man could vote who did not believe that Christ was the Son of God. This meant it was a Christian colony. It did not offer the true dissenter—the Jew, Moslem, or atheist—that freedom of conscience ensured by Roger Williams' theories of government in Rhode Island.

William Penn's colony opened its arms to virtually anyone seeking the twin goals of cheap land and freedom of worship. They came from England and Scotland and Ireland, from Holland, France, the German principalities, and Switzerland. Some had the means of paying for their passage and their land, but there were hundreds who had nothing more than the dream of a new life. For these, the picture was grim.

A German writer of the time described the suffering on the crowded ships bringing such impoverished colonists to the Delaware. Six hundred were crowded into the ship on which he was a passenger, although it was built to carry three hundred. Smallpox, then rampant in Europe, took the lives of scores of migrants. When storms lashed the Atlantic, the suffering, especially among those already ill and weak, was unendurable. Every day, it seemed, services were held for those who succumbed and were buried at sea. Women in childbirth suffered the most, and many died. The bodies of mother and offspring were thrown over the side at once. The author of this gruesome personal history recorded that thirty-two children died of hunger, thirst, contaminated food, or disease and were all thrown into the ocean.

More misery awaited these unfortunates when they landed in Pennsylvania. The passengers had to agree to work without pay from three to six years to reimburse the ship's brokers for their passage. If a man died at sea his widow had to assume the debt for his passage as well as her own. Children were bound to work until they reached eighteen or twenty-one years of age, and many a family that had survived the ocean's storms was separated at the pier, the members forced to go off to work for different "owners."

It is difficult to understand how the early Quakers could have permitted such traffic in human misery. The Society of Friends forbade such normal expressions of pleasure as dancing, sports, hunting, going to theaters, and reading novels. Their dress was plain and unadorned. Yet with all their rules for what they deemed good conduct, the Quakers were able to stand by and see children torn from their parents' side and condemned to labor as indentured servants.

The Friends were kindly, forward-looking in their concept of what government ought to provide for the people, and far from oppressive, yet every good Quaker was supposed to keep an eye on other members and report misdemeanors to the congregation. This surveillance technique has been used by other people in other eras, including Nazis and the Russian and Chinese Communists.

On the other hand, Penn was proud enough of his constitution to want it extended to all who lived within the colony's boundaries. This obviously meant the Indians, but this posed many problems. To iron them out, Penn called together the Shawnees, Lenni-Lenapes, and other tribes who met with him at Shackamaxon, outside Philadelphia. He parleyed with them about the equality of all mankind. While he could not see his way clear to giving them an actual voice in government, he did enter into a covenant of eternal friendship with the Indians, a compact "never sworn to and never broken." As long as the Quakers played the dominant role in governing Pennsylvania, there was never a violation of the covenant.

Mixed juries of white men and Indians were established to handle complaints between individuals or races. Incredibly, in an era when other colonists were either hounding the Indians off their ancestral acres or defending themselves to the death against hostile tribes, the Indians in Pennsylvania lived in harmony with the colonists for more than half a century. The intellectual climate in the colony fostered the generation of progressive ideas. Less than eight years after Penn had been granted this vast portion of North America some of his colonists, the Mennonites, had voiced a formal ecclesiastical protest against the institution of slavery in America.

Penn had been most fortunate in his founding of the province. First of all, the Swedes and Dutch who were there ahead of him had bought their land from the Indians and had treated them fairly. And his own religious teachings ensured a continuation of these friendly relations. Penn himself made a trek clear to the Susquehanna River; a white man going that far inland anywhere else from Canada to Florida would have been in great danger of Indian attacks.

Europe soon learned of Penn's success. Voltaire was so impressed by the covenant with the Indians that he almost espoused Quakerism. Other men hurried to migrate to Pennsylvania. Within four years of the first landing on the west shore of the Delaware, Penn could boast that 72,000 people lived within his colony. And they dwelt in peace.

This did not mean they had no problems. The border dispute between Maryland and Pennsylvania dragged on for years. It was eased, but only partially, when the king issued new charters that established Delaware in 1703 and separated it from both Maryland and Pennsylvania.

Another continuing problem involved Penn's constitution. His original draft had set up a system that was top-heavy and clumsy. When Penn returned to England seeking to secure the rights of his colony against attack from Lord Baltimore and others, stresses born of the constitutional faults became worse. Thomas Lloyd, Penn's representative, was an able, honest man, but he was no William Penn.

The assembly, which could introduce no laws, became sullen and refused to approve bills proposed by the council. The number of members in the two legislative bodies went up and down in rapid succession. At one time as many as five hundred were entitled to sit in the assembly and seventy-two in the council. At other times they were cut to a more reasonable size. During a period of ten years Penn changed the form of the government, drastically or not so drastically, six times.

For a colony devoted to peace and brotherly love, it frequently behaved in a querulous manner. Not one of the constitutional changes pleased the Pennsylvanians. At different times the council was shorn of authority, had it restored, ruled with Lloyd as lieutenant governor, and ruled with Captain John Blackwell when

Lloyd withdrew. Blackwell was a Puritan and tried to carry out Penn's entreaties to collect quit-rents. The colony needed income. But both the council and the assembly refused to permit the collection, holding by some perverted sense of logic that the paying of the legitimate fees would "arrest the improvement of the colony."

Until just before Delaware had been made a separate colony, the legislature had met alternately at Newcastle and Philadelphia. After the separation the Pennsylvanians suddenly refused to abide by any laws enacted in Newcastle unless they were subsequently reenacted in Philadelphia. Further roiling the waters, the Society of Friends became disputatious and its ranks riven by disagreement. The group dismissed George Keith, a great leader and teacher, calling him a wanderer from the true faith. Many followed him out of the Society, forming a rump movement and building meetinghouses of their own. Eventually the parent Friends Meeting in London ruled against Keith, who promptly joined the Church of England, became a minister, and evened the score with his enemies by returning to Pennsylvania as a missionary for his new sect.

These were serious matters, but only gnat bites to what befell Penn next. Charles II had given Penn his colony and had remained his close supporter. James II had been less solicitous, because of his strong Catholic leanings, but had still been a powerful patron. Suddenly James was overthrown by William of Orange and his wife Mary.

The new monarchs were Protestants, but were not swayed by this when dealing with the Quaker proprietor. In 1691 the king took over the colony, though he did nothing to damage Penn's personal rights as proprietor. William's decision was based on hard reasoning. While Penn had stayed in England the province had become torn with dissension, rents had not been paid, the parent colony had fought with the stepchild colony of Delaware and, most serious of all, had not organized any defenses against the Indians and the French, who were threatening most of the other American colonies.

It was a noble concept that all men should love each other and that armies and navies are unnecessary. But such an idyllic situation did not exist, and New York, Massachusetts, and Virginia in particular saw no reason why they should carry the burden of protecting everyone.

It was decided to put Benjamin Fletcher, royal governor of New

York, in charge of Pennsylvania too. Fletcher was many things, none of them worth emulation. He was a thief and conniver, brutal and ruthless with those in his disfavor, and an official who betrayed his trust by dealing with pirates. As Pennsylvania possessed no armed forces, pirates had made the many streams leading into the Delaware havens for their ships, glad to escape from places like Charleston and Pamlico Sound where more militant colonists had made it too hot for them. In the little ports frequented by the pirates, debauchery and vice became common, to the consternation of the highly moral Friends.

News of this distressed Penn, far away in London. He went to the king and the Privy Council, argued that only he could correct the deteriorating conditions in Pennsylvania, and won their support. When he promised to contribute a sizable sum to help pay for forts being erected on the New York frontier, William gave him back his powers and restored all his proprietary rights.

For several years the Quaker leader tried to manage things from England, but discord persisted. Finally the assembly was given the right to participate in the enactment of laws, and Penn could spend more time making the colony a profitable one. Towns were established far in the interior, and agricultural products, lumber, and furs funneled into the port of Philadelphia. Shipping revenues grew until the Pennsylvania city threatened to become a larger commercial center than New York.

A few months before the turn of the century Penn brought his family to the fine country house he had built upriver and called Pennsbury. There, in what may have been the most pretentious brick mansion in the colonies, surrounded by pleasant walks and hedges, flowering shrubs and fruit trees, Penn lived in a manner beyond the reach of any other colonial governor. Just before moving into his country place his wife had presented him with a son, John. Penn was inordinately fond of the boy, especially as his first son, William, had become something of a wastrel.

Pennsbury was designed by an architect who was told not to spare expense. The grounds were laid out by a landscape gardener used to working for royalty. Fine oak paneling made the main rooms as handsome as any in the palaces of Europe. Poplar trees lined a broad walk up from the Delaware, and the many buildings behind the main house sheltered servants, carriages, horses, weaving looms, wine presses, and tools. The cellar was stocked with the finest Madeiras, sherries, clarets, and rums his agents could buy. All this cost a pretty penny, and after a time Penn went into debt to finance his princely style of living. But this did not deter him. When he wished to confer with his aides, he sent a vessel he called his "barge" down the Delaware and brought them twenty miles up the stream to dine on wild turkey, venison, wild duck, and other luxuries served on Wedgwood china with sterling silver utensils.

As Penn grew older he mellowed, and many a Quaker eyebrow arched when he was seen riding with his wife on fine horses imported from England, dancing by candlelight in his ornate drawing room, or supervising sports competitions between white youths and Indian braves. Had he not been as wise, as just, and as deeply interested in the welfare of the colonists as he was, a rebellious spirit might have sprung up, but even the most waspish adversary could not overlook what Penn had done for Pennsylvania. They had only to look at Philadelphia, with its fine streets, pleasant homes, and busy piers and warehouses to sense how well off they were in comparison with most other colonies. Out in the hinterland new villages were springing up everywhere, the inhabitants free from worry and living in peace with the Indians. The Quakers in general abhorred the idea of human bondage, and not too many of them owned slaves. Enough did, however, to lead the government to enact laws giving Negroes the right to trial and to arbitration of complaints, and establishing rules of conduct for those who did own slaves.

Penn never wavered from the basic purpose of improving conditions among his people. When the downriver "territories" were given the right to break away and form a distinct colony, Penn was unhappy but he interposed no objection, and when the separation came, he remained as governor of Delaware, although it was little more than a personal tribute on the part of the new colony.

Not long after this division took place Penn gave his colony still another constitution, the best one yet. In the years since the first settlement the colonists had come to feel their own strength, confident of their ability to rule themselves. They had been years in which democracy had started to work, even if weakly, and Penn saw the need for giving more power to the citizens themselves. His last constitution left considerable power in the hands of the governor—a post he held until his death—but the assembly was given rights formerly held by the council. Elected representatives would henceforth wield the real power. The council remained as an appointive body named by Penn and his heirs, but the lower house would now speak in the name of the people.

The City of Brotherly Love also benefited from Penn's eagerness to serve his people in his last years. He gave Philadelphia a charter, which in itself vested the city with no great privileges, but in an era when kings ruled with little check upon their whims and fancies, it was a token of self-rule, a symbol that the citizens of the capital city were entitled to establish regulations for their own better governance. Like the new constitution, it was a sign of the times, another event casting a long shadow ahead toward 1776.

XI

Georgia: One Man's Dream

IF ANY OF the thirteen original colonies was the projection of one man, the fruition of a dream nurtured in the heart of a single individual, that colony was Georgia.

This statement may seem to do umbrage to the memory of Roger Williams and William Penn, both of whom exerted powerful influence in the settling and early growth of Rhode Island and Pennsylvania. But Williams found his colony almost by happenstance while he was a fugitive, and Penn's colony fell into his lap like a ripe plum because of an earlier kindness done a king by his father. Georgia was conceived by James Edward Oglethorpe alone, who in 1732 won the consent of George II and the financial support of influential backers, who led the first party of settlers across the Atlantic, and who kept his little colony intact against both the connivance of ill-wishers and the attacks of the Spanish in Florida. Oglethorpe was a man among men.

He had spent his early years in the English countryside and then fought the Turks under Prince Eugene as the prince's aide-de-camp. He won a seat in Parliament, which provided him with a vantage point for planning his great project: alleviating the misery of men rotting in debtors' prison.

In England at the time when the American colonies were being established, debtors were hounded, cast into jail, and left with no hope of freeing themselves unless friends came to their aid. There were scoundrels and deadbeats in every prison, but for each one of these there were dozens of decent men who were thrown into cells simply because they could not raise enough money to support their families or pay their bills.

Oglethorpe was neither a religious activist nor a soft-hearted do-gooder. He believed that the system was unfair, that it penalized good men, and that it robbed the country of the productivity of able workers. As a member of Parliament, he investigated the prisons and was shocked at the utter brutality of the jailers and wardens.

When he went to George II with his proposal that debtors be allowed to settle the frontier territory between South Carolina and the Spanish holdings in Florida, the wily monarch saw that he could hardly fail to benefit by giving Oglethorpe a charter. It would create a buffer area to protect the rich plantations of lower Carolina from Spanish incursions and would rid him of men who were a drain on the home economy.

Georgia, the last of the thirteen colonies, was the only one that was not begun in the seventeenth century. By now it was apparent to everyone that the settlement of North America had been an economic bonanza for England. Slowly at first, and then with breathtaking swiftness, commerce had burgeoned as flour, furs, lumber, salt fish, tobacco, cotton, rice, cattle, and other goods moved in a great stream across the Atlantic. Manufactured goods without number had gone back to the colonies, lining the pockets of many an Englishman.

Oglethorpe sweetened his proposal to the king by holding out the lure of financial gain for the nation: "When hereafter it [Georgia] shall be well-peopled and rightly cultivated, England may be supplied from thence with raw Silk, Wine, Oil, Dyes, Drugs, and many other materials for manufactures, which she is obliged to purchase from Southern countries."

That was the bait in the trap, and it was all that was needed. George granted to Oglethorpe and his nineteen associates, called trustees, all the land between the Savannah River and Florida. They were to colonize it, make it secure against the Spaniards, and turn it back to the king after twenty-one years. No settler was to have more than five hundred acres, slavery and liquor would be banned, all forms of Christianity except Catholicism would be protected, and the colonists would enjoy all rights held by Englishmen in England.

Perhaps the strangest clause in the charter was the one forbidding the trustees from owning any land. They were to be trustees in fact, not just in name, holding the land only for the benefit of the colonists. This was a most important point, and made it easier for Oglethorpe to raise funds from wealthy merchants with philanthropic leanings, from clergymen and churches, even from that stalwart source of economic power, the Bank of England.

Oglethorpe set out on the good ship *Anne* with 114 settlers, touched in at Charleston to pick up gifts of cattle, food, seeds, and farm implements, and then entered the mouth of the Savannah River in January 1733.

With a scouting party lent by South Carolina, Oglethorpe studied the lay of the land from Port Royal to the St. Mary River to select a defensible site for his first settlement. Finally he chose a sandy bluff on the Savannah, about twenty miles in from the sea. The escarpment in front made attack from the water unlikely, and the swamps ringing the area to the rear provided a barrier against land attacks.

Luck played into Oglethorpe's hands when he met his first Indians. The Creeks had not been particularly cordial to the Carolinians and might have been expected to oppose further white incursions on their homeland. But a woman named Mary Musgrave helped convince the Indians that Oglethorpe's people would be friendly. Mary was the daughter of a Creek squaw who had had a passing romance with an English fur trader from Charleston. She had married a Creek warrior and lived in a village near the Savannah River, but she harbored no dislike or distrust for white men. Between Mary Musgrave and Tomo Chichi, chief of the Creeks, the tribe was won over, and gladly sold the colonists the land on which to build their first homes. Oglethorpe told the Indians he wished to live in peace with them, and for all the time he was associated with the colony of Georgia this friendly relationship was maintained.

Considerable confusion has always existed about the caliber of the men and women Oglethorpe took with him on the *Anne*. They were industrious, law-abiding Englishmen who had been thrown into debtors' prison for reasons of financial distress only. The men were carpenters, weavers, bootmakers, and farmers for the most part, although there were also penniless merchants, clerks, and even a few clergymen among them. Later groups of colonists may have been called "the scourings of London's streets," but not those on the *Anne*.

Everyone turned with a will to building the village called

Savannah. Cannon were placed downstream from the settlement, and tents were pitched to house people until wood cabins could be erected. The plan for the town was well thought out. It called for a large central square with four square sections, or wards, around it, each with its own central plaza. Each family was given a small plot for a home, a garden plot at the edge of town, and farm acreage outside the village limits. Provision was made for a series of outlying hamlets, each built on the same plan as Savannah, when the colony received more settlers from England. Oglethorpe's military mind conceived of the central squares as places to which the colonists could retire if danger threatened the outlying houses.

The new colonists had valuable cooperation from the rich plantation owners of South Carolina. The planters were quick to see the advantage of having a buffer province between them and the Spanish, so they lent what support they could. They promised to send militia in time of emergency, dispatched laborers to help in building Savannah, and armed several small sloops for the purpose of patrolling the waters off Florida.

Back in London the other trustees had not been idle. More money was raised by popular subscription and more colonists solicited. A group of Scottish families from the Highlands crossed the ocean under a Captain McPherson and built a town called Fort Argyle on the Ogeechee River, the next important stream below the Savannah.

Other boatloads of debtors, carefully screened to keep out the ne'er-do-wells, increased the strength of the burgeoning settlement. To the surprise of everyone, an unexpected addition arrived—about half a hundred Jews from Pernambuco, Brazil. They had migrated to South America soon after the Portuguese began colonizing Brazil, but restrictions imposed by Catholic governors and churchmen led them to try again elsewhere. After some early friction, they became valuable and respected members of the new province.

Protestants from all over Europe, especially Switzerland, Austria, and Germany, joined Oglethorpe's company, drawn by attractive proposals made by the trustees. Notable among these were Salzburgers fleeing the greed and cruelty of their bishop, who combined the functions of religious and political ruler. The Salzburgers founded a town called Ebeneezer, and two years later had grown numerous enough to help Oglethorpe start a second town, Frederica, at the mouth of the Altamaha River, well down the coast.

Success bred success, luring new colonists, but it also brought trouble. The English trustees became careless, or were swept away by their own enthusiasm and faith in good works, and they let down the bars on new settlers. A scrofulous lot of debtors arrived at Savannah, determined to make trouble. They refused to work, grumbled about the regulations against slaves and liquor, and injected, for the first time, a feeling of disunity.

One would expect that the clergy would have been strong supporters of the governor, but they were thorns in his side from the outset. One preacher, the Reverend Mr. Samuel Quincy, wrote home long-winded complaints picturing the colony as on the brink of failure. "I may venture to say," he wrote, "that there is not one family which can subsist without further assistance." It wasn't true, of course, as any observer could have noted, but it upset the trustees in England.

So Oglethorpe went home to tell the true story, taking with him a sample of silk grown in Georgia (from which a gown was woven for the queen). He also took Tomo Chichi and a couple of other Indian chiefs, who were presented at court and enjoyed being lionized by everyone. The governor convinced the king that things were going well and returned to Savannah with so many new colonists that the operation was called the "Grand Embarkation." There were three hundred English people and a large number of Moravians. Within weeks they were at work establishing outlying villages, some at Darien and some on St. Simons Island.

Two of the passengers on this trip were the brothers John and Charles Wesley, founders of the Methodist Church. The trustees asked John to serve as chaplain to the new colony, and Charles functioned as Oglethorpe's secretary for a time. The arrival of these men of the cloth in Georgia should have been highly beneficial, but aside from making some conversions among the Indians, they created only bitterness and disharmony.

John Wesley was truculent and opinionated, believing his way was the only way and quarreling with everyone over the correct interpretation of God's word. The Moravians were anathema to him, and the Salzburgers, he thought, were ignorant and backward in all religious matters. Wesley complained that there was "neither man nor woman in the town who minds a word you say."

What spilled the fat into the fire was the sudden intrusion of romance in the young minister's life. He fell in love with Sophia Hankey, a pretty young woman in his congregation, who turned him down flat and married a parishioner named Williamson. In a titanic peeve, Wesley refused to allow the young bride to take communion at the Lord's table. Naturally, her husband considered this an affront to his wife's reputation and brought an action against the preacher.

While the suit was pending, the court ordered Wesley not to leave the colony. An entry in his *Journal,* which he kept with meticulous care, reveals what happened next:

> Being now only a Prisoner at large, in a Place, where I knew by experience every Day would give fresh opportunity, to procure Evidence of words I never said, and actions I never did; I saw clearly the Hour was come for leaving the Place: And as soon as Evening Prayers were over, about Eight o'clock, the tide then serving, I shook off the dust of my Feet, and left Georgia, after having preach'd the Gospel there (not as I ought but as I was able) one Year and nearly Nine Months.

The colony survived his departure with no apparent trauma.

Georgia had been established, in part, to serve as a bastion against the Spanish. In 1738 and 1739 it had a chance to show its usefulness. England declared war on Spain, and Oglethorpe was ordered to attack St. Augustine. While he was gathering together a rather ragtag and bobtail force of six hundred men, the Spaniards attacked his outer defenses on Amelia Island. It was a standoff engagement, followed by a gallant but futile attempt on the colonists' part to capture the Spanish capital. South Carolina, despite its earlier promises, sent a small armed sloop and nothing else, letting the Georgians down badly.

Wars in the colonies reflected the larger conflicts in Europe. Crisis followed crisis, but often with long periods of stalemate between. Things were quiet in Georgia until 1742, when Oglethorpe's Indian allies brought word that the Spaniards were about to launch a large-scale assault on the young colony.

The governor had built Frederica on St. Simons Island not only as a satellite town, but as his main fortress for the defense of the entire colony. Gathering troops, Oglethorpe hurried there just in time to meet the enemy's van. His men were ill-trained but brave. In the midst of the battle he sent a small company to attack the enemy from the flank. Shouting like demons, the Georgians fell upon the unsuspecting Spaniards, routing them with heavy casualties.

Oglethorpe, remembering what he had learned fighting the Turks, used a ruse to clinch his victory. He let a deserter overhear a plan for a heavier attack, and let word drop that an English fleet of men-of-war was just over the horizon. The deserter carried the false news to the enemy troops, regrouping a few miles down the coast. If miracles do happen, Oglethorpe profited by one within the hour. Totally unknown to him, several English warships had been cruising in the vicinity on the watch for a Spanish fleet carrying reinforcements to St. Augustine. The deserter had no sooner peddled his false rumors than the English ships hove into sight off St. Simons Island.

Oglethorpe had outmaneuvered and outfought the enemy; the young colony had come through its test with flying colors. The Moravians, abhorring war, had refused to send men to march under his banner. The long-established colonies to the north, such as Virginia and the Carolinas, had played no part in the defeat of the Spaniards. Oglethorpe and Georgia together had stood off the challenge.

If only the governor had been as successful in small matters as he was in large ones. While he was away defending them, a handful of his followers sent a list of grievances to London, complaining about the lack of hard liquor and urging that the restrictions against owning slaves be lifted. Other dissident colonists carried tales to Parliament that the governor was pocketing public funds and wasting money with extravagant schemes. None of these charges held up under scrutiny, and the authorities in England gave Oglethorpe a clean bill of health. But the petty nagging went on. Rum was smuggled over the border from South Carolina, and some years later—after Oglethorpe had gone—slaveholding became legal.

As the colony prospered, religious groups in the home country sent more missionaries to convert the heathen Indians. A rebelliousness against both the Catholic and Anglican churches in England provided the motivation for establishing new forms of worship.

One of the most notable preachers of the time was George Whitefield, who had been an itinerant minister in Ireland, making many converts to Methodism. Fresh from his success there, he crossed the ocean and undertook the winning of souls in the new colonies. He was a brave man, and wandered up and down the land, preaching in churches when allowed, or in open fields when local pastors shut their doors to him.

Whitefield was a powerful evangelist. Whether in wilderness outposts or the large cities on the coast, people flocked to hear his revivalist message of salvation through faith and love. On one of his long walking trips he reached Georgia, where he was dismayed to find scores of children orphaned by disease, by the war with the Spaniards, or by the arduous labors that had proved fatal to their parents. The roving revivalist determined to build an orphanage for these children and undertook to raise funds at a series of public meetings.

When he reached Pennsylvania, Benjamin Franklin took note of his appeal for funds and, being the realist he was, asked would it not be less wasteful to bring the orphans to the older colony, where buildings were available, than to buy and transport materials to far-distant Georgia. Franklin's advice was brushed aside, so he refused to donate funds to the drive.

But that was not the end. Whitefield continued with his golden oratory, and it happened that Franklin attended a later meeting. Of it the sage of Philadelphia wrote a humorous, and revealing, anecdote:

> I happened soon after to attend one of his sermons, in the course of which I perceived he intended to finish with a collection, and I silently resolved he should get nothing from me. I had in my pocket a handful of copper money, three or four silver dollars, and five pistoles in gold. As he proceeded I began to soften, and concluded to give the coppers. Another stroke of his oratory made me ashamed of that, and determined me to give the silver; and he finished so admirably that I emptied my pocket wholly into the collector's dish, gold and all.

Back in Georgia with ample funds, Whitefield built his orphanage.

Although he preached of Jesus' commands to look upon each person as a brother and to be that brother's keeper, Whitefield somehow found it in his heart to espouse the cause of slavery. He saw no conflict between the evils of human bondage and the teachings of Christ.

Businessmen in Savannah petitioned the trustees for the right to import Negroes, pointing out that without this cheap labor they could not hope to compete either with the Spanish colony to the south or the older English colonies to the north. The trustees denied the petition, calling slaves a "baneful commodity." There the matter stood for a time.

Oglethorpe was to undergo one final disappointment. His nearest subordinate, who owed everything to the governor, complained to Parliament that Oglethorpe had committed new acts of disloyalty to the Crown. The Privy Council called Oglethorpe home to answer the charges. It required but a few days to prove every last accusation false, but Georgia was to suffer immeasurably because of the trumped-up case: Looking about for a man to command the royal army mustering to oppose Charles Stuart, the Pretender, the king's advisers reached out for Oglethorpe. They raised him in rank to major general and sent him hurrying off to Scotland to fight Bonnie Prince Charlie. He never saw Georgia again.

James Edward Oglethorpe had conceived a noble project and had given of his time and personal funds to make the dream work. He had nurtured the infant colony and made it strong, defending it against a powerful and crafty enemy. Years later, when Georgia and her sister colonies banded together in their struggle for independence, General Oglethorpe was offered command of the British army sent to quell the rebellion. In a decision that will forever ennoble his memory, he turned it down.

XII

Bacon's Rebellion: Sign of Ferment

WHILE THE YOUNGER English colonies in America were being organized, Virginia, the first one, was growing healthier and stronger, but not without turmoil. Acrimonious conflicts flared between royal governors, the new assembly, and the people. It was bad enough that the colonists had to cope with privation, Indian attacks, and squabbles among themselves, but on top of this was the dissension and bickering that went on in England.

Many Englishmen—James I included—feared that the Virginia Company had usurped too many powers. In fact, it had overcome most obstacles, had done its best to support the settlers, and had sent thousands of new immigrants to Jamestown and the neighboring towns. Yet people cried "monopoly" at the company.

At one time a hurried census indicated that of five thousand colonists sent to Virginia, only one thousand could be accounted for. Charges of misfeasance and neglect were hurled by people who did not realize that already an out-migration from the villages on the James had begun. Some had gone upriver and others had gone into the country around Albemarle Sound.

There had been losses, of course. When the old chief, Powhatan, died, younger bloods in the tribe began to foment trouble. His successor, Opechancanough, seizing upon the death of an ally as a pretext, attacked the plantations. Terror reigned for weeks until the Englishmen gathered their puny forces and inflicted serious defeats upon the natives. But victory did not come until nearly four hundred whites had been massacred.

James I arbitrarily decided that the Virginia Company was mismanaging the new colony and abrogated its charter. The king did not realize it, but his action unfettered the little colony. There would be royal governors and appointed councils, but hereafter the Virginians would look to their own devices. In the process they would grow stronger and more self-reliant.

The first governors were decent men, but they were soon followed, in 1627, by the notorious Sir John Harvey. This man, whose career as a sea captain hardly prepared him for his task, issued a veritable blizzard of orders and proclamations under which he took to himself most of the powers of the assembly. He levied additional taxes, all of them illegal, and set aside the functions of the courts. Patiently, the Virginians did their best to live with this mountebank. It was no use. Nothing could be done to alter his greed and his lust for power. Then the colonists handled the problem in their own way: they bundled him onto a ship and kept him incarcerated until the ship reached England.

Charles I, who had ascended the throne, toyed with the idea of giving the Virginia Company its charter again and was amazed to find that his subjects across the ocean wanted that no more than they wanted Harvey. Tact was never an outstanding characteristic of the Stuarts, so he sent Harvey back to Jamestown. Harvey assumed that this endorsement gave him carte blanche, and whereas before he had been arbitrary and willful he now became ruthless and cruel. Even the king sensed the change, and in 1641 sent over a replacement, the capable but tough Sir William Berkeley. Behind this appointment was the hope that a firm hand, but an understanding one, might quell the rising insistence among the settlers that they have a greater say in their government. It was a common error of the times. Kings, blinded by their philosophy of divine right, failed to sense the burgeoning power of those they governed.

Berkeley was a bluff old Cavalier and a stout Royalist. He upheld the king whenever possible. He had been instructed to have the assembly convene once a year, but to hold on to his veto power, to sit with advisers as a sort of supreme court, to have all tobacco sent to England and nowhere else, and to prevent foreign ships from carrying on any substantial trade with the new colony. If there were riches in Virginia, the king wanted them for himself.

Oliver Cromwell's overthrow of the Stuarts caused consternation on the James River. Many of the more powerful landowners were

Royalists at heart. The establishment of the Commonwealth was gall to them. Berkeley did his best to nullify the Parliamentary party's instructions, but when Cromwell sent commissioners to take over the colony there were enough colonists who disliked Royalists to force Berkeley to knuckle under to the assembly, now called the house of burgesses. The burgesses announced that they would serve only Cromwell and his agents. Then they elected a governor of their own, Richard Bennett, who was smart enough to state publicly that he was only acting under powers held by the assembly and that his own tenure was dependent upon the house of burgesses.

This indication that elected men hold power from those who put them into office was another sign that the Virginians cherished their independence and would someday be willing to fight for it.

Berkeley had led the people's militia against the Indians when Opechancanough took to the warpath, and the Virginians had a kind regard for him because of it, but this did not keep them from brushing him aside in favor of their own governor. Self-government, even as limited as this regime was, was heady stuff, and the colonists liked it. But it was short-lived.

Even before the Restoration, Berkeley had assumed his old powers, and in his second period in office he was more irascible, motivated undoubtedly by a desire to even a few scores. What was much worse, however, was a growing inefficiency on his part and among those to whom he delegated power. He worried about Indian attacks and spent too much money building forts. His underlings wasted or stole tax money, imposed poll taxes, and interpreted other tax laws in such a way that the poor were ground down and the wealthy favored. The tobacco-growing interests were particularly hard-hit, which even Berkeley admitted in a report sent to England in 1671. But instead of realizing that this inequitable policy was undercutting the economy, he reasoned that it was due to the rebellious spirit abroad in the colony: "I thank God there are *no free schools, nor printing,* and I hope we shall not have these hundred years; for *learning* has brought disobedience, and heresy, and sects into the world, and *printing* has divulged them, and libels against the best government. God keep us from both."

It is easy to be misled about these early Virginians. There has been so much talk of Cavaliers and gentlemen and landed aristocrats that the cold facts are often overlooked. For every country squire there were a score of farmers with less than five hundred acres of land, and there were tradesmen, artisans, and laborers in the towns as well as merchant princes. There were a few wealthy plantation owners who wore brocaded silk waistcoats and silk hose, powdered wigs and lace cuffs, but they were far fewer than those who dressed in homespun, leather jerkins, and hand-knit woolen stockings.

All these Virginians, rich and poor alike, were now imbued with a feeling that they had conquered a wilderness, established a government with considerable home rule, and were contributing greatly to the home government. In the 1670s the colonists paid £150,000 in customs duties each year on tobacco alone.

If the king had left well enough alone he would have been wise, and profited more handsomely. One of his mistakes was sending felons to Virginia as a source of cheap labor. At one period in the mid-seventeenth century so many of these hardened criminals arrived at Jamestown that the authorities passed a law prohibiting the landing of any jailbirds and put teeth in the law by declaring that any shipmaster who tried to controvert the edict would have to carry the felons to another country.

By this time in its colonial history, Virginia did not have to rely upon such outpourings of English prisons for a source of cheap labor. Slaves had been brought in from the West Indies in a constantly mounting number. The less fortunate white settlers, who had small holdings or worked as field hands for the large landowners, could not or would not compete with black slaves. These men, termed "mean whites" by their fellows, lived on the ragged edge of poverty all the time. They, more than anyone else except the slaves themselves, were the victims of the inhuman system of slavery.

A second mistake made by the king was at least more understandable. It grew out of the common philosophy in court that colonies were established, supported in their early days, and defended against enemies for one purpose only: to pour wealth into the monarch's coffers. In the first few years after a colony won a toehold on foreign soil this was a fair bargain for the settlers, but once the colony began to produce goods in excess of local need it became a barrier to economic growth. Colonies sought the best market for their products, and that best market was not always the mother country.

The Dutch had always been in the forefront of seaborne commerce. Their ships touched in at any port where cargoes were waiting for bottoms to take them overseas. Some indication of this far-ranging trade can be gained by studying the operations of just one family, the Philipses, of New Amsterdam.

Frederick Philipse and his son Adolph owned a fleet of ships that took flour, lumber, furs, hides, and cattle out of the Hudson Valley to Europe, the West Indies, Africa, and Madagascar. These ships brought back spices from the East Indies; dishes, pewterware, furniture, arms, gunpowder, and building brick from Europe; slaves from the coast of Africa; silks and other fabrics trans-shipped at Madagascar; and rum and slaves from the West Indies. Before the English conquered New Netherland the Philipse family was one of the most powerful in the New World. After the English seized the colony the Philipses continued to thrive, and at one time owned one-third of all the land now contained in the Bronx and Westchester County.

Men like these were looking for trade everywhere, including Virginia. Because their rates were lower than those of English ships making the same ports, the men at Jamestown welcomed them and offered them many cargoes. Charles II would not brook this rivalry. To handcuff the colonists and at the same time break Dutch control over world shipping, he had Parliament enact the Navigation Acts, a set of laws that unquestionably hastened the day when his colonies would break away.

The Navigation Acts, in brief, forced almost all products of English colonies to be exported only to England. They had to be carried on English ships or on those of the colonies—of which there were very few—and these vessels had to have English masters and at least three-fourths of their crews had to be English. Any manufactured goods for consumption in the colonies had to be bought in England, even if made elsewhere. This made the colonists dependent on England, protected English merchants, and raised the prices of everything needed in the New World.

News of these restrictive regulations fell upon the Virginians at a time when the economy was turning upward and prosperity seemed within reach of all but the slaves and some of the "mean whites."

The colony had grown and spread out in all directions. It had been divided into eight shires, five of them—James City, Henrico, Elizabeth City, Warwick, and Charles City—along the James

River's north bank and one of them, the Isle of Wight, on the south bank. Farther north lay Yorkshire, and on the peninsula between Chesapeake Bay and the ocean was the "Kingdom of Accomac." Each had a typically English government, with a sheriff, bailiff, and sergeant, and a lieutenant commanding the local militia.

Indians had refrained from attacks on the settlements after Berkeley's victory over Opechancanough and his war party. Thousands of indentured servants had worked out their passage payments and had picked up the hundred acres of virgin land to which each was entitled. The temperate climate and rich soil rewarded many a plantation owner with bumper crops.

The early days of malarial fever, starvation, and Indian forays seemed far away now. Fine farms stretched down to the edges of the rivers, the bay, and the sea, and most of them had their own wharves where ships tied up to unload furniture, tools, clothing, and other needs before taking on board tobacco, sugar, and lumber. Some of the inbound cargoes gave evidence of the good life enjoyed by many Virginians: wines, whisky, china and silver dishes, thoroughbred horses, fowling pieces, books.

The Virginian was growing proud—proud of his worldly station and proud that he had overcome the wilderness and created the first English colony in the New World. He went to church on the Sabbath, happy for the most part to be a supporter of the Church of England. He was more than a little pig-headed, having no use for dissenters, and did not raise his hand in protest when Governor Berkeley drove four thousand Puritan nonconformists over the border into Maryland.

Nor did the average Virginian protest when the profligate Charles II came up with an unconscionable plan for lining his pockets: he formed the Royal African Company and made the Duke of York, his brother, its chief officer. The African Company sent ships down the coast of Guinea to Lagos and the mouth of the Congo to steal black men and women for the sugar fields of the West Indies and the tobacco fields of Virginia.

When Indians were driven from their ancestral lands, when slaves were traded like bundles of lumber, or when dissenters were fined, imprisoned, and finally driven from the colony, few voices cried out against man's inhumanity to man. But when the Navigation Acts began to chip away at their profits the colonists rose in anger. For perhaps the better part of two decades it did them little good. Charles was adamant. To make matters worse, he gave the northernmost section of the colony, along the Chesapeake and Potomac, to a court favorite, Lord Culpeper. Then he named Culpeper and Lord Arlington royal proprietors of the entire colony. Two men were thus made virtual owners of a province containing forty thousand landowners, thousands of indentured servants, and at least two thousand black slaves. New taxes were devised to enrich the two noblemen, and Berkeley, by now an old man, did his best to collect them.

Bad examples are easy to follow. The venality at the court in England was reflected in Virginia. Berkeley received pay equal to at least $20,000 today, and the burgesses, who had started out serving without salaries, demanded, and got, regular stipends. Residents noticed that the burgesses were holding their meetings in alehouses and taverns rather than in the state house and were picking up perquisites right and left. When they objected, the burgesses passed laws that took the right to vote away from all persons who had started life in the colony as indentured servants and had bought their way to freedom.

It was behavior like this that gave Virginia a reputation as a haunt of arrogant aristocrats and heightened the feeling of distrust that existed on the frontier. Men facing the exigencies of life in the wilderness bridled at the thought of their governing officials wasting tax money and wining and dining in luxury down on the tidewater.

Then events happened that crystallized the hatreds, and boded ill for the governor and his clique.

England had managed to embroil itself in another war with Holland. The Dutch were having the better of it. Their men-of-war were blockading American ports, and other vessels sailed boldly into Hampton Roads and seized eighteen English merchantmen loaded with tobacco.

Far away in New England an Indian outbreak had set the northern colonies ablaze. King Philip's War, as it was called, sent reverberations all along the frontier, stirring the warlike Susquehannocks into open rebellion. War parties swept down upon the northern and western outposts of Virginia, laying them waste and killing scores of colonists.

By this time Virginia parishioners were going to church to pray for better times. Crops had failed, disease had wiped out at least half the cattle in the province, and now they were threatened with massacre by the Indians. It seemed as if the dark days of John Smith had returned, but with no John Smith to rescue the colonists. They were wrong. There was a man, named Nathaniel Bacon, who strode upon the scene in their hour of need as if sent by a Divine Providence.

Governor Berkeley was beseeched to send soldiers but he refused, for reasons even his supporters could not understand. Finding no help in tidewater towns, young Bacon raised a body of "well-armed housekeepers" and marched after the Indians. The home-grown troops found the Susquehannocks and defeated them roundly at the Battle of Bloody Run. Bacon came back a hero. He was elected a burgess and rallied support so easily that the next session of the house was called "Bacon's Assembly."

Bacon was only thirty-three years old, but he had traveled widely before becoming a plantation owner in Virginia two years before. He knew tyranny when he saw it, and he hated it. Berkeley did not know how to handle him and the threat he posed. At first he invited him to join the council, thinking to get him away from his cohorts. Then he gave him a commission to lead another body of soldiers after Indians who had not learned a lesson at Bloody Run. Vacillating to the end, Berkeley then withdrew the commission, called Bacon a traitor and his men rebels, and hastened across Chesapeake Bay to raise an army of his own in the Kingdom of the Accomac.

Bacon and his militant force of supporters marched from the frontier to a point between Jamestown and the York River then called the Middle Plantation. There each man took a solemn oath to support their leader against Berkeley and his "wicked and pernicious counsellers." Overnight the movement became known as "Bacon's Rebellion."

Word came from the outlying plantations that the Indians were on the move again, and the little force took time out to whip the warriors once more. When they returned, they found Berkeley and his adherents defending Jamestown. There was a sharp, bitter battle, which Bacon won; but his men, happy at victory over the hated governor, set the town on fire. Before anything could be done, Jamestown was nothing but a smoking shambles.

Berkeley sent men to round up Bacon's followers, who had scattered to their homes. Dragging them into court, the bailiffs barely

waited to hear the pronouncement of guilt before hurrying the victims to the gallows. The governor was so vindictive that he had
already hanged thirty-two Virginians before word came from London to cease the proceedings. "Had we left him alone longer," said
one member of Parliament, "he would have hanged half the country." Charles II was even more direct: "The old fool has taken
away more lives in that miserable country than I for the murder
of my father."

What happened to Bacon is still not certain. Some said he died
of malaria, caught while campaigning in the low country around
the capital. There were rumors of poison, countered by charges
"that he had dyed by imbibing or taking in two [sic] much brandy."
Loyal supporters took Bacon's body away and buried it so secretly
that it has never been found.

Bacon's Rebellion, like many another abortive uprising in history, led to even more restrictive government. The king sent commissioners with instructions to manacle Berkeley, and British soldiers, symbols of tyranny and oppression, to put down any signs of
public opposition.

Psychologically, it was a mistake to quarter the redcoats on the
Virginians. The colonists saw that they could hope for nothing
from the throne: their economy would continue to work for the benefit of England, and they could expect political interference, backed
by arms, to contravene any move toward greater self-determination.
Royalist and Parliamentarian, aristocrat and freeman, town merchant and upland homesteader, all knew now that liberty was
anathema to the king. Any political gains would come, not through
petition, but by force of arms.

There was still a hundred years to go, but the Virginians could
see, no matter how long or devious the way, what lay at the end of
the trail.

XIII

King Philip's War and
the Salem Witches

THE COLONIZATION OF Rhode Island, Connecticut, and the region that became Maine and New Hampshire by the Massachusetts Bay settlers did not slow down the growth of the parent colony. In the early decades of this expansionist activity, four or five new arrivals from England replaced every person who left the towns around Massachusetts Bay. Because of the pressures put upon the dissenters by the king and church in England, thousands of Puritans really had no choice but to migrate. Life at home had become so unbearable that the worst hardships in the New World could not stop the movement westward.

The reverse was true in New England. Each year brought better conditions. Defeat of the Indians in the Pequot War brought about peace that lasted for several decades, during which the small towns grew larger and outposts were thrust still farther into the wilderness. A natural yearning for land and the security that went with it led men to strike out from Salem, Charlestown, Dorchester, Boston, and Plymouth and move on to settle Worcester, Springfield, and Dedham. From Hartford other men moved up and down the Connecticut Valley. Down on the shores of Long Island Sound towns called Stamford, Milford, and Guilford were settled by Englishmen who had but a few years before founded New Haven.

As early as 1634, fourteen years after the landing from the *Mayflower*, four of the larger colonies—the Massachusetts Bay towns, Hartford, Plymouth, and New Haven—felt they would be stronger if bound together by an agreement (largely a military-assistance pact). Later, calling themselves the United Colonies of New England, they organized the New England Confederation, which was a forerunner of other unifying steps to follow much later. It was not entirely democratic, for only Puritans could hold office, but it functioned more or less successfully for forty years, providing for a common defense against Indians, settling boundary disputes, and, most important of all, giving the colonists a feeling of self-government.

No such movement toward managing its own affairs was manifested in Virginia until much later, mainly because of the preponderance of Royalists in that colony. The Puritans had no reason to feel any warmth toward those who had oppressed them.

Busy with the wars that tortured Europe all through the colonial period, torn by conflicts between the Cavaliers and the Roundheads, bitter over religious strife between Protestants and Catholics, England could not devote much time to the fledgling settlements three thousand miles away across the Atlantic. Left to their own devices, except for occasional interference, the settlements matured swiftly. And as they matured they grew increasingly independent.

The New England colonists were strong-willed people. They provided for the building of churches just as soon as a village could afford a pastor, yet they kept Rhode Island out of the confederation because of its religious independence. They made it mandatory that as soon as a settlement numbered fifty persons it must arrange for a school for boys. (Girls, the Puritans thought, could take care of themselves without too much learning.)

During the Commonwealth in England, although New Englanders favored it over the Stuarts, this spirit of independence led them to ignore the Parliamentarians. As Cromwell was so busy at home, almost no attention was paid to the colonies, and the men of the New England Confederation made the most of it. They enacted regulations for raising forces to fight the Indians and the French, blocked the Dutch from expanding into Connecticut, and entered into a busy trade with the West Indies.

Industrious, brave, thrifty, and righteous, the Puritans were capable of thoroughly un-Christian behavior. They robbed the Indians, punished them for small malefactions, and drove them from their homes. Though they had fled Europe to escape oppression, they used their power to persecute others. When they kept Rhode Island out of the confederation they said they wanted nothing to do

*French military posts

French Forts

with that colony "further than necessity or humanity may require."
But there was precious little humanity in their dealings with
Quakers, Anabaptists, and others who would not knuckle under
to the Puritan clergy.

It was in the middle of the seventeenth century that the New
England colonies began to hear rumors of turbulence in the motherland in reaction to a new sect, the Quakers. Each vessel arriving
from England brought stories of strange events. Women belonging to the sect walked naked through the streets of several cities
as a protest, men claimed that preachers had no right to take pay
for ministering to their parishioners, and officials reacted by throwing the Quakers into jail or branding them and cutting off their
ears. Such news frightened the authorities in Massachusetts into
passing laws forbidding Quakers to set foot in the colony. The teachings of Roger Williams and Anne Hutchinson had been bad
enough: the Quakers must be kept from preaching their doctrine
at all costs.

In the summer of 1656 the ship *Swallow,* out of Barbados, docked
at Boston with two women passengers, Mary Fisher and Anne Au-
stin, both ardent Quakers. Lieutenant Governor Richard Belling-
ham ordered the sheriff to throw the women into jail. They were
stripped of their clothes to see if their bodies bore any mysterious
signs marking them as witches. For five weeks they were held in
dank, unlighted dungeons and were branded with hot irons on their
backs. Then the master of the *Swallow* was ordered to take them
back to Barbados.

Stark, inexplicable fear goaded the Puritan authorities into passing harsh laws. Any Quaker, once banned, who dared to return to
the colony was to be hanged. Others were to have their ears cropped
off as punishment for a first offense of preaching or of even being
present in the colony. Women who insisted upon preaching when
ordered to desist were to have their tongues pierced through with a
hot iron.

None of these barbaric measures kept the Quakers from trying
to spread their particular brand of religion. They arrived on ship
after ship, willing to suffer for their beliefs. Their sympathizers also
felt the colony's wrath. An old man who befriended several Quakers was shackled to an iron bar with heels and head bent nearly
together and left to lie that way for sixteen hours. When he was
freed he was whipped 117 times with a tarred rope.

Quaker men went from village to village to "testify" to God's will. Lydia Wardell, saying the Lord had given her the order, removed all her clothing and attended divine service at the Newbury church, and Deborah Wilson walked stark naked through the streets of Salem.

The gallows was no answer to such foolishness. Extremists among the new cult refused to leave the colony, preached in the village commons, and repeatedly stripped off their clothing, as if that act somehow would restrain the officials. It had no effect at all upon men so fearful of dissension that they sold one Quaker's children into slavery as a means of collecting his fine.

For three years the madness persisted. The Quakers would not give up, and the authorities insisted on brutally punishing all who entered Massachusetts. The terrors of the Spanish Inquisition were duplicated by men who themselves had known the horror of religious persecutions. Whippings were inflicted over a period of days until the victims' bodies were little more than pulp.

In October 1659, Bay Colony magistrate John Endecott sentenced Mary Dyer, William Robinson, and Marmaduke Stevenson to hang for having returned from banishment. The three were led to the gibbet, the nooses were put around their necks, and they were then given a chance to "confess" their heresy. The men declared they were glad to die for the truth, and the traps beneath them were sprung by the sheriff. At the last moment Mary Dyer was pardoned, provided she would leave the colony.

But Mary could not forget the sight of her companions dying on the gallows. She returned to Boston, was arrested, and led through the streets to the cadence of muffled drums. Once again, the hempen rope was fastened about her neck.

"Repent, and live," the sheriff whispered to her.

"I come here not to repent," cried Mary Dyer. "I have already been in paradise." The trap fell and she died for her faith.

Before reason prevailed, hundreds of Quakers and other nonconformists had been arrested, forty-seven banished, scores branded with burning irons or mutilated in other ways, and four had been hanged.

Charles II, who did few things in his life worth praising, played a major role in stopping the hideous mistreatment of dissenters. He was petitioned by Quakers to intervene, and he chose a most dramatic way of making his power felt: he sent word to Governor

Endecott commanding him to halt all persecution and, to make it
even more forceful, sent the order by a Quaker who had been banished twice and whipped cruelly.

It is hard to understand how decent men could have been moved
to such extremes. The only reassuring aspect of this horrible epi-
sode is the fact that both Puritans and Quakers later found it wise
to steer away from such irreconcilable positions.

Those colonists who had left the Bay Colony to settle Rhode Island and Connecticut had other problems. They could claim support from the older colony, but would that protect them against
Dutch claims? And how much could the dissenters of Providence
and Newport expect from those who had driven them into the wilderness? These satellite provinces needed some sort of recognition
of their own status and, having nowhere else to turn, they sent
delegates to London to get charters from the king.

Connecticut's governor, the talented son and namesake
of old John Winthrop of Boston and Salem, was astute enough to
convince Charles II that the men of Hartford, Saybrook, and New
Haven were loyal to the Crown. On that premise the king could
afford to be lenient. In 1662 he granted Connecticut a charter. Its
provisions were unusually liberal, especially as to boundaries. No
one had bothered to give the king any lessons in geography, so he
granted the colonists "all the land between Narragansett Bay and
the South Seas," including much territory claimed by the Dutch.
It caused consternation in New Haven because it made unity with
Hartford inevitable, and it disturbed Rhode Islanders because that
colony had started several towns on the western shore of Narragansett Bay.

More important, at the moment, were the political clauses of the
charter. It provided for a governor and assistants, and a house of
deputies elected from each town by the freemen of the colony. Aside
from forbidding any laws contrary to those in existence in the
home country, the charter gave a great degree of home rule: it
required no approval of local laws by the king, and it established
perhaps the most advanced form of independence then possessed
by any colony in the New World.

Rhode Island's charter was equally generous. No person was to
be denied his rights; he could not be molested or questioned because of his religious convictions, or for any matter of personal
conscience.

One might have thought Charles II was suffering from an over-abundance of Christian charity were it not for another step he took about this time. Vengeful at those regicides who had brought about the overthrow and beheading of his father, he sent word to New England that he had information that two of the men had taken refuge there. Edward Whalley and his son-in-law, William Goffe, were in fact hiding in the Bay Colony at that time. When the king ordered them arrested and brought back to London, the Massachusetts General Court turned the task over to two young Englishmen only just arrived from England. They knew so little about how to get around in New England that Whalley and Goffe were easily spirited out of Boston and down to New Haven, where they hid in a cave until the king's messengers gave up the hunt.

No king, no matter how stupid, could have failed to notice the growing spirit of independence in the Bay Colony. This was why Charles favored the Connecticut and Rhode Island delegations with far better charters than he did the representatives of Massachusetts when they went to London to get a new one. And it also explained why he sent royal commissioners to Massachusetts to inquire why he was not receiving more revenue and, working secretly, to curb the willful spirit of the colony.

The commissioners sent back reports telling the king how prosperous the Bay Colony was and how it was shipping salt fish, corn, lumber, iron, and naval stores to many foreign ports at a nice profit, the Navigation Acts notwithstanding. Strong measures might have been taken to channel more of the profits into the royal treasury if two events had not occurred: the outbreak of war with the Netherlands and a sudden, ferocious assault upon the colony by the Indians.

Wiser men would have seen the Indian outbreak coming. When Massasoit, friend of the Pilgrims, died, his son, Metacom, assumed the leadership of the tribes living around Massachusetts Bay and upper Narragansett Bay. For a reason lost in the past, the colonists called this Indian "King Philip." Philip was not the man his father had been—patient, forgiving, and eager to assume that the whites would someday recompense the Indians for the land they were taking: Philip knew better.

Then, too, in the advancing years the picture had changed. Instead of a few acres given the Pilgrims at Plymouth, the Indians had now lost hundreds of thousands of acres of their homeland.

The probing fingers of white settlements had reached all the way up the Maine coast, along the Kennebec, Merrimack, and Connecticut rivers, even to the lowlands of the Berkshires.

As one historian, Herbert Aptheker, has pointed out, the Indians had lent invaluable help in overcoming the wilderness. They supported the early settlers when famine threatened. They showed the newcomers how to plant corn and tobacco, squash, pumpkins, peas, and beans, how to make corn pudding, and how to use a fish head or seaweed as fertilizer when the seeds were buried. The Indian taught the settler how to trap animals and fowl for food, how to tell the good mollusks from the bad, and how to boil maple sap to make sugar. The Indian's trails became the white man's early roads.

"In a word," Aptheker wrote, "the Indians taught the Europeans how to live in the New World, and were repaid by having that world taken away from them."

King Philip's home was at Mount Hope, near Bristol, Rhode Island. From the hill where his wigwam was pitched he could look out upon the waters of Narragansett Bay and, in the other direction, across the hills and cranberry bogs toward where the Plymouth settlements had been built. Philip had sold much of his land, and had come to realize that the payment could never make up for the loss. Yet he had held his hand for years.

When the missionary John Eliot had gone to live among the Indians to teach them English and to compile an Indian dictionary, Philip avoided him but did nothing to stop him. One of his men, Sassamon, became friendly with the whites, and it was this that saved the colonists.

Warlike Narragansetts urged Philip to lead his Wampanoags on the warpath. Philip demurred for a time, while more of his land was callously and ruthlessly taken by the same white men who had previously bought some of it. When the white man paid anything for the land, it was with trinkets that had little value or, worse, with liquor and arms.

Finally Philip conferred with the Narragansetts again, and later with the Nipmucks and the Nashuas. The bloody stick went from village to village. War, Philip said, was the only solution. Sassamon took word of the coming attacks to the whites.

The spark that ignited the conflict called King Philip's War flared up in June 1675. A farmer at Swansea wounded an Indian who had shot one of his oxen. It was all the natives needed. A few days later bands of warriors burst out of the woods surrounding outlying settlements and massacred all who could not flee in time.

Drums beat on Boston Common, fires blazed on a dozen hilltops in a signal mustering soldiers, and bands of troops moved out of the villages to defend their women and children. From the Merrimack in the north to the shores of Narragansett Bay in the south the flames of burning cabins, the cries of tortured whites, and the war whoops of the Indians told of spreading war.

Captain Thomas Savage with 120 men marched swiftly to Mount Hope, where Philip had remained, waiting for news of the initial attacks. So sudden was the appearance of Savage's force that Philip barely escaped. Fifteen Indians were killed, and all of Philip's cattle were taken away. His headquarters was burned and his cornfields set afire.

Mendon was burned in July with a heavy loss of life. Next on Philip's plan was an attack on Brookfield, a Massachusetts village with a strong garrison house. Eighty villagers fled to the fort as their homes went up in flames. Against burning arrows, the men of Brookfield held out until a rescue column of soldiers fought its way through the Indians. It was only one battle among dozens, and the white men were not always so lucky.

Hiding in the wilderness, Philip sought other allies. The Mohegans, living on the border between Rhode Island and Connecticut, refused to break their treaty with the settlers. Their leader, Uncas, sent warriors to fight with Governor Winslow, who gathered an army of 1,100 whites and Indians. In a swampy area near present-day Kingston, Rhode Island, the Indians had built a fortified retreat, and Winslow determined to destroy it. The village had been planned by Indians who had learned from the white man's engineering and was a formidable place to attack. A palisade ran around the encampment on a hill rising out of the bogs. A single path made of logs was the only way to enter the fort.

On a bitter, snowy December afternoon the colonists and their Indian allies launched an attack in the face of murderous fire from behind the palisade. A dozen soldiers died on the log path, but others took their place, and finally the village was taken. Some warriors escaped, but others, and all the women and children, were trapped when soldiers set the wigwams and log cabins afire. When the sun went down that bitter afternoon more than three hundred Indian corpses lay in the embers of the fort. With them, and on the frozen floor of the forest outside, lay the bodies of scores of white men. The Great Swamp Fight was over. It had been a costly victory.

Word of this ghastly defeat hardened the hearts of every Indian under Philip's command. Leaving their villages, they roamed in the forests and attacked white settlements whenever the prospects of victory appeared good. Massachusetts suffered the most. Groton, Weymouth, Medfield, Lancaster, and Marlborough were burned. Then Warwick and Providence felt the wrath of Philip's avenging force. Having carried the war to the enemy near his home, Philip slipped away from his pursuers and struck at settlements on the Connecticut River. There were bitter battles at Springfield, Northampton, and Hatfield, with heavy losses on both sides.

All the bloodshed, all the tragedy, was for nothing. The whites, with better arms and better tactics, survived as the war dragged on during 1675 and 1676. Philip, his men decimated in battle, sought aid from the Mohawks and was turned away. This so disheartened many of the braves that some of them went to their leader to ask him to sue for peace. Furious, Philip killed the foremost warrior.

Twice Philip's tribesmen attacked the village of Deerfield, in Massachusetts. Each time they burned cabins, massacred some of the residents, and carried others into captivity. The second time, Philip ambushed a column of sixty whites sent to relieve the beleaguered town and killed nearly every one of them. Behind his back, however, forces were at work that would bring an end to the war. A brother of the Indian struck down for suggesting a negotiated peace deserted to the colonists and led a party to Mount Hope, where they captured Philip's wife and child. When the Indian leader learned that his wife and son had been sold into slavery in Bermuda he returned to his home, disheartened and crushed. A few days later he was found and shot to death, the mortal bullet fired by the Indian traitor.

Philip's death did not end the conflict immediately, but it sounded the tocsin for the Indians. A few warriors joined northern tribes in attacks on Berwick, Maine, and Dover and Exeter, New Hampshire, but by the end of 1676 the war was over to all intents and purposes. Thirteen white villages had been burned to the ground and many Indian encampments were put to the torch.

More than six hundred New England colonists lost their lives, and far more than that number of Indians were dead.

For the colonists the war was a unifying experience, as men from different provinces fought side by side. For the Indians it was total defeat. Remnants of the various tribes wandered close to starvation on the fringes of white civilization, their cornfields gone, many of their women sold into slavery. The way to further expansion was now open to the settlers, but for the Indians between the Hudson and the Atlantic it was the end of traditional tribal life.

The archives hold a document describing Philip's death, written in the pious phrasing of an English colonist, Benjamin Trumbull. It rejoices in the killing of the chieftain, whom it accuses of malice and wickedness, but says nothing at all of the wrongs inflicted by the white man. Nor does it hesitate to quote sanctimoniously from the Bible, employing these words from the Prophet Isaiah: "Woe to thee that spoileth, and thou wast not spoiled, and dealest treacherously, and they dealt not treacherously with thee; when thou shalt make an end to deal treacherously, they shall deal treacherously with thee."

Only an Indian could sense the irony in such words, coming from those who had despoiled his home, his fields, his family, and his hopes.

New England suffered from many ills besides the tomahawk and the flaming arrow. In his everyday existence the Puritan was denied pleasures common to other people. He had to devote time and money to the welfare of the church or he had no say in communal affairs. Sermons were long, and full of the threat of hell's fire for wrongdoers. Students who attended classes at Harvard spent as much time on theological matters as they did on mathematics and science. A Puritan worried not only about his own conscience and behavior, but also about his neighbor's. The clergy did its best to convince the people that God's way was arduous, sober, and boring. In England men had been imprisoned, mutilated, and executed for petty offenses. The Puritans carried this moral and penal code to the New World, never hesitating to use horrible punishments in an effort to curb dissension and nonconformity.

Some idea of the strait-laced morals of the Bay Colony and other New England provinces can be gained when it is remembered that men and women were branded with hot irons, had their tongues bored through, their ears lopped off, and were fastened into cruel positions in the stocks for such minor actions as speaking in an unmannerly fashion about the preacher, swearing in public, or missing divine service. Nathaniel Hawthorne's novel *The Scarlet Letter* notwithstanding, only a few women had to wear a red *A* for "Adulteress" on their bosoms, but many a colonist did have to wear a *T* for "thievery" or a *D* for "drunkenness" upon his outer garments. To the hard-core Puritans it was good penology to make malefactors suffer public scorn. Punishments were aimed at preventing such misdemeanors among the populace, never to help the sinner correct his ways.

Perhaps it was this constant concern about sin and punishment that created an emotional climate that could permit an entire colony to be disturbed by witchcraft. To a Puritan, the Devil was forever skulking just behind the door, or just down the lane behind the barn, waiting to catch the unwary and the un-Godly. A good Puritan was always at war with the Devil and, as everyone knew, or thought he knew, witches were the Devil's handmaidens.

The colonists had heard stories about witches in Europe. They were as much a part of their lore as elves and fairies are in the fantasies of children. In the early days of the Bay Colony an occasional cry of "Witch" had been raised by the ignorant or the fearful, but it was not until the late seventeenth century that supernatural manifestations came to be accepted on a wide scale.

The hunt for witches really began in 1692 in Salem, and, of all places, in a preacher's home. The Reverend Mr. Samuel Parris, shepherd of a flock in that town, employed a Negro slave, a woman named Tituba, who had been brought up from Barbados. Tituba was well loved by the children of the neighborhood, and she filled their heads with tall tales. One must assume that she delighted in teaching the girls who gathered at her skirts how to mew like cats, bark like dogs, and otherwise act as if possessed by Beelzebub. And one must also assume that the girls enjoyed it, for they remembered these things the next time they went to church: at the service they went into what seemed like spasms, and Abigail Williams, only eleven, shouted to the parson that a yellow bird was sitting on his hat.

Matters grew worse after that. Neighbors called at Parson Parris's home to see the girls behaving like animals, crying out as if in pain, and otherwise behaving as if in the clutches of Satan.

A committee of ministers asked Abigail, Anne Putnam, Mary Wal-cott, and others among the girls who had bewitched them. "Sarah Good, Sara Osburn, and Tituba," replied the girls, forgetting the servant's many kindnesses.

Sarah Good was a penniless old lady who went from door to door begging for scraps of food, and the Osburn woman was remark-able only because she was an ancient crone, wrinkled and lame.

Sheriffs and constables rounded up the accused, judges and cler-gymen gathered to sit in judgment, and the girls testified that the three women had bewitched them, stuck pins in them, and pinched them while telling them the Devil's instructions. It was palpably false—the mouthings of children frightened at their own misdoings —but everyone seemed to take it seriously. Tituba compounded the felony by telling silly stories of how the Devil came to visit her and how she could ride a broomstick over the clouds.

The townspeople shook their heads at this sign that Satan had invaded their devoutly Christian village. After the three accused women were taken to jail in Ipswich, the girls dreamed up charges against others in Salem. One was a child of five years, accused of having bitten one of the girls, and so fearful were the Puritan officials they threw mother and child into prison, chained together.

From this beginning, the frauds were multiplied. Men settled grudges against others by accusing them of witchcraft. People who should have known better testified to such "facts" as having seen a woman slip through a keyhole, seeing an imp three feet tall and covered with hair standing by the fireplace in the Parris house, and seeing a wealthy man conversing with Satan in the moonlight. The entire community lost its sense of reality. Hysteria swept over the colony like a storm, leaving people unable to think sensibly. Judges, ministers, and officials—the very men who should have re-mained calm—added fuel to the fire.

Then an accusation of witchcraft was made against the wife of the minister at Beverly. This, more than any other event, stemmed the madness and brought the colonists to their senses. Mrs. Hale, the pastor's wife, was one of the most respected women in the prov-ince, honored by rich and poor, powerful and lowly alike. How could such a woman be in league with Satan, they asked, and the answer that came at last to their puzzled minds proved the turn-ing point in the whole affair. The judges had erred legally in ques-tioning the accused and not the accusers, and thus had not discovered how baseless was the evidence on which charges were made. Had they examined the girls with any real determination, they would have discovered that the children were playing a game or were, at best, deluded.

Increase Mather, president of Harvard, drafted directives for future examinations of accusers, and one of the judges, Samuel Sewall, made a public confession in Old South Church in Boston before the entire congregation, admitting that he had failed to weigh correctly the testimony of impressionable children and vicious or frightened adults.

So, like a dark cloud blown away from the face of the moon, the horror passed away in Salem. But before it did, more than 150 innocent persons had been thrown into prison, one victim who would not answer questions had been crushed to death under a great pile of stones to keep the Devil from getting his body, and nineteen other men and women who had done no wrong to anyone had been hanged.

These unfortunates lost all their household furnishings, and their cattle and money, if they possessed any, and they were forced to pay for the food they ate in jail and the fuel used to heat their cells. If they could not, their children had to assume the debt. Only a depraved society could have gone so far as to charge these persons fees for the very writs that imprisoned them, for reprieves, for discharges, for the price of their chains and manacles, even the fees to be paid to the hangmen who took their lives.

But such was the hysteria that these nineteen were dragged into carts that rumbled over Salem's cobbled streets like the tumbrels of the French Revolution, up to the brow of a hill overlooking the town, and there hanged on a gallows.

In later years many of the accusers, particularly the children, confessed what every sensible person should have known: that they had no evidence beyond their own wild imaginings. The guilt they felt can only be guessed at, but how much worse was the communal guilt of those who thought they saw the hand of God at work on the hill where nineteen swaying forms hung for days on the gibbet.

XIV

Massachusetts:
Bad Apple in the King's Barrel

Ⅰɴ ᴛʜᴇ ᴇʏᴇs of the Stuart kings Massachusetts was the bad apple in the barrel of American colonies. Tensions had begun to build up almost as soon as the first colonists landed on the shores of Massachusetts Bay, taking their charter with them and making the company headquarters Boston instead of London. From then it had gone from bad to worse, so far as the English rulers were concerned.

It was bad enough, thought Charles II, that the colony was trying to rule itself, passing its own laws and establishing procedures for officeholding and voting. What must have galled him more was the effrontery of the colonists: they refused to pay taxes, violated the Navigation Acts, and traded with other colonies and other countries, without any of this benefiting the royal exchequer.

As a means of handling the obstreperous colonies, the affairs of all New England were handed over to the Privy Council, which sent Edward Randolph to America to conduct an inspection. Randolph found little to praise. On his return to London he submitted a long denunciation complaining that the colonists denied appeals from court decisions to higher authority in England, evaded the Navigation Acts, coined their own money without the king's likeness on it, gave refuge to the regicides, and punished people for religious reasons, even putting some to death.

Randolph returned to Boston to put the squeeze on the colonists, to collect more taxes, and to bring the dissidents to heel. It was a task he enjoyed, at least up to a point. Then the colonists—whom he usually referred to as smugglers—got their backs up and sent representatives to London in an effort to negotiate a settlement. One of them was Increase Mather, a fiery orator and strong supplicant, but it did Massachusetts no good.

The Privy Council objected to the way the Bay Colony had taken over Maine and New Hampshire, the way it had imposed taxes and fines of its own, for its own fiscal benefit, and the way the Puritans were oppressing other sects. When James II came to the throne the situation deteriorated rapidly. Finally the king decided to recall the charters and appoint a royal governor to rule all New England. Behind his statements was a barely disguised threat to send redcoats to Boston to enforce his rule if the colonists did not come to terms.

Before executing these drastic plans, however, James made New Hampshire a royal colony and sent Edward Cranfield over to run the government. Cranfield may well have been the worst royal governor in the colonies. He imposed taxes to line his own pockets, sold pardons, confiscated real estate illegally, and antagonized every man in the colony.

Cranfield's behavior led the colonists to look upon royal interference as cruel and unfriendly. What little hope of settling the disputes that may have existed was now dissipated. The colonists believed that only by their own strength and will power could they survive with any freedom. In many ways, it was the beginning of the polarization that led to the war of independence.

Confronted with the colonists' intransigence, James II dropped the other shoe. He used the Court of Chancery to revoke the Massachusetts charter. Then he sent Sir Edmund Andros to New England as the new royal governor, with instructions to consolidate all the New England provinces into one. Andros, already governor of New York, bravely undertook the assignment.

Andros is often depicted as a ruthless agent of royal power, and he did do his best to execute his orders. At the same time, however, he established a system for the defense of the colonies against the French and the Indians, building forts and raising troops to serve on the border. But even if Andros had been a saint, the tasks of reconciling the colonists to the king and of building adequate defenses would have been too great. Events had moved ahead too fast.

With the Massachusetts charter abrogated, Andros demanded

that of Connecticut, riding down to Hartford from Boston with the panoply and pageantry one would expect at a royal investiture. In one of the great dramatic episodes of the colonial era, he convened the council and asked for the charter. It was evening, and the chamber hall was illumined only by candlelight. Officials brought out the polished wooden box containing the document John Winslow had won from Charles II. Suddenly, by prearranged signal, all the candles flickered and went out. There were no matches in those days, so a soldier hastened next door to get a flaming brand from the fireplace. When the candles were lighted again the box was empty, the charter missing. Captain James Wadsworth had seized the document, made off with it, and hidden it in the hollow of an old oak. The tree, called the Charter Oak, remained standing until 1865. A chair made from the tree is now in the senate chamber of the state capitol at Hartford.

It was a brave gesture, but nothing more. On October 31, 1687, Andros annexed Connecticut to Massachusetts.

Tensions grew and friction worsened between Andros and the people of New England. The governor was accused of trying to introduce the Church of England as a state church, of censoring the press, reducing the powers of town meetings, and otherwise oppressing the colonists. Perhaps his most hated act was the raising of an army of six hundred men which the people had to support with special taxes. He used these soldiers in a swift attack on the French settlement at Castine, Maine, and without such a force the northern frontier might have been endangered.

On April 4, 1689, word came by a ship entering the harbor from Nevis that a revolution in England had brought William and Mary to the throne. Overnight pandemonium broke out. All through Boston the sound of drumbeats echoed as companies of colonists mustered and marched toward the state house. A force of militia trained its guns on the armed frigate *Rose,* riding at anchor in the outer harbor. In from Newton, Salem, Medford, and other outlying towns marched other New Englanders, armed with muskets and powder horns. Edward Randolph, the king's tax collector, English bailiffs and sheriffs, aides to the governor—all found themselves arrested and tossed into jail. Andros tried to stem the rioting but was himself arrested. He tried to escape, dressed in women's clothes, but an alert soldier noticed his heavy boots and he was seized again and held for trial.

Simon Bradstreet was elected governor by the people. New England had won what old England had won through the ascendancy of William and Mary: the end of absolute rule by kings.

Andros was sent to London under guard of a group of colonists. He was not tried in a court, but examined by the lords sitting as overseers of Trade and the Plantations. Naturally he was released at once.

William and Mary granted Massachusetts a new charter in 1691. It provided for a governor, a lieutenant governor, and a secretary to be appointed by the Crown, but this was a minor point compared to a clause granting the franchise to vote on the basis of property qualifications. A man with sufficient land had the right to vote and hold office. The old rule about belonging to a church—that is, the Puritan church—was ended for all time.

Thus the charter became a double-edged sword: it gave the people a greater measure of freedom from the divine right of kings, and it ensured freedom from control by the clergy. For the first time since settlers stepped ashore to found the Massachusetts Bay Colony, the hidebound, bigoted, and cruel dominance of the Puritan theocracy ceased to be a major force in the colony.

When the excitement died down, the new monarch selected—for the first time—as royal governor a man who had been born in the colonies. He was Sir William Phips, a fabulous character, born in Maine to parents with twenty-five other children, who began his checkered career as a sheep herder. Later, as master of a merchant vessel, he was lucky enough to stumble upon a wrecked ship fairly bursting with treasure. Naturally such wealth belonged, for the most part, to the man who ruled England. Instead of running off with the treasure, Phips turned it over to the Crown. This pleased James II so greatly that he wined and dined the captain, knighted him, and later named him royal governor of all New England except New Hampshire. So were great decisions made in the days of the Stuarts.

Phips began his tenure happily, well liked because of his romantic background, but before he was recalled he was at odds with everyone. It wasn't easy to preside over a colony that wanted the right to representation and that took advantage of every loophole to win more privileges for the common people.

It was no solution to the problem when in 1698 the king, deciding there were too many governors and too many colonies, tied all the New England provinces, New York, and New Jersey into one huge territory. The Earl of Bellomont, then serving as governor of New York, would assume the combined command. Bellomont had spent a great deal of his time hunting down pirates who infested out-of-the-way inlets and coves of North America, preying on the growing commerce of the colonies. It had been hard work, but he and his successors were to find it was nothing compared to governing the restive, independent, and militant residents of New England.

While major attention had been given to Massachusetts, bellwether of the northern colonies, other provinces in the area had been growing, some faster than others, but all benefiting from the Bay Colony's efforts. After the first movement into Connecticut there had been a slowing down of settlement, due to many reasons. The very unanimity represented by the Puritan church in Massachusetts was lacking below its border. Men and women from the Bay Colony had settled Hartford, but the towns of Wethersfield and Windsor owed more allegiance to Plymouth than to the larger province. Saybrook and New Haven, for their part, had a strong infusion of Presbyterianism in their makeup, and no barriers had been erected against other sects. This should have appealed to many refugees from Europe, but instead dissidents preferred the out-and-out freedom of worship guaranteed by Pennsylvania and Maryland.

As a result, the population in Connecticut grew rather slowly, new inhabitants trickling in from Massachusetts and overseas, but never in the large groups that landed by the thousands in Philadelphia. There was even some out-migration in the early days. Connecticut residents sought to establish towns in New Jersey, and a number of inhabitants of Branford moved out of Connecticut to start again near the Swedes on the Delaware.

This independent spirit actually had a good effect on those who remained in Connecticut. Each town, while prideful of the colony's charter, tended to stand alone. The town became a self-sufficient unit where men took upon themselves all the functions of government that were not withheld by the Crown, and even some of those. They had banded together to fight the Pequots, but after that each community managed its affairs without much interference either from other towns or from the king. Men gathered at the town meeting, selected their own officials, called selectmen, and met everyday problems by their own courage and wisdom. The town-meeting form of government was surely one of the most independent and democratic ever established. There were churches in every town, usually Congregational, but whatever the particular religion happened to be, attendance at service was voluntary and, perhaps for that reason, commendably high. There was also a school in every town, as the people had a reverence for education hardly second to that for religion.

Geography and topography did much to make town government nearly supreme in Connecticut. There were no roads, only a few Indian trails over rugged terrain connecting the new towns with older ones in Massachusetts or with the few in Rhode Island. Much travel had to be done by sloops that rounded Cape Cod and tacked laboriously up the Connecticut River. It was often far easier to sail across the sound to Long Island than to get from one town to another in the province, and this led eventually to the settlement of numerous villages on eastern Long Island by Connecticut men. This didn't sit well with the Dutch, who claimed the entire island, but the handwriting was already on the wall, and the English towns were not molested.

The settlement of eastern Connecticut was delayed by the presence of the Mohegan Indians, who lived along the Shetucket and Thames rivers. This tribe had been loyal to its treaties with the whites during the Pequot War and King Philip's War, and the colonists felt some hesitance about taking their land, though willing to pay for it. So this barrier existed for many years between the main settlements of Connecticut and those in Rhode Island.

Turmoil was the midwife presiding over the early days of Rhode Island. Roger Williams, motivated by the purest of ideals about religious freedom, had started Providence, and Mrs. Hutchinson, far less idealistic, had founded Portsmouth. Heresy bred heresy, and the lady's unfaithful followers promptly established Newport. Later still other dissidents founded Warwick. Williams tried to rule Providence in a most democratic manner, with all freemen convening to sit as a court and five selectmen handling everyday affairs. Over the other towns William Coddington served as governor, having jurisdiction of the territory east of Narragansett Bay, but the brand of democracy practiced fell far short of the ideal. Ardent religious protagonists seem to make poor civic leaders.

Rhode Island was looked upon with suspicion by nearby colonies.

The people of Plymouth, Boston, Hartford, and Saybrook had all sought new homes in which to worship as they saw fit, yet they eyed the small province with distrust because it refused to deny anyone, of any religious belief, refuge within its borders.

Roger Williams was adamant on one point. He had gone to England and obtained a charter containing many privileges. He had allowed the towns to manage their own affairs, and before he obtained the charter, he had failed to set up a cohesive government for the whole colony. But he insisted that the only requirement any man needed in order to vote and have a say in government was that he "live civilly."

After most of the religious squabbling died down and Mrs. Hutchinson shook the dust of the new colony from her skirts to try again in New Hampshire, the colony was organized as "Rhode Island and the Providence Plantations." Williams served as governor for three years, leaving that post before James II took away the charter and tucked Rhode Island into the giant complex handed over to Edmund Andros.

Once William and Mary came to the throne, the tiny colony settled down to a period of steady growth and less turbulence. But two things never really changed: religious freedom remained a way of life, and the colony adhered to the belief that Indians were entitled to honorable and fair treatment. It was an example lost upon most of the English colonists in North America.

XV

Royal Governors and
King William's War

WHEN THE DUTCH colors came down from the fort at New Amsterdam and were replaced by the Union Jack, half a century of Dutch rule ended in this rich province. For the next 113 years the English ensign would fly above the greatest port in the New World.

Actually there was a fourteen-month hiatus when the Dutch recaptured the town, but this would have little effect on the course of empires or common men. What mattered was that from New Brunswick to Florida the Atlantic coast became an English stronghold. There would be memories of Dutch influence in New York and Swedish and Finnish influence on the Delaware, but from the day in 1664 when Colonel Richard Nicolls came ashore at the Battery this part of the North American continent would use the English language, abide by English common law, and, in the process, forever halt the expansionist dreams of the French and Spanish.

A lesser man than Nicolls would have found the task assigned him too great. The documents by which he ruled as royal governor seem to have been drawn up purposely to create confusion, quarrels, even warfare. Most important was the patent itself, by which Charles II arranged to give to his brother, the Duke of York, all that land from the Delaware to the Connecticut, from the Atlantic to Canada, and Long Island, Nantucket Island, and Martha's Vineyard. If Charles had wracked his brain for a way to cause future trouble, he could not have succeeded better. The colonies of Massachusetts, Connecticut, the Jerseys, Pennsylvania, Maryland, and Delaware all saw their boundaries infringed upon. Maine, struggling to keep out of the Bay Colony's clutches, learned that the Duke of York had also been granted a dubious claim to an area called Cornwall, lying between the Kennebec and St. Croix rivers. It mattered not at all to the king, but his assumption of ownership of the hinterland beyond New York also angered the French.

So it was no sinecure awaiting Nicolls. To his other burdens was added one of great psychological importance: he took ashore with him from the English fleet 450 redcoats—the first body of troops permanently assigned to service in the colonies. Their presence was an open, suppurating sore that would not heal until excised by revolution.

With evil men like Cranfield oppressing New Hampshire, stubborn men like Andros taking away the charters, and rascals misgoverning northern Carolina, it is easy to assume that all the English officials in the New World were selected not for their ability but for their lack of it. But Nicolls, although faithful to the Crown, was a fine man and when he failed it was because of interference from his superiors.

Within days of the takeover from the Dutch the people of the colony knew that life would not be greatly different than it had been under Stuyvesant. All the Dutch burghers had to do was swear allegiance to Charles II and then go about their former occupations. The common man saw little real change, and the wealthy landholders, who had purchased the patroonships and other large estates, were allowed to keep them intact. Instead of "patroons" these men became known as lords of the manor, and their influence was as great under the Crown as it had been under the Dutch West India Company's aegis. The Van Rensselaers, Van Cortlandts, Philipses, and other Dutch families lived on in their fine mansions along the Hudson or in their beautifully furnished townhouses in Manhattan, almost unaware of the change in government. Nicolls naturally replaced the officials of the two largest towns, New York and Albany, putting Englishmen into the posts of mayor and aldermen. But power based on wealth is hard to overcome, and it was not long before Dutchmen were sitting with their conquerors in the aldermen's chambers.

The new governor was astute enough to send emissaries to the Iroquois, promising them the same support and friendship that they had enjoyed with the Dutch. He did more than that. He sensed how eagerly the French were pushing southward from the St. Lawrence and assigned some of his troops to stations above the Mohawk River. Their military presence meant more to the Five Nations of the Iroquois than any number of parchment treaties.

The king and the Duke of York undercut Nicolls time and again. As has been seen, the Jerseys were taken away from his domain and given to Carteret and Berkeley. Worse yet was the imposition of new codes and regulations, which retained in the hands of the proprietor all powers of taxation, appointment, and court control. The duke looked upon his new province as a means of support, and the taxes he imposed were cruel and confiscatory.

The bubble burst when England again went to war with Holland. Trade fell off alarmingly, and what business was not diminished by the war was nearly paralyzed by York's taxes. But New York was a cosmopolitan town even then, a city where eighteen different languages could be detected by a careful observer, where ships of many nations came and went with cargoes for the whole world. If normal commerce could not be maintained, the merchants reasoned, they could turn to illegal devices. Barefaced piracy became a way of life. Even Nicolls, who was spending much of his personal wealth on such things as food and powder for the troops, turned to privateering.

Nicolls was so disheartened by York's greed and lack of interest in the colonists that he wrote to the duke, telling of the starvation on Long Island, of the sorry lack of commerce in the capital city, and of the hardships borne by the soldiery. Nothing happened, and Nicolls went home in 1668, disillusioned and far poorer than when he arrived in the colony.

Sir Francis Lovelace took up the chores Nicolls had put aside and improved things but little, suffering in the bargain from the ignominy of being run out of office by the short-lived return of the Dutch. Lovelace is perhaps best remembered for the small achievement of initiating the first mail service between New York and Boston. Once a month a post rider put the letters into his saddlebags, mounted his horse, and started up the shore to Massachusetts Bay. As far as Pelham the road was not too bad, but from there on the rider had rough going on paths that were nothing more than Indian trails. Only a stout-hearted man would volunteer as a mounted mailman in those early days.

When Lovelace returned to New York to find the flag of the Netherlands raised over Fort James, he scurried out to Long Island, where the English villages had prevented any Dutch intrusion. He could not escape the shame of losing his headquarters town and went home, to die in disgrace.

Next to try his hand at governing the colony was Sir Edmund Andros, who assumed power in 1674. The king and duke had handed him far too much responsibility, which Andros would find out for himself when he went to Boston to rescind the Massachusetts Bay charter. The people there were far more obstreperous than those in New York. One can only imagine the joy of New Yorkers when word was brought from Boston that William and Mary were now on the throne and that Andros—the charter thief—had been clapped in jail.

Governor Thomas Dongan followed Andros. He spent considerable time fortifying the northern frontier against the French and became a temporary favorite of the New Yorkers because he handed over to the city a new charter of incorporation in 1683. Known as Dongan's Great Charter, the instrument remained more or less in force without alteration until the Revolutionary War.

In the kaleidoscopic procession of governors, all more or less detested by the people, England gained little beyond the taxes squeezed from the unwilling colony. It mattered but little who sat in power in New York City; the people sensed that government was inevitably forced down upon them, never built up with their consent or cooperation. In dozens of ways the inhabitants grew more and more restive. Those wealthy enough to feel kinship with the throne, including such Dutch worthies as Stephen Van Cortlandt and Frederick Philipse, together with Anglican churchmen and government officials, found themselves bound together as royalists or Episcopalians. The majority of the people, both Dutch and English, felt no such loyalty to British institutions, and their patience was wearing thin.

The change at the seat of power in London was reflected in all the colonies. Francis Nicholson, the deputy left in command in New York when Andros went to Boston, stood on particularly shaky ground. His commission had come from a Stuart king, the people had no love for him, and the French were threatening again on the northern borders. Conditions were ripe for an uprising, and it came with surprising success.

A German brewer, Jacob Leisler, was captain of a company of the City Guard when in 1689 the militia was called up because of the French threat. There may have been a verbal insult hurled by Nicholson at the irregulars, or there may not have been, but Nicholson was understood to have snubbed the soldiers, and that was all that was needed to precipitate action. There was a sudden appearance of City Guard forces at the governor's door, a demand for surrender, and Leisler found himself in possession of the keys to the fort. Nicholson fled to England.

Leisler convened the council and, with the indulgence of ten of the eighteen members, assumed dictatorial powers. Foolishly, he thought he could keep London ignorant of his assumption of power—he had all letters to England searched and censored to prevent news from reaching the throne—but of course this was futile.

Stupid and arrogant both, Leisler took one very significant step when he called representatives from all the colonies to meet at the first colonial congress in Albany. They did not talk of rebellion or independence, but they did speak of ways to work together to defend their borders from the French and the Indians. The conference had been called because of an attack in February 1690 upon the village of Schenectady and the massacre of many of its inhabitants.

For nearly two years Leisler maintained his position as governor of New York, but he quickly lost some of his popular support to a point where one New Yorker referred to the brewer and his minions as a pack of rascals "herded together out of Hell." Leisler, wrong in his assumption of power, shortsighted in his arrogance, evil in his appointment of his son-in-law as lieutenant governor, nevertheless still had considerable support in the streets. Common people had so little love for monarchs that Leisler's rule took on a specious glow of righteousness.

Leisler's Rebellion ended in 1691 with the arrival of British troops under a new governor, Colonel Henry Sloughter. The German brewer-turned-autocrat resisted arrest at first, and his supporters fired at the redcoats, drawn up on parade. The inevitable followed. Leisler was seized, along with his son-in-law and those councilmen who had voted him into office. The councilmen were spared, but the ringleader and his relative were hanged.

New York's next long-term governor (Sloughter died shortly after Leisler was hanged) was Colonel Benjamin Fletcher, good friend and crony of pirates everywhere. There may have been a touch of opéra bouffe to it all, but it was also immoral.

William of Orange, at war with the French, issued letters of marque authorizing his people, including the colonists, to seize enemy vessels on the high seas. Business was particularly good in New York, yet ships left port with empty holds and returned with rich cargoes. No one was rude enough to ask where the riches came from. Fletcher himself outfitted vessels for privateering adventures. Everyone able to charter a ship became, for the nonce, a privateer or, to use an uglier word, a pirate. Besides sending his own ships out, Fletcher made deals with masters of legitimate vessels who were happy to double as pirates. Captains Tew, Hore, and Glover were particularly amenable.

The Earl of Bellomont, who in 1698 followed Fletcher as governor of New York, was of an entirely different stripe and wrote at length about his predecessor's shady dealings. Besides telling of how cargoes were shifted from licensed to unlicensed vessels at Sandy Hook, at the entrance to New York Bay, and how Madagascar had become a smuggler's nest known to half the ships sailing from New York, Bellomont added this long-winded sentence in a letter home:

> It is likewise evident that Tew, Glover and Hore had commissions granted them by Coll: Fletcher when none of them had any ship or vessell in Colonel Fletcher's Govern^t, yet they had Commissions and were permitted to raise men in New-Yorke, and the design publique of their being bound to the red sea, and Captn Tew that had been before a most notorious Pirate (complained of by the East India Company) of his returne from the Indies with great riches made a visit to New York, where (although a man of most mean and infamous character) he was received and caressed by Coll: Fletcher, dined and supped often with him, and appeared publickly in his coach with him and they exchanged presents, as gold watches etc, with one another, all this is known to most of the City and on this Coll: Fletcher gave him his Commission.

Men looked upon as decent by their fellow citizens engaged in this illicit traffic not only to make a profit, but because the Navigation Acts and other English regulations would otherwise have strangled commerce. Piracy was one way of getting around English oppression. It should be said that much of the privateering was not the old brand of cutlass-and-dagger operation where victims were slaughtered on the decks or forced to walk the plank. The piracy business had become more sophisticated.

St. Mary's, a small island off the northern coast of Madagascar, was a rendezvous for many ships out of New York. There cargoes were transferred from ships sailing from the East Indies and India, as well as from Arab dhows whose freight, although it may have been legitimate, was more likely stolen from any of a hundred East African ports.

Records of fleet operations run by the Philipse family reveal how widespread commerce had grown. Their vessels carried furs, hides, tobacco, sugar, rum, whale oil, copper, cocoa, sassafras, and logwood from New York to London; peas, salt, hardtack, flour, wine, rum, lime juice, and gunpowder to Madagascar; and manufactured goods from Europe back to the colony.

Some ship captains actually seized vessels on the high seas and made off with their cargo, but most of them evaded the laws in less bloodthirsty ways. It was easy to buy and sell at St. Mary's Island, far from the eyes of English customs officers. It was also easy to switch freight from an inbound vessel to one lying at anchor off Sandy Hook. Then the first ship would declare what cargo it wished to pay duty on while the second one, known to have been in port the day before, would unload its transferred cargo at a dock without customs men overseeing the operation.

Quite obviously, with the local governor financially involved in such an operation, it was easy to prevent prying eyes from being where they were not wanted. Whatever the moral judgment on such operations may be, they were just another facet of colonial rebelliousness and of the growing feeling that England was dipping too greedily into the cash drawers of colonial enterprises.

By 1699 England had added the Wool Act to the notorious Navigation Acts, forbidding the colonists to manufacture finished articles made of wool or to sell it outside the provinces. Three decades later the screws were tightened even more; the hatters of Danbury and Norwalk in Connecticut were forbidden to make hats. Englishmen, proud of their self-reliance and prouder still of their success in establishing new homes in the wilderness, were not the sort of people to put up with such restrictions. They made what they wished, sold it locally, loaded it on vessels in Boston, Newport, New York, Charleston, and other ports, and dared the English fleet to catch them once they had sailed out of harbor.

Fletcher was certainly no fool. He had seen what happened when the French and Indians attacked Schenectady and knew that one reason why the English colonies were vulnerable to such raids was their lack of unity and failure to coordinate defenses. He made this clear in a letter written in 1696:

> The Indians, though monsters, want not sense, but plainly see we are not united, and it is apparent that the stronger these colonies grow in parts, the weaker we are on the whole, every little government setting up for despotic power and allowing no appeal to the Crown, but valuing themselves on their own strength and on a little juggling in defeating all commands and injunctions of the King.

Fletcher had little opportunity to further his plan to unify the colonies against the enemy creeping down from Canada: word of his traffic with smugglers and pirates led the Crown to remove him in favor of the Earl of Bellomont.

Bellomont found New York on the wave of a prosperous period of expansion. The docks were busy, with slaves working hard to handle the cargo and warehouses bursting with goods from all over the world. There was plenty of hard currency available, but a man had to be sharp of eye and well versed on the various exchange rates because the coins might be Spanish doubloons or pieces-of-eight, Dutch guilders, French louis d'or, or pieces from Portugal, China, and the East Indies; there were never enough English shillings, however.

Although he governed virtually all of New England and New York, Bellomont devoted much of his time to ending piracy and smuggling. He arrested suspects, seized goods that were of questionable origin, and put his own men into posts where they could keep a weather eye on misdoing. Poor old Bellomont worked so hard that he wore himself out and died in office in 1701.

There is no need to detail all the inept, profligate, and stupid governors set over the people of the northern colonies. They came and went, some enriching themselves and others losing their fortunes. None of them had much love or respect for the men and women they governed.

When Queen Anne came to power at the death of William III in 1702, she chose a cousin, Lord Cornbury, to govern New York and New Jersey. He deserves mention mainly because he was such a scoundrel that his sponsor had to recall him. Cornbury showed his colors when a new war with France caused fear all along the American frontier. After asking for money to build defenses at New York Harbor, the governor must have pocketed the funds, as not one cannon was mounted. His greatest duplicity was a scheme contrived with Governor Joseph Dudley, of Massachusetts, to annex Rhode Island to the Bay Colony and Connecticut to his own. This was what convinced Anne that her cousin would be safer at home.

Frontier policies of the various colonies created an atmosphere for wrong-doing on the part of governing officials and individuals of lesser stature alike. Coastal settlements urged men to settle on the frontier as a means of protecting the older communities. So deeply interested were the established towns in having such bastions erected on their borders that they issued orders forbidding the settlers to leave their villages, even in the face of Indian attack.

In view of the French effort to restrain any outward migration from the English colonies and their use of Indians to do the lion's share of the fighting, it was no wonder that friction between frontiersmen and governors or colonial assemblies grew.

King William's and Queen Anne's Wars put the burden of survival on the border settlements themselves. In 1690 Schenectady was sacked in an Indian massacre planned by the French. The blow was avenged a few months later by the capture of Port Royal in Nova Scotia. It was a typical reaction, repeated later on many occasions, but the year-by-year attrition resulting from attacks and skirmishes on the border fell more heavily on the settlers than on the residents of the coastal cities.

Conflict between France and England as their colonies expanded grew out of European wars, religious and behavioral differences, and the friction born of trying to colonize the same territory.

The English colonists, after the early fiasco at Jamestown, went about establishing new settlements in North America with hardheaded, businesslike determination. They put seeds in the ground even before they built homes. They carried on a busy fur trade but permitted nothing to get in the way of settling new territory, building permanent towns, and strengthening political control over their territories.

It was different in Canada. The French kings sent over many pioneers, but most of them were men without wives or families. These men thought more of the fur trade than of empire, and most of their inland settlements were forts or fur-trading posts rather than seats of agricultural activity.

Englishmen had learned at Jamestown that women were needed to create viable colonial towns. The French, on the other hand, roamed the forests at will, carried on amours with Indian squaws, and put in few crops. It was a romantic life, of course, but it had its duller side. Samuel Champlain established Port Royal, on the Bay of Fundy, with an all-male society. When the men grew homesick for the attentions of women, Champlain formed what was the first social club in the Western Hemisphere, "L'Ordre de Bon-Temps," the Order of the Good Time. The year was 1606, before a single permanent English settlement had been established on the North American continent. Each night the men met in the main building to dine. The meals were planned and cooked by members in rotation. All this is mentioned only to emphasize the difference between such an existence and that in the later colonies to the south where English men and women built homes, tilled the soil, and sat down at table together with children who would carry on the work of colonizing the new land.

Because the French fraternized with the Indians and wanted little of their land, relations between the two groups remained friendly. Catholic missionaries went everywhere with the French colonists and were indefatigable at converting the Indians both to Christianity and to the French cause in the struggle with the English. Jesuit priests played almost as important a role in ruling Canada as any governor.

The fur trade blossomed into a tremendously important source of revenue for France, and the French kings hated to see Englishmen chopping down forests and spreading out into the wilderness from which those furs came. Needing more furs all the time, the French expanded farther and farther into the wilderness. Before the first English settlements had been planted on the edge of the Atlantic, the French had ventured clear up the St. Lawrence and Ottawa rivers; and long before the English had spread inland more than a few miles, there were French forts at Pittsburgh, Detroit, the Straits of Mackinac, and Lake Champlain.

By the time William of Orange ascended the throne, the French had explored and laid claim to most of the land between the St. Lawrence and the mouth of the Mississippi. Moreover, they showed every intention of surging southward from the fortified cities of Quebec, Montreal, and Trois Rivières to try to drive the English into the sea. That they were badly outnumbered and scattered made no difference to them. They could rely on their numerous Indian allies to turn the trick for them.

In their greed for land, the English colonists had antagonized most of the tribes from Maine to Georgia. The Mohegans were friendly, but were so small in number that their allegiance meant little. But in the Iroquois the English had powerful allies. This was a direct and immeasurably valuable bequest from the Dutch in New York. So the Iroquois, who hated most of the tribes friendly to the French, stood guard against incursions on the New York frontier. When William declared war with the French—another in the endless conflicts over world commerce—the New Englanders, with no such friendly bastion on the border, were exposed to attack.

The Jesuit missionaries had been busy urging their Indian allies to repel enemy encroachments upon their ancestral lands. For years the Jesuit cry had been "Destroy the heretics!" War in Europe was all the tribes in Maine and Quebec needed.

Count Frontenac organized a war party under Francis Hertel and sent it up the St. Francis River to what is now northern New Hampshire, across the forests of Maine, and down the Piscataqua. On a bitter March night in 1690 the French and Indians fell upon Salmon Falls, killed thirty whites, captured fifty-four women and children, and fled to the woods. Another party sent out by Frontenac rendezvoused with Hertel's group and attacked Portland. This time the English had been forewarned, and they sought refuge in the fort. The French offered to protect the settlers if they surrendered. The minute the Englishmen opened the gate of the palisade the Indians rushed in, killed all but five people, and wiped the settlement from the face of the earth.

Haverhill, Massachusetts, felt the wrath of the Indian attack, as did other towns from the Hudson to the Penobscot. Sir William Phips tried to capture Quebec City, but his fleet was wrecked in a storm that lashed the Gulf of St. Lawrence. Finally the conflict in Europe died down and King William's War ground to an end in the colonies as well.

This was the background of the situation that confronted the northern provinces when Queen Anne became embroiled with the French.

During the four-year lull between the wars the French had not been idle. Father Sébastien Rasles, missionary leader of the Indians

ROYAL GOVERNORS AND KING WILLIAM'S WAR

on the Kennebec, had exhorted his charges to prepare for battle. No sooner had word of new hostilities on the Continent, the War of the Spanish Succession, reached the New World than the Christian Indians, who promptly forgot whatever mercy and brotherly love they may have learned, struck at the northern New England outposts. For eight years, from 1702 to 1710, it was tomahawk against flintlock, flaming arrow against water buckets, savage brutality against raw courage. On the fourth try Port Royal, rebuilt by the French, was recaptured by the English, burned to the ground, and all of Acadia ravished.

Most tragic of all was the second visitation of Indian terror at Deerfield, Massachusetts. Scene of the massacre in 1675 during King Philip's War, the little settlement had remained an exposed outpost, far up the Connecticut River near present-day Vermont. To the French, it was a plum waiting to be plucked. On a freezing, snowy night in 1704 French soldiers and their Indian allies swept down on the little town, shouting with glee at the thought of quick victory. When the battle was over, only the church and one house remained unburned. Forty-nine people were shot or hacked to death and ninety-five others dragged off to Canada as captives.

Massachusetts had suffered the most, but all the northern colonies had spent time and energy and lives without altering the basic problem. The frontier still existed, fear tormented every settler in the hinterland, and the colonial governments had shown no aptitude for working together in the face of a common danger. Ahead of them was the grim specter of an even worse conflict, the French and Indian War.

XVI

Ever Westward

As THE EIGHTEENTH century advanced, the colonies felt themselves growing stronger in a hundred different ways. Massachusetts
had carried the brunt of a war with the French and the Indians.
Virginia, remembering Bacon's Rebellion, demanded from the
royal governors more rights for the house of burgesses. New York
was becoming wealthy with its growing commerce, and Pennsylvania, free of worry from Indian attacks, was expanding westward to the Susquehanna.

People whose parents and grandparents had faced the dangers of
the wilderness found that their little towns and fast-growing cities
now gave them a measure of security everywhere except on the
frontier. Whereas before their concern had been self-protection,
now they thought of commerce, expansion, home manufacturing,
and escape from the oppressive measures imposed by the Crown.

Despite disease, deaths at sea, Indian attacks, and the rigors of
life on the frontier, population had mushroomed, and with it came
wealth. Although the early discoverers were disheartened at not
finding gold as the Spaniards had, the richness of the North
American continent was nevertheless awesome. The fur trade was
an endless source of wealth, the forests yielded lumber, spars for
the sailing ships of the era, tar, pitch, turpentine, and other naval
stores. New England harvested the seas for a rich profit. In the
South cotton and tobacco were beginning to replace indigo and
rice as the main cash crops. Grains were the principal income-pro-
ducing crops in the middle colonies.

Overseas trade flourished despite the Navigation Acts and other
restrictions. Boston, New York, Philadelphia, Charleston, and the
Chesapeake Bay ports were booming as ships came and went by

the hundreds. Northern New England took an early lead in shipbuilding, supplying merchants with their own bottoms for international trade. By the early years of the eighteenth century the old
dependence on the English and Dutch merchant marines had begun
to diminish.

Given things to sell and ships to transport them, the people
took to the sea, and colonial ships were seen in every port on the
globe. When they couldn't be escaped, taxes were paid to the
Crown, but many a ship sailed and returned with no money going
to the royal tax collector. England called it smuggling, of course,
but the colonists looked upon it as a natural right and a sign of
their independence.

In virtually every colony this independent spirit led to conflict
between the elected assemblies and the royal governors. Connecticut
and Rhode Island, which had not surrendered their charters, were
more fortunate than the others, but friction was unceasing. The
royal governor became the target of colonial hatred, but it was his
subordinates—customs collectors, attorneys general, surveyors of
the king's forests, admiralty judges—that prompted the enmity.
If they had been paragons of virtue they still would have been disliked because of their duties. These were the men who prowled the
docks checking what cargo had been brought into port and insisting
on payment of customs duties, who dunned settlers who had gone
out into the wilderness for their quit-rents, and who interpreted
most laws for the benefit of the throne.

It was not all one-sided, however. The colonists insisted upon
their inherent rights as English subjects, but they disliked helping
to pay for the fleets and armies England maintained in Europe and
in North America. Without such forces Spain and France, and
possibly even little Holland, would have gobbled up the defenseless
colonies.

If the English kings had selected their representatives with
greater care, much of the difficulty might have been avoided. But
appointments went for the most part to political sycophants, to
friends, or to those to whom the monarchs were indebted. It was a
way of paying off obligations, and the colonists were made to suffer a long succession of inept, greedy, and vicious officials, most
of whom were trying to repair their own personal fortunes.

Perhaps the main cause of friction between the colonies and the
home country was the restlessness of the times. All over the civ-

ilized world the common man was throwing off his yoke and becoming more and more convinced that he had an inalienable right
to a voice in the laws that governed him. This does not mean that
the cry of independence was on every tongue. Most of the colonists
thought of themselves as Englishmen, wanted to remain tied—if
somewhat loosely—to the Crown, and had as much difficulty getting
along with the other colonies as they did with the king and his
representatives.

A shortage of currency hampered commerce, and this was
another source of friction. It seems incredible today that for generations the Dutch and early English colonists in New York used
Indian wampum, colored beads strung on threads, as a medium of
exchange. Soon after the English seized New York the prominent
merchants of that city hoarded great casks of wampum, just as
today's millionaires hide funds in Swiss banks. This currency shortage led to demands for the issuance of paper money—a demand
supported by the popular assemblies and opposed by the royal
governors.

It did not help matters when many of the governors stole tax
revenues, or spent them according to whim. In New York the assembly claimed that it held an "inherent right" to govern expendi-
tures of tax monies.

The problems were aggravated by the very growth of the colonies.
In Massachusetts Bay more and more people were leaving the settled areas to stake out new homesites in central and western Massachusetts. New Yorkers were settling the Mohawk and upper
Delaware valleys. In Pennsylvania many residents, particularly the
Germans, were moving out into the lush farmlands along the Susquehanna and its tributaries. Scots-Irish families, most of them
hardy folk with antiroyal leanings, filtered through the coastal
towns and made their way into the Piedmont of the Carolinas and
into the foothills of the Appalachians in Maryland, Virginia, and
Pennsylvania.

These people differed in many ways, but all were infused with a
strong feeling of independence. The Germans were good church
members, usually belonging to the Mennonites, the Dunkers, or an
offshoot of these sects. On the other hand many of the Scots-Irish
frontiersmen cared little for organized religion and supported their
churches poorly. These people were at first equally impatient about
supporting schools but later became strong proponents of public

North America, 1650

education and contributed far more than their share to the teaching professions.

Like hill people everywhere, uplanders looked askance at the folk in the lowland towns. In Virginia and the Carolinas the owners of large plantations adopted many of the ways of English landed gentry; this was anathema to the men living in log cabins and grubbing a precarious living from hill farms. And the residents of the established towns did not like the idea that the frontiersmen would eventually build towns and demand a voice in the government. In Massachusetts the royal governors tried to whittle down the number of assembly seats accredited to new communities. In most of the other colonies conservative merchants and landholders on the coast attempted to reduce the influence wielded by the newer settlements.

Among the tricks played by the older communities was the gerrymandering of the frontier country into abnormally large counties. Thus an upland county in the Carolinas might be the size of Connecticut or Rhode Island yet have the same number of representatives in the assembly as a much smaller county along the Atlantic. Even the God-fearing, pure-of-heart Quakers were not above political trickery; they saw to it that Pennsylvania's three "Quaker counties"—Philadelphia, Chester, and Bucks—each with eight representatives in the assembly, could outvote all the other counties in the colony.

Thus the seaboard counties had the upper hand and enacted laws that tended to favor men with property over those without land. This disenfranchised many freemen who had not yet purchased a homesite or who could not afford one, and it kept power in the hands of the wealthier families in the cities. It was no different in the other colonies. Boston, New York, the tidewater region of Virginia, and Charleston all exerted far stronger influence on legislation and fiscal control than did the regions back from the coast. The very men in the coastal cities who were fighting England for more liberty from royal oppression were trampling on the rights of men in their own colonies.

This conflict of interests would have led to an explosive situation at a much earlier date had it not been for the exigencies of the struggle against the French. On the frontier this conflict never really came to a halt, even when peace treaties were signed.

Count Frontenac had seen the value of establishing frontier

posts and had erected several in the seventeenth century. Samuel Champlain extended this program, building forts in northern Maine, along the Richelieu River and Lake Champlain, and on Lake Ontario. French *coureurs de bois* and their Indian allies were constantly forging southward, keeping English frontier settlements on edge. Jesuit missionaries, who had converted thousands of Indians to Catholicism, spurred their adherents to attacks against "heretics."

Led by courageous men like Joliet, Marquette, and La Salle, the French turned the corner of the English territory, bypassing the western stronghold of the Six Iroquois Nations at Niagara, and followed the Ohio and Mississippi clear down to the Gulf of Mexico. This was a clear threat to continued English expansion westward. Most of the royal charters had given the colonies western borders that were completely indefinite or that extended to the Pacific Ocean. French expansion south of the Great Lakes nullified the charters and put the French clearly on the frontiers of the English colonies.

As pioneers moved into exposed positions in the highlands or close to Canada, they asked for help from the assemblies and governors, but their requests were usually buried in committee. Residents of the coastal cities were largely uninterested in the problems of their friends and relatives who had moved on in the never-ending push to the west. Only when the threat became serious enough to involve the coastal towns was there any real coordination of defense measures. In this respect the New England colonies were better than those to the south. Pennsylvania, in particular, earned the dislike of other colonies—New England and New York more than the others—because the Quakers abhorred war and would not contribute money or men.

Friction marred all efforts at unity. Maine and New Hampshire were alternately happy and unhappy about the way Massachusetts tried to control or absorb them. When the Indians threatened they were glad of support. At other times they wanted to go their own way. Connecticut and Rhode Island argued over where their joint boundary should be between the Thames River and Narragansett Bay, and Maryland and Pennsylvania did not resolve their border dispute until the eve of the Revolutionary War.

Despite these differences there was a constant exchange of population. One example will show this incessant movement as men sought better conditions. The town of Dorchester in Massachusetts had not been settled more than a few decades before some of its residents pulled up stakes and sailed down to the Carolinas, where they established another Dorchester. Some years after this there was still another move and a new Dorchester was settled in Georgia.

Germans and Moravians found their towns near Philadelphia growing too crowded (although there were only a few thousand in the largest) and trekked westward in search of new homes. Hardship on the trail never seemed to deter them. Some of their members finally found land to their liking in the verdant valleys of the Appalachian range in the Carolinas. Other Germans, aware of the friendly attitude of the Iroquois, moved out along the Mohawk River from Albany.

The Scots-Irish, perhaps the most venturesome of all, were responsible for extending civilization farther from the Atlantic coast than any other ethnic group.

Although all thirteen colonies owed varying degrees of allegiance to England, the New World was already proving itself a vast melting pot. Outside of New England the English were outnumbered by other groups, including the Dutch, Swedes, Germans, French Huguenots, and Scots-Irish. Many others, including Austrians, Swiss, and Jews, saw the new provinces as a place to seek a better life and escape religious persecution. They did not always find the latter, but oppression was seldom as stringent as in their homelands, and Rhode Island, Pennsylvania, New York, Maryland, and Georgia were earthly paradises compared to most countries in Europe.

These people contributed immeasurably to the wealth and well-being of the growing colonies. Huguenot settlers were indefatigable workers and became important citizens of towns in Westchester County, New York, Charleston, South Carolina, and in Virginia. In the Carolinas at first they cultivated silk worms and wine grapes but soon shifted to the trades and professions. Because they assimilated easily, they lost most of their national characteristics in a few decades.

German princes were often so ruthless in stamping out religious sects other than the state church that many residents of the Rhineland sought refuge in the English colonies. Queen Anne was particularly solicitous of people from the Palatinate and helped many of them to migrate to her possession across the sea.

Her kindness was marked by a great tragedy, but in the main the Palatine Germans benefited enormously from the offer of land and the opportunity to worship as they wished. The tragedy grew out of one migratory surge across the ocean when three thousand persons were embarked in ten ships for the long and tempestuous crossing. Before the vessels reached New York, 773 of the migrants had died at sea. This was one of the worst incidents of its kind, but it was far from unique. Seldom did any ship make the crossing without a considerable loss of life, either because of storms, disease, or hunger.

It was hunger and lack of opportunity more often than religious oppression that led the Scots-Irish migrants to leave northern Ireland, but there were religious overtones. England passed laws unfavorable to the Presbyterians. No Presbyterian pastor was allowed to perform the marriage ceremony, tithes were collected for the Church of England even from dissidents, and dissenters could not hold government office. These reasons, added to the everyday difficulty of gaining a decent livelihood in a depressed economy, pushed many Scots-Irish into seeking a new home overseas. No single ethnic group was scattered so widely throughout the colonies. Whether the climate was hot or cold, the economy based on agriculture, shipping, or manufacturing, the Scots-Irish could be found hard at work. More often than not, though, their independent spirit led them to quit the towns where they first settled and strike out for virgin land in the wilderness.

The courage of these immigrants cannot be stressed too strongly. Men and women in their middle years, often with large broods of children, submitted to indenture to pay for their passage to the colonies. As soon as they freed themselves of their debts they hiked off through the forests, usually with one horse and one cow, making their arduous way over rivers and mountains, and building crude homes of felled trees. All they took with them were a few tools, pots and pans, and the clothes on their backs. But every man had a German-made gun from Pennsylvania: the life of his family often depended upon his ability to shoot it accurately.

The flow of immigration in the late 1800s reached such a tidal wave that one might assume most of the migrants arrived long after the nation was founded. But the figures show how erroneous this belief is. Germans numbering close to 100,000 were residents of Pennsylvania and New York fifty years before the Revolution.

Around the time of the Irish famine in the early 1700s each year saw ten or fifteen thousand Scots-Irish arrivals on American shores.

New England received small influxes of settlers from other lands, but not to the degree common in other provinces. Most of the people landing in Boston, Providence, Newport, and New Haven were Englishmen from England, although there was a small flow of English people who had left their homeland and gone to the West Indies, especially Barbados. Not liking the climate or the frequent hurricanes, these families left the Caribbean islands after a generation or two to try again in New England.

Promotional literature and handbills appeared in Europe to attract immigrants to the American colonies. The English monarchs appealed for settlers. So did the trading companies and the proprietors who wished to populate the lands granted them by royal edict. Church leaders, especially the Huguenot and Puritan ministers, urged their followers to seek freedom in the New World. Influential men obtained large grants of land on the frontier and then canvassed their home regions for settlers. In the Carolinas parcels of fifty thousand and more acres were often deeded outright to favorites, who then brought over thousands of settlers to populate the region.

Arrival of new immigrants by the tens of thousands over a period of thirty or forty years created serious problems. New colonists wanted a voice in the affairs of their provinces, and the entrenched settlers were loath to surrender power. Many of the later immigrants were poor, having nothing in common with those who had been established in the country long enough to own plantations, manufacturing establishments, shipping firms, stores, print shops, and thriving professional practices.

Language caused more trouble than any other single factor. Differing accents among those who used the English language could be accepted, but when the Huguenots spoke French and the Germans and Swiss spoke German, there was friction. Nowhere was this more evident than in Pennsylvania. The Palatine Germans, the Moravians, and the Swiss migrated to the land west of Philadelphia and built communities in what became known as the "Pennsylvania Dutch" country. They had little need to use English. In addition to coming in large numbers from Europe, these Germans were a fecund people, proliferating rapidly. English Quakers in the eastern counties and other English-speaking people feared they would be swamped under the Germanic language and customs. Even Ben Franklin, normally a clear-headed, calm thinker, wrote in his newspaper of the dangers threatening the English language and the very government itself.

One obvious reason for Franklin's concern was the provincialism of the provinces. Each one operated more or less in a vacuum except in times of extreme danger. When the idea of union finally became important, this isolationism would have to be overcome.

Transportation between the colonies was difficult and time-consuming, and this contributed to their isolation. It required a week to drive between Boston and New York or between Monticello and Philadelphia. A man on horseback could make it in less time, but anyone relying on a stage could expect the trip to consume the full week.

A hundred years after the Pilgrims landed at Plymouth a single trail wound its way from Boston to Providence and on to New York. Trenton, New Jersey, was connected with the twin capital of the Amboys by a road that meandered through virgin forests and crossed streams at fords that were impassable in the spring. A biographer of John Stevens, one of the fathers of steam transportation in North America, described a stage that connected Burlington and the Amboys in 1728 as a clumsy vehicle that imperiled passengers and damaged freight and was so unstable that the driver had to ask for assistance from his passengers to avoid tipping over. It was "All lean to the right now, gentlemen, if you please" or "All to the left here, thank you." When a Philadelphia paper advertised a "summer stage fitted up with Benches and Cover'd over, so that the Passengers may sit Easy and Dry," this was cause for high praise.

Wretched roads and slow communication meant that goods could pass from one colony to another only with difficulty, and news was almost as slow. Only the most vital intelligence was relayed by fast post riders, so Savannah and Charleston did not learn of events in Boston and New York until weeks after they occurred. With other communities weeks away over horrendous roads, little thought was given to union.

If transportation and the dissemination of news were slow between large cities on the coast, there is no word to describe the delays between those cities and the frontier settlements. A family living along the Juniata River in central Pennsylvania might learn of an event in Philadelphia months later, and a person in the hill country of Carolina might not learn of a relative's death in Charleston until the relative had been buried half a year.

Yet with all these difficulties the colonists steadily grew in number and scattered farther and farther beyond the lowlands. After the penury that dogged the common man in the Old World's crowded cities, the English colonies held out rich hope.

With all its drawbacks, the New World was a paradise to most colonists.

XVII

Evil Times:
America and the Slave Trade

PARADISE IT MAY have been for white colonists, but America was something totally different to the black slaves brought from Africa. For them it was a cruel, inhumane place where they were deprived of every right, worked to the point of exhaustion, and made to support an economy from which they derived no benefit.

Black slaves had been introduced into the English colonies even before Jamestown had ceased to be a precarious outpost in the wilderness. Tobacco growers had need for cheap labor, and the Negro filled that need. Long before the end of the 1600s slavery was an accepted fact in most of the colonies and was the very basis of the successful plantations in those colonies south of Maryland. The rice, indigo, and cotton crops depended upon slave labor, either black or indentured white. The indentured white man could eventually buy his way to freedom, but for the black there was no way out.

Nowhere was the importance of the black slave more vividly shown than in Georgia. Slavery was outlawed at the beginning, and Governor Oglethorpe fought it until he left the colony, but the planters, looking at the economic well-being of the Carolinas and knowing that Spanish Florida thrived because it used slaves, finally won out, and Georgia became a slave-owning colony. In the opinion of the whites it was impossible for Georgia to compete successfully with other producing areas unless costs could be driven down through the use of slave labor.

In the early years the supply came entirely from Africa. Raiding parties went ashore, seized any able-bodied adults they could lay hands upon, and shanghaied them aboard ship. It is irrelevant that certain natives of Africa were themselves often as cruel and immoral as the slave traders; the white man's culpability is no less. Stronger tribes preyed on weaker ones, gathering in their victims and selling them to the slavers at the water's edge all along the west-central coast of the continent. At first the trade was poorly organized. Ships that could not find cargoes often took on slaves to avoid going home empty. But as the sugar plantations of the Caribbean islands wore out or killed off the Indian natives they had used as a labor supply, the great demand for black slaves fostered more efficient methods.

Ships flying the flags of most of the civilized nations turned to "blackbirding." Vessels were altered to carry hundreds of victims, chained in rows in the holds and 'tween-decks, where they suffered the tortures of thirst, hunger, and disease during the long voyage from Africa to the West Indies. They died like flies, and their bodies were flung to the sharks. The only reason any care was taken of them was the simple economic one that enough had to be alive at the port of arrival to make the trip profitable.

A ship could carry a cargo to Europe, drop down to the African coast, load up with slaves, and then deliver them at a fine profit in the West Indies or southern ports. On the last leg of the voyage home the hold, so recently crowded with human freight, often held another rich cargo, this time sugar, cotton, or rice. Blackbirding meant fabulous returns on a small initial investment.

When the southern colonies turned to a plantation type of economy, thousands of blacks were brought into the port cities of Savannah, Charleston, Wilmington, North Carolina, and those on Chesapeake Bay. Hardly a sizable city in the South was without a slave market, where planters went to purchase field hands, examining them carefully to determine if they were healthy, testing them for their strength as farmers did draft horses, and haggling over the price asked by agents of the blackbirding captains. Males brought the largest sums, and healthy women of child-bearing age almost as much. Children and old people were sold for much less or "thrown in to make the pot sweeter." At the height of the importation slavers, wanting to ensure a source of supply nearer the market, turned the island of Barbuda in the West Indies into one vast breeding farm for human beings.

There are no statistics to show how many thousands of Negroes were imported as slave laborers. It is known that some plantation owners owned as many as a thousand. Few whites, except the indentured ones, were without at least a few slaves, and even in the North many blacks labored in warehouses, on the docks, and in the homes of well-to-do city residents. Quakers, who behaved admirably in their relations with the Indians, often owned slaves, although many abhorred the practice and it was eventually outlawed.

White indentured servants endured untold hardships. They worked fourteen and more hours a day, existed on the smallest amounts of food that would keep body and soul together, had no privileges, and were beaten for the simplest infractions of rules laid down by their employers. Horrible as this existence was, it was nothing compared to the conditions under which black slaves existed. The slaves were deprived of all rights. A slave could not vote, could not appeal to the courts for any redress, was denied the right to bear arms, could not own land, could be bought, sold, and trafficked in like any chattel, and was under the complete authority of his owner. Most lived in hovels no better than pig sties.

There are many examples of owners who treated their slaves with kindness. Some even provided weather-tight housing and reasonably adequate rations. But for the vast majority of the blacks life was a daily struggle just to stay alive, what with poor and insufficient food, beatings, and oppressive measures for every real or fancied infraction. Worst of all, possibly, the blacks were ignored. They were considered of no more importance than the cattle in the barn or the chickens in the henhouse. Such indifference demoralized them.

Slavery also did great damage to the character and morals of the owners. Many became depraved and heartless. The degradation was insidious, often leaving the white masters unaware of their own inhumanity. In a diary kept by William Byrd, for thirty years a member of the Virginia council, owner of thousands of acres of land where Richmond now stands, possessor of a library equaled by few in the New World, and the very epitome of the aristocrat of tidewater Virginia, there are forty-three entries over a three-year period in which Byrd wrote that he, his wife, or other close

relatives whipped, beat, chained, or put a bit in the mouth of
black servants. As one historian said, this was the true picture behind the "moonlight and magnolia fantasy," as it has to be assumed that if one of the most cultured men of his time stooped
to such measures, less enlightened owners must have been a hun-
dredfold more brutal.

Slavery's contribution to the early economy was so enormous it
can only be imagined. It made many a white man wealthy beyond
his dreams. It helped the South to become prosperous. In the
North it sustained the shipbuilding and shipping industries in
times of recession, creating fortunes in New England, New York,
and New Jersey that were astronomical at the time and impres-
sive even by today's standards.

A few decades after Georgia reversed itself and opened the flood
gates to slavery, the Quakers, Mennonites, and Moravians of Pennsylvania took various steps to forbid this immoral institution, but it
remained a potent force in the southern economy until the Civil
War, and much later.

Repressive measures were often so brutal that rebellion seemed
the only way out for some blacks. As early as the 1680s there were
insurrections in Virginia and Maryland, and in the first half of
the eighteenth century more than a score broke out elsewhere, mostly
in the South.

New York did not go unscathed. In 1712 a slave rebellion led
to the wounding or killing of fifteen whites. Retribution was swift;
twenty-one slaves were executed, the more fortunate by hanging,
the less fortunate by being burned at the stake, broken on the
wheel, or hanged alive in chains. Tensions remained high through
the years, and in 1741, when New York was a city of about twelve
thousand inhabitants, there was another outburst of white repression, born for the most part of fear and ignorance. A storekeeper
discovered her shop broken into and looted. It was rumored that
several Negroes had been overheard whispering about new-found
riches, and half a dozen or so blacks were put in jail. Facts differ
somewhat as to later events, but a series of fires broke out and suddenly the whites were convinced that Negroes were conspiring to
burn the city down.

In the next few days a warehouse, the soldiers' barracks, several
barns and residences, and the governor's home were reduced to
ashes. For no sensible reason suspicion fell upon seven Negroes

brought into port on a Spanish ship. Two garrulous old women thought they heard the Spanish slaves say something about "Scorch a little—but by and by," and panic swept over the town. Vigilante bands roamed the streets watching every black. A grand jury was convened, attorneys rushed to offer the governor their services in any inquiry, and finally the supreme court, the justices bewigged and black-robed, went into session. Someone with a calmer head asked one of the Spanish slaves what he had meant by his remark. He said he was talking about how the Spanish at Porto Bello had been "scorched" by Admiral Vernon, who had won a great victory. It did no good; fear was everywhere. A reward of £100 was offered to any person giving evidence of a conspiracy.

A fifteen-year-old wench who served grog to sailors in a tough waterfront saloon was one of the witnesses. She told a fantastic tale of Negroes planning to burn the city and take over the government. She was probably half-witted or worse, but solemn judges listened and gave credence to her story. It was not unlike the testimony of the foolish girls in Salem against old women accused of witchcraft. The judges heard only what they wanted to hear.

In the midst of the turbulence Governor Oglethorpe sent a message to the New York authorities about a Spanish plot to burn English colonial towns. There were other unfounded rumors in the letter, including one that Catholic priests were to be the agents, doffing their clerical garb to pose as physicians and dancing-masters. Through the town ran frightened people shouting "The Papists!" "The Romans!" "Fire!" and anything else they could think of. A schoolteacher who had never harmed a child in his life was accused of being a priest in disguise and was hanged, protesting his innocence. A Negro slave was burned at the stake after confessing to something he hadn't done. Before the madness died down, nearly two hundred people had been thrown into jail, eighteen had been hanged, twelve burned to death, and thirty-two sold as slaves in the West Indies.

There had been no slave rebellion; that was certain. The reprisals were manifestations of rank, unbridled fear that had been nurtured by earlier stories of slave uprisings. Without fear, the lies would have fallen on deaf ears.

Some of the tension grew out of economic rivalry between black slaves and white indentured servants. Despotic owners used the blacks to depress wages, and hatred mounted on both sides.

There are many instances of indentured whites seeking redress from owners who starved or beat them. Some had to wear iron collars because they had tried to run away, and many a servant girl, bound out to an immoral master, found that she was fair game in his eyes and was in constant fear of sexual assault. In most colonies once an indentured servant had worked off his debt he was free to claim a piece of land, usually on the frontier, and start life over as a freeman. Many of them, remembering their own servitude, abstained from using black slaves, but others, less humane, counted slavery as a blessing to help them to get rich in their turn.

The disparity between wealthy and poor was as evident in colonial days as at any time in history. For every landed aristocrat with his fine team of horses, his town house, and his big plantation or farm there were hundreds of men barely meeting the needs of their families. In the cities conditions were worse than in the villages and rural districts. Housing for the poor was generally indescribably wretched. Sewage ran in the gutters of many cities, streets were unpaved, muddy morasses, and living quarters were crowded and verminous. By the year 1700 the large seacoast cities were already blighted by slum districts. Poorhouses existed for those who had neither the strength nor the heart to continue fighting for a marginal existence. Some colonies made the poor wear badges of their misfortune, just as two and a half centuries later the Nazis forced Jews to wear symbols of their religion on their clothing.

Those at the top of the social hierarchy had little concern for those at the bottom. Cotton Mather, a cleric whose heart should have been torn by the inequities of the period, wrote of the danger presented by the growth of the poorer classes and had no use for those whose lot was poverty. Starvation, in his mind, was a natural force essential to maintaining a proper social balance.

The situation in the port cities caused many men to lead their families into the wilderness in search of better lives. Records show that within fifty years after the *Mayflower* landed, workmen in Maine, Massachusetts, and New York had struck for better pay. As no unions existed, employers often beat down these efforts by hiring from the ranks of the unemployed or by using slave labor.

In the popular mind, the colonists are pictured as wearing satin and velvet, silver buckles, and powdered wigs, but only a small percentage of the people knew such luxury. Or we think of the frontiersman, rugged and self-sufficient, feeding his family on game and enjoying the freedom of the open spaces. All too often we forget the masses in the crowded little cities who worked on the piers, in the shops and factories, or as servants, always on the very fringe of economic disaster.

Yet, although grim conditions were all too prevalent, they were never as bad as in the cities of Europe. The American colonists had one asset that was missing in the Old World: hope. They could look about them and see others who had improved their lot by dint of hard work. They saw indentured servants who had won their freedom and they knew that somewhere beyond the cruel cities, perhaps many days' journey into the hinterland, there was land to be had for a song. There might be Indians to reckon with, drought, bad winters, and lost crops, but their horizon was illumined by the bright sunlight of hope. For the poor of Europe there was not even a glimmer.

By the middle of the eighteenth century most of the colonies were Crown colonies. The king ruled with little interference, despite the effort of the assemblies to protect the colonists' rights. But London was many months away from the large cities, and much more remote from the frontier settlements. A man who lived in the interior could live his own life with little worry about royal proclamations. His life was harsh and rigorous, and devoid of many of the pleasures of civilization, but his self-sufficiency liberated him from many of the concerns that plagued city people.

Where the pinch came was in the cities. Commerce and trade affected almost everyone, from the highest to the lowest. When the Navigation Acts circumscribed colonial commerce, everyone suffered. When England tried to set aside a Virginia law favoring debtors and permitting payment of taxes, rents, fees, and debts at a figure that the mercantile interests in London thought too low, plantation owners and servants alike found their purses pinched.

In Virginia this latter move led to court action, known as the Parson's Cause case, in which the name of Patrick Henry was raised as the people's champion. Henry, a young attorney of only twenty-seven, held in 1763 that in colonial matters the colonial legislature had supreme power. He saw no reason why the king and Privy Council should control funds raised in the colony and spent in the colony. At this, Henry's opponent shouted "treason." The vested interests wanted everything their way, but Henry won his case. The same cry of treason would be raised again, but then it would be Patrick Henry himself who threatened the status quo, and in an entirely different manner.

One wonders whether the colonists would have demanded independence from England if the king had not insisted upon turning the screws on trade and commerce. Men are quick to anger when their pocketbooks are emptied by unfair and confiscatory taxes.

The Carolina and Virginia tobacco growers took all the risks of raising their crops and hated to see England lay a heavy hand on their profits. The upland weavers saw no reason why they should not fashion their own fabrics and clothing from wool instead of sending the raw material to England and then having to buy it back as finished goods. In the New England colonies the economy was based on shipping, trading, and the distilling of rum from molasses imported from the West Indies. Cargoes could be purchased from Dutch and French Caribbean possessions at prices more advantageous than those existing in the English islands. In the mid-eighteenth century Rhode Island was buying five times as much molasses from foreign islands as from those under the Crown, and that most obstreperous of all colonies, Massachusetts, was importing thirty times as much from sources held to be illegal by the English.

The Parson's Cause case was small potatoes compared to the court fight that grew out of England's attempt to curb illicit purchases of molasses.

The king's surveyor general in Boston applied to the home government for writs of assistance with which to search homes for smuggled goods. These writs, in the nature of court warrants, differed from true search warrants in that any official could pick them up with little trouble and then invade a man's home to see if he was trafficking in contraband.

The rum distillers and other merchants in Massachusetts retained James Otis, Jr., to defend them against the writs. His arguments made him famous overnight. Otis argued that a man's home is his castle and that British law itself mandated that a search warrant had to be sworn out individually and only after evidence of well-grounded suspicion. From his defense motions and summations we have phrases that foreshadowed the American democracy: "A man who is quiet," he said, "is as secure in his house, as a prince in his castle." The power of the writ of assistance "is a power that places the liberty of every man in the hands of every petty officer" and if not curbed would exalt the informer, make officials vindictive, and eventually lead to a situation where society would "be involved in tumult and in blood."

Otis did not win his suit, at least not in the technical sense, but his arguments were so forceful that few writs of assistance were ever issued. News was slow in traveling from colony to colony in those days, but eventually James Otis' words were known from Maine to Georgia. When the colonists murmured his words about the "liberty of every man" they were unwittingly thinking of rights they would demand not too many years later.

A wise man must have seen as early as the 1730s that there was a spirit of independence abroad in the American colonies that boded no good for England. He might not have foreseen an actual struggle for independence, but he would have had to be myopic indeed not to see the way the winds were blowing.

When the Massachusetts assembly tried to have the upper hand in planning a common defense against the Indians before it would vote the governor funds with which to fight the war, that spirit was surely visible. When the New York assembly threatened it would starve the royal governor into agreeing to bills passed against his will, the handwriting was on the wall for all to see. James Glenn, governor of South Carolina, wrote home complaining that the assembly had usurped many of his powers, even to naming the treasurers, controller of duties, Indian commissioners, and a military officer responsible for maintaining defense supplies. Governor Clinton of New York was equally quick to complain that the assembly was "wresting his Majesty's authority out of the hands of the Governor."

Yet dislike for English oppression was by no means universal in the American colonies. The landed aristocracy, particularly in the South, had far more in common with their brothers at home than they did with servants, poor farmers, and freemen that were the majority population in the colonies. These men, and the wealthier merchants in the cities, read English books and journals. They bought their clothes and furniture in England, and such luxuries as fine crystal, dishes, and silver for the table. Their cellars were filled by wine exporters in London, their library shelves were kept up to date by shipments from the Old World, and their fine guns, blooded stock, and breeding cattle all came from England. Many sent their sons to English universities. Men of this walk of life had little in common with the working-class people living in the cities, and even less with the rough-and-ready pioneers living in log cabins on the distant frontiers.

At the same time there were factors driving the diverse elements of colonial society together. When a bearded rifleman marched in the company led by Nathaniel Bacon to overthrow a tyrannical governor, he was on the same side of the ideological fence as the rich tobacco grower stirring uneasily under the heel of the royal tax collector. They were not ready to think of themselves as Americans yet, or to entertain a positive feeling for rebellion, but they thought of themselves as American colonists, different from the West Indian colonists and different from the inhabitants of England.

This slowly growing feeling of oneness might have spread more rapidly if it had not been for the friction and oftentimes open hatred that existed between the different segments of the population. Anglicans had little use for Baptists, Methodists, and Quakers. Germans formed their own communities and kept away from the English. Southern colonists found the New England trader too shrewd and quick for their liking, although they used his ships in preference to English bottoms. The tidewater resident, whether a plantation owner with a thousand acres of rich black soil or a cobbler on a Charleston side street, felt little sympathy for the problems of the man clad in deerskin and linsey-woolsey picking out a slim existence high in the Smokies or in inland Pennsylvania or New York.

As the colonists moved farther inland and took up new occupations, and thus were no longer dependent on the seaboard cities for their livelihoods, they had little patience with the powermongers on the coast.

The fur trade remained a vital business right up to the Revolution. Albany was the largest fur-trading center on the North American continent until the Hudson's Bay Company was formed to collect pelts in the Canadian far north. Each summer men working for the fur companies left Albany and went to Fort Oswego on Lake Ontario to barter for furs with the Indians, who brought their pelts from as far away as the shores of Lake Winnipeg. In the fall the fur traders returned to Albany with their purchases, there to sell them for use in the colonies, or more often, for shipment to the markets of Europe.

Thousands of men were engaged in one way or another with this brisk and remunerative trade. They had little in common with landed gentry in the Virginia Piedmont or in the Carolina lowlands. Nor did they have much to do with the traders and merchants of New England. It was only when the Indians threatened or the

Crown imposed restrictions that the fur traders, the shipwrights of
Maine, the merchants of Salem, the tobacco growers of Maryland,
and the plantation owners of Carolina realized their common interests.

In a pioneer society it is always thus. There is so much to be
done each day to provide food for the table, shelter for the family,
and perhaps to start up a new trade that cultural and political in-
fluences have limited effect. The intelligentsia of the period were
concerned with the scientific discoveries being made in Europe,
but progress had little meaning to a man in a cabin on the Kennebec or on a hillside in western Virginia.

Considering these truths, it is significant that as many new ideas
were born in the New World as there were. Certainly the religious
freedoms fostered by Roger Williams, Anne Hutchinson, and the
other liberals of the church were unique. And just as surely, the
growing dissatisfaction of men like Nathaniel Bacon, Jacob
Leisler, Patrick Henry, and James Otis showed how inevitable conflict with England was becoming.

Most colonists wanted to be left to their own devices. Ties with
the home country were still strong, but they were emotional rather
than political. What sufficed in England was not good enough for
Englishmen who had uprooted themselves and struck out in the
wilderness. But with security and prosperity came a stratification
of society. When a few hundred souls live in a community of log
cabins there is a unanimity of purpose and little difference between
men. Once villages become cities and some residents grow wealthy,
attitudes change. This could be seen in the churches, where men like
Cotton Mather were moving away from the original Congregation-
alist concept of local control and trying to set up centralized
supervision. Power, Mather thought, ought to be kept out of the
hands of the "mean poor" and reserved for those worthy of ruling,
whether in business, politics, or religion.

By the early decades of the eighteenth century the power of the
press had become an important factor in the unrest, particularly
in the northern colonies. Benjamin Franklin's half-brother, James,
edited a small paper in Massachusetts that attacked the church
hierarchy, and he was arrested for sedition as a result. Cotton Mather wrote that Franklin was a "wicked printer" who published the
weekly only "to lessen and blacken the Ministers of this town, and
render their ministry ineffectual; a wickedness never paralleled anywhere upon the face of the earth." These hysterical words reveal

how alarmed the theocracy was. Franklin evaded serious punishment by leaving the colony without being brought to trial, so the
case was never truly adjudicated, but its significance was not lost on
the power elite: The government had not taken any steps to hush the
opposition.

A much more important example of the influence a paper could
wield came during the regime of Governor William Cosby in New
York. Cosby was a reactionary, corrupt official whose tyranny was
fought valiantly by the Popular party. The party started the New
York *Weekly Journal* in 1733 and gave the task of editing it to
an impoverished printer, John Peter Zenger. When the Popular party
handily won the 1734 election, Cosby tried to even scores. He asked
the assembly to agree to an indictment of Zenger. The legislative
body refused. He asked the grand jury to indict the printer for
seditious libel. It refused. Finally he arrested Zenger on an information returned by the council. Zenger was tossed into jail but
went on editing the paper with the help of his wife, who conferred
with him through the cell bars.

The trial that grew out of Zenger's indictment is one of the most
important in the nation's history of civil rights. Zenger was defended by Andrew Hamilton, of Philadelphia, who was astute enough
to realize that he would have to argue along political lines rather
than legal ones. He cited the growing freedom of speech in com-
menting upon the church and urged the jury to ponder criticism
of the governor in the same vein. Hamilton's summation contained
these words, which won over the jury:

> The question before the Court and you, gentlemen of the jury,
> is not of small nor private concern, it is not the cause of a poor
> printer, nor of New York alone, which you are now trying. No!
> It may in its consequence, affect every freeman that lives under a
> British government in America. It is the best cause. It is the cause
> of liberty . . . of exposing and opposing arbitrary power (in these
> parts of the world at least) by speaking and writing truth.

In effect Hamilton was saying that in a trial involving libel, the
truth was an effective defense. The jury found Zenger not guilty,
and cannons boomed all over town. It was a serious setback to
tyranny and one from which the English never really recovered.
Its full effect was not felt for decades, but royal governors were
forced to be mindful of a colonial jury's refusal to find a fellow
citizen guilty when his only crime was telling the truth.

XVIII

Indian Sun on the Wane

BEGINNING IN 1740, the War of the Austrian Succession tore across Europe. The hostilities were reflected in the American colonies and were, in fact, a prelude to the French and Indian War. It gave the English colonists a taste of what was to come.

In May 1744 a French force from Louisburg on Cape Breton Island raided Canso, Maine, captured most of the inhabitants, and transported them to Boston. Within a few weeks the whole frontier in New England and New York was aflame with Indian raids.

By this time the French held possession of everything north and west of the thirteen colonies, with forts at the headwaters of the Ohio, on the Great Lakes, and along the entire length of the Mississippi. Military men, looking for a way to strike a blow at this vast empire, considered attacks on many places, including Quebec and Montreal. But it was a New Hampshire militiaman who conceived the idea of attacking the strongest point of all, Louisburg.

For more than thirty years the best engineers in the French army had been building and fortifying a giant enclave guarding the entrance to the St. Lawrence River. There were thick stone walls, a central keep, outlying bastions and rifle pits, storehouses, homes, and armories. In the shadow of its great cannon the French fleet could anchor in safety. It was unthinkable that the colonists could capture such an impregnable place, but the Massachusetts authorities proposed to try, and asked for four thousand men to make the effort.

William Pepperell, of Kittery, Maine, was given command of the militia. Five ships from the English fleet in the West Indies sailed north to help. On April 29, 1745, the French at Louisburg awoke to see an armada of more than one hundred vessels riding in the sea south of town and soldiers coming ashore in boats.

The French engineers had planned well, even to setting up outlying batteries to help defend the main fort, but this played into the English colonists' hands. Under cover of night a party of militia set fire to houses near the royal battery and drove the artillerymen into the fortress. Then the thirty heavy guns were maneuvered over the marshes until they could be fired into the fort. Other guns, buried in the sand, were found and added to those brought from the captured battery. Then cannon from the warships were taken ashore.

It was a time of horrible hardship for the English soldiers. Disease struck down many of them, but the work went on day after day, week after week, with the cannonading going on during every daylight hour. Solid shot crashed against the granite walls, slowly and inexorably pulverizing them. No help came from France, and on June 17 the French commandant surrendered what had been considered the most powerful fortress in the New World.

Peace treaties seldom please any of the belligerents, but the one that ended this short war was anathema to the colonists: the great fort at Louisburg was given back to the French. This rankled in the hearts of many militiamen who had left their homes to fight for the mother country's interests. Unable to do anything about it, they went back to tilling their farms and working at their trades, but their hatred toward the French grew ever stronger. They heard stories of friends who had migrated westward over the Alleghenies, and had found the French already strong along the banks of the Ohio. Virginians among them gloried in the news that the Ohio Company had been formed to develop the new paradise over the mountains, but they were forgetting that France had sent a new leader to manage affairs in Canada. This new governor general was the Marquis Duquesne, who lost no time in preparing the French outposts for a war he knew was inevitable.

To the English leaders in London it seemed obvious that when war came again much of the fighting in America would have to be done by the colonists themselves. The redcoats were spread too thin, from Scotland to the Ganges; few could be spared. The Privy Council turned to Benjamin Franklin and asked him to convene a meeting of the various colonies to discuss mutual defense.

Franklin issued a call for convention at Albany, New York. The shrewd printer-turned-statesman did not go to the session empty-handed. He had drawn up a plan for a super-government, with each colony raising troops, taxing its residents to buy arms and supplies, and agreeing on the government of any new communities to be established on the frontier. It was an elaborate effort at unification within the structure of the British empire. There was to be a president general appointed by the Crown and a grand council chosen by the people of the colonies. Basing his figures on the population, Franklin proposed that the council have 48 members, divided as follows: Massachusetts Bay 7, New Hampshire 2, Connecticut 5, Rhode Island 2, New York 4, the two Jerseys 3, Pennsylvania 6, Maryland 4, Virginia 7, North Carolina 4, and South Carolina 4. Georgia was considered so newly established, and so busy with Spanish incursions, that it should not be asked to join the organization.

Poor Ben Franklin. He was years ahead of the times. No one evinced strong liking for his plan. Virginia refused even to send delegates to Albany. Worse yet, the king and his ministers were aghast at the thought of a super-powerful organization of colonies acting without direction from the throne. The plan fell through. The colonies were still a long way from seeing the wisdom of working together in their own self-interest.

The collapse of the unification must have been sweet music to Duquesne's ears. He promptly ordered the building of a fort at the site of present-day Pittsburgh, where the Monongahela and Allegheny form the Ohio River, as well as other forts between the Great Lakes and the Ohio Valley. The first assignment could not have been easy, as English forces already manned a small outpost there. This fort was tangible proof that at least one colonial official sensed the danger from French expansion. It had been established by Governor Robert Dinwiddie of Virginia, a man of action who didn't mind building a fort or two in territory claimed by Pennsylvania.

Dinwiddie had picked for his military commander in the field a young commander of militia named George Washington. The outpost had been erected at the confluence of the Monongahela and Allegheny rivers, and another, called Fort Necessity, built farther south. Young Washington was forced to surrender the fort on the Ohio and later was defeated by a superior force at Great Meadows. The date is interesting: July 4, 1754. Perhaps the most important thing to emerge from this unfortunate beginning was a diary

Washington kept, in which he detailed the French operations beyond the mountains. When the king saw the diary, which created a
furor when published in London, he ordered ten thousand British
regulars to America and moved to oust the French from the Ohio
Valley.

Faced with such a critical situation, the Crown should have used
all the wisdom it possessed, but it selected the king's young brother,
the Duke of Cumberland, to supervise the war overseas, and that
worthy, who knew no more about military affairs than he did about
astronomy, sent Major General Edward Braddock of the regular
army to defend the border.

Braddock was an arrogant, bull-headed, indifferent leader who
scoffed at the idea that his brilliantly accoutered soldiers should
"skulk" along in broken ranks to take cover among trees and rocks.
Washington, who knew how to fight Indians, pleaded with Braddock to break his force into units and to fight as the frontiersmen
fought, but what English general of that era would listen to a mere
colonel of colonial militia? The inevitable happened. Out in the hilly
forests of western Pennsylvania Braddock's force was attacked by
French and Indians who hid behind natural shelter and cut the
redcoat companies to shreds.

When Braddock fell, mortally wounded, Washington took command and salvaged what he could, but it was a bitter defeat for the
English and their colonists. Legend has it that Braddock whispered
an apology to Washington as he lay dying.

England now decided it was time to play a larger role in defending the American colonies. It had become apparent that their disunity was playing into the French hands. And the disunity was
truly unbelievable. The Quakers of Pennsylvania, although the
enemy had erected a fort directly in their path westward, acted as
if they had never heard of the war. New York, which had financed
the Iroquois, thought the Indians could handle the French with little
help from the whites, and only the military acumen of Sir William
Johnson in the Mohawk Valley saved the colony from a deep invasion. Maryland, sheltered by Virginia and Pennsylvania, tried to
sit out the conflict, and the Carolinas gave only token support.

Through the years leading up to the French and Indian War a
few men had shown brilliance in confronting the French, but most
were inept or slothful. Governor William Shirley of Massachusetts
had kept the enemy off balance in northern New England and Nova
Scotia, and Major Robert Rogers and his Rangers performed in-

valuable service in New Hampshire around Lake Champlain and Lake George. Despite these efforts, the French had forged an iron barrier that stretched from Louisburg on Cape Breton Island all the way to the lower Mississippi. It seemed in the early 1750s that English expansion westward would be halted at the crest of the Appalachian range.

Washington returned from the campaign with Braddock to warn Governor Dinwiddie that all the back settlers were now menaced by the French. He, at least, saw the threat inherent in disunity. For a young man in his twenties, this militia colonel was singularly astute and already sensed the need for concerted effort to save the colonies.

Dinwiddie had chosen wisely when he selected the young surveyor. Washington was the great-grandson of John Washington, who had migrated to Virginia during Cromwell's regime. None of his ancestors had been devoted to the military life, although his half-brother Lawrence had served with Admiral Edward Vernon in 1741 in fleet and land actions against Cartagena, a Spanish port on the Caribbean. Lawrence had inherited the beautiful family property on the Potomac, which he named Mount Vernon in honor of the admiral, and his younger brother busied himself in his late teens as a surveyor in the Shenandoah Valley.

At first neither Washington's warnings nor Dinwiddie's pleas for help aroused any sympathy in the middle colonies, but Shirley, who had taken command of the forces in New England and New York, prepared to resist the French. William Johnson erected forts at Lake George, and in battles near there defeated Baron Dieskau of the French army. It was some recompense for Braddock's defeat, and Johnson was knighted.

Shirley next turned his attention to Nova Scotia. In June 1755 he sent John Winslow with two thousand men to Acadia, who, with the help of British regulars, defeated the French. Acting under orders from Shirley and the Privy Council in London, Winslow rounded up thousands of Acadians and transported them southward, scattering them from Massachusetts to Georgia. Every school child knows the story of the Acadians from Longfellow's poem "Evangeline," but few realize that the dispersion was essential to the survival of the northern English colonies. The chore was distasteful to Winslow, and he acted with great kindness and understanding in executing it.

There was one more campaign under Shirley's aegis, an attempt to seize Fort Niagara, but an early winter frustrated the effort and 1755 ended with the border still insecure.

Braddock's defeat near Pittsburgh, the failure to capture the cornerstone fort at Niagara, the continued evidence of French pressure, and, at home, the Seven Years War, led King George II to appoint William Pitt as head of England's war effort. This concession to the parliamentary leader left a bitter taste in George's mouth, but it was a wise move. Pitt acted swiftly. He sent word to the American colonies that England would repay the colonies for expenses incurred in putting militia into the field, and he ordered that provincial officers were to rank equally with those in the regular army. The wisdom of this order was apparent in every campaign that followed.

Pitt's appointment came not a minute too soon, for the French had named the Marquis de Montcalm as leader in Canada. Before the English knew of the appointment, Montcalm had captured Fort Oswego on Lake Ontario, giving the French undisputed control of the Great Lakes, just as Braddock's defeat had left them in command on the Ohio.

While the Earl of Loudoun dallied in an attempt to seize the fortress of Louisburg, Montcalm swept down Lake Champlain and captured Fort William Henry. Indians massacred most of the defenders despite Montcalm's attempt to restrain them. It now seemed that Albany would fall; no frontier settlement felt secure. But it was the crest of the wave for the French in North America. William Pitt would do what had to be done, and it would prove more than enough.

First he summoned the lumbering Earl of Loudoun home and sent Lord Jeffrey Amherst to Nova Scotia to seize Louisburg. In 1758 Amherst and General James Wolfe defeated the forces under Drucour, and the great fort guarding the entrance to the St. Lawrence fell to the British. The massive fortification that was the greatest triumph of Vauban's engineering skill could not stand up to the pounding of Wolfe's artillery and the guns from Admiral Edward Boscawen's fleet.

News of victory on Cape Breton was a tonic throughout the American colonies. The colonists needed good news, for they had just been defeated badly at Ticonderoga, a defeat that had cost the life of Lord George Howe, their leader. Assemblies hurried to appropriate funds for new militia units, Washington and General

Joseph Forbes led a combined regular and colonial force west toward Fort Duquesne, Colonel Bradstreet captured Fort Frontenac, and Amherst was named commander in chief of all English forces in North America.

At once things started turning toward the better. General Forbes, with Washington at his side, mustered six thousand men, mostly from Virginia and Pennsylvania, but with a Highland Scots regiment to give it starch, and marched over the mountains toward the headwaters of the Ohio. Washington commanded two thousand of the troops. At first there was some friction between the two men. Forbes, who was known as "Iron Head," ridiculed the colonial uniform as unsoldierly, but before many days on the march the regulars envied the long shirts and deerskin trousers of the irregulars.

Forbes's first assault on Fort Duquesne was repulsed. He drew back to lick his wounds and fell ill, prostrated by the strenuous service in the wilderness. He turned over command to Washington, who led an advance force in a new attempt. To his surprise he found the fort abandoned and put to the torch, the French having no stomach for a large-scale battle with such a sizable force. Forbes ordered a rough stockade erected on the site and named it Pittsburgh in honor of the man who had infused the empire with a will to win over the French.

Troops gathered from the southern colonies, joined those from Virginia, and helped wipe out one enemy stronghold after another all the way to Lake Erie. Lord Amherst had not been idle meanwhile. He sent General Prideaux and Sir William Johnson to capture Fort Niagara. Prideaux died in a preliminary engagement and Johnson took over. First he overwhelmed a French force sent to relieve the fort and then led his Mohawks and the colonials in a successful attack on the fort. It was a victory that echoed even in the House of Commons. Edmund Burke cited it as severing "that communication so much talked of and so much dreaded between Canada and Louisiana."

With a large force of regulars Amherst undertook an invasion of Canada from Albany. For the first time in his career in the New World, he failed to sense the urgency of the occasion. When he found Ticonderoga and Crown Point abandoned, instead of double-timing to Quebec, where the English fleet had gone from Louisburg, he dilly-dallied, cutting roads and improving defenses at the forts.

Amherst lost a chance to go down in history as the captor of the French stronghold—an honor reserved for General Wolfe.

Pitt knew the time was ripe to end French influence forever in North America, and he gave Wolfe plenty of men and supported him with a strong fleet. In June 1759 Wolfe sailed up the St. Lawrence, disembarked his troops on the Ile d'Orléans opposite Quebec, and emplaced his big guns within range of the city. Montcalm's position was almost impregnable. The city and fortifications were atop a huge bluff protected by water on two sides. Any frontal assault would have had to be made up precipitous cliffs almost overhanging the St. Lawrence.

Wolfe spent weeks bombarding the city, hoping to draw Montcalm from his refuge, but the French general was too wily. Even a poorly timed assault by English grenadiers failed to lure the French from their position. Montcalm was banking on the approach of winter to drive the enemy fleet out to open water.

Wolfe, suffering from an incurable illness, spent his daytime hours looking for a way up the bluff. On a day in early September he found what he was looking for. A soldier told him about seeing a trail leading from the shore upriver from the city. It was little more than a goatpath, clinging to the face of the escarpment, but Wolfe recognized its potential. Preparations went forward during the following week, and on September 13 Wolfe was ready.

While the fleet maneuvered as though to land troops below the city, Wolfe with 4,500 men in small boats and on rafts drifted downstream well above the city until they reached the point where the narrow path started up the hill. It is said that Wolfe sat in the sternsheets of his boat reciting stanzas from Thomas Gray's "Elegy Written in a Country Churchyard," particularly the one about the paths of glory leading to the grave. When he was done he said, "Gentlemen, I would sooner have written that poem than take Quebec."

All through the dark night English soldiers followed one another in single file up the steep path. The men in the van overpowered the sentries at the top before an alarm was made, and when dawn broke the English lines were drawn up and ready on the Plains of Abraham behind the fortified city. It was too great a shock, even for the brilliant Montcalm. Instead of waiting for an attack behind his walls, he sent out troops piecemeal, and Wolfe won the battle that ended France's glory in the New World. Both generals died from wounds received that day; neither witnessed the changing of the flags above the walls.

The next summer—almost exactly one year after Wolfe's great victory—Montreal surrendered to a combined force of British regulars and American colonials. It had to be surrender, for the heart had gone out of the French on the Plains of Abraham. In 1763 all of French Canada was ceded to the British by the Treaty of Paris.

By the time Wolfe captured Quebec there were more white men in each of the thirteen English colonies than in all French Canada from Cape Breton to Louisiana. Neither the French kings, the governors on the St. Lawrence, nor the men themselves, moving happily through the forests and fraternizing with the Indians, saw the wisdom of putting down roots in the New World. It may have been, too, that their very reliance upon the Indians helped bring about their downfall. The cruelty and bloodthirstiness of the redskins who fought under the lilies of France created in the minds of the English settlers an implacable hatred for all things French. One example will suffice to demonstrate this smoldering rage.

For nearly a century the St. Francis Indians, who lived on the southern banks of the St. Lawrence above what is now Vermont and New Hampshire, had been the most brutal of the tribes that ranged along the New England frontier inflicting one massacre after another. While Wolfe was capturing Quebec, Lord Amherst asked Major Rogers and his Rangers to punish the tribe. The Rangers, numbering under two hundred, made their way up Lake Champlain and then overland toward the St. Francis River. Their route took them through one of the most impenetrable areas in the east, much of it a swamp where they had to walk in water up to their waists, a morass as trackless as the ocean wastes.

For twenty-two days they made their way through the swamp until they reached the St. Lawrence and the main village of the St. Francis Indians. Rogers and two companions sneaked up to the edge of the village and saw the Indians dancing around a pole on which there hung more than six hundred scalps taken from white settlers. Late at night the Rangers attacked the village and set it afire. More than two hundred braves were slain; but the women and children were spared. Five English captives, awaiting torture on the morrow, were rescued.

With this blow, which cost Rogers heavily in men, the St. Francis Indians were wiped out. The most evil tribe in Canada disappeared from the pages of history. If the French had fought their own battles and controlled their native allies, the English colonists, busy with their settlements and their trade, might never have risen in wrath to extirpate the enemy.

With the French defeated, peace settled over the English colonies—unbroken except for the bloody rebellion led by Pontiac, the Ottawa chieftain. Pontiac, disgruntled over the Treaty of Paris, organized a simultaneous attack on eight English forts and settlements, using Indians from tribes that lived all the way from Tennessee to Lake Huron. It was a shrewdly planned assault and was temporarily successful, but Pontiac himself, leading the attack on Detroit, was betrayed by an Indian maiden who was in love with a British soldier. Detroit held out for five months, and the rebellion collapsed.

The way westward for white expansion was opened in a poignant ceremony. Sir William Johnson, who had lived with the Mohawks as an Indian and who had fought the French allies so successfully, called all the tribes east of the Mississippi together at Fort Oswego. The Indians, including the chastened Pontiac, gathered by the hundreds in the summer of 1764 and smoked the pipe of peace and buried a symbolic hatchet. Hundreds of white captives, held prisoner for years, were surrendered by the Indians. There were speeches of everlasting peace and amity, and treaties written on deerskin and birchbark were signed by all the important notables. Then Pontiac led his delegation to the shore, where they embarked in war canoes. At a signal from the old rebel, the canoes headed into the sunset and the white man's path to the west was opened to the Mississippi.

To the farmers of New England and New York, the war-hating Quakers of Pennsylvania, and the planters and husbandmen of the South it was good news. They had had enough of fighting the Indians. Now there were crops to be harvested, burned towns to be rebuilt, and new families to be formed to replace those decimated by the years of frontier warfare. The trails over the mountains to the promised land of the Ohio were open again. There were a few Indians to be reckoned with of course, but peace would bring an end to their activities in time.

The Indian had ceased to be a major factor in colonial history. In the beginning he had lost only a few hundred acres near Plymouth and Salem, but then lost everything in New England when King Philip failed to expel the white intruders from his hunting grounds. The Tuscaroras had been forced to flee Carolina, and the Creeks and Cherokees would soon be driven beyond the Mississippi. True, the Iroquois considered themselves the white man's friend, but time would reveal to them too that where the settler cut down trees for his cabin there was no longer any room for the Indian. He could rebel, and he did on occasion, but the curtains were drawing closer and closer about him. There was no stopping the English colonist. He had survived shipwreck, starvation, disease, and Indian massacre. He had stood up to the French and driven them off the continent. The Pacific lay far to the west, beckoning to the white pioneer. Nothing would stay his inexorable steps toward the setting sun.

XIX

It Was Never an Easy Life

A SWEDISH TRAVELER and writer, Peter Kalm, journeyed far and wide in America during the mid-1700s and left behind many observations about life in the colonies. One of his most interesting comments was the suggestion that the French empire in the New World was, in fact, highly beneficial to England because it kept the colonies from uniting against the mother country. When the French and Indian War was over, any such influence was dissipated.

Almost at once the colonists looked to the land beyond the mountains, knowing that the French were no longer a restraining factor. Along the Atlantic seaboard the first signs of urban crowding were bringing new problems to the fore. In Virginia and Maryland tobacco planters were discovering that yields were shrinking as the soil became depleted. The farmers of the era knew little about crop rotation, and fields that had produced rich harvests in the early years were now yielding far less. One way of meeting this problem was to take up new land, far to the west.

Slavery brought benefits to the plantation owners but not to the small farmers. Competition for wages became fierce in the older settlements, and freemen dreamed of new homes in the forests where they could make a fresh start. But for others, life on the coast was still all they wished it to be. The wars may have slowed down expansion and decimated the population of many of the frontier towns, but in the cities it was business as usual.

The colonies had grown up in many ways. The old days when each family eked out a precarious existence from a small plot just outside the palisade had disappeared. Industry had come to the provinces, and with it came trade, commerce, and shipping.

New York was a cosmopolitan city, as were Boston, Philadelphia, and Charleston. Through these harbor cities passed the produce of fisheries, forests, and farms. Millions of board feet of lumber went to Europe from all the colonies. In the South the forests gave bountifully of tar, pitch, turpentine, and other naval stores, and when tobacco fields were left unseeded cattle became a source of revenue for the planters. In the middle colonies hogs were a profitable asset. Roaming at will in the woods and fields, they ate nuts, roots, seeds, and other pasturage that cost their owners nothing. When they were fattened they were slaughtered and salted, and traded in the West Indies.

But it was New England that profited most from commerce with the Caribbean region. The Grand Banks off Newfoundland are one of the richest sources of fish on earth. As early as 1750 more than four hundred vessels sailed out of Massachusetts to the Grand Banks. Codfish, their main catch, were salted and packed in barrels made during the winter. The best of the fish went to European markets, and the less valuable to the West Indies, where it was traded for sugar and molasses for the many rum distilleries operating in New England.

The New Englanders early turned to shipbuilding to provide craft for their own trade. With abundant wood in the forests nearby, shipwrights produced many bottoms for the trade to the West Indies. Yankee ingenuity was already at work: in the early eighteenth century men in Gloucester, Massachusetts, designed a new and swifter vessel called a schooner. It was handier to sail in narrow waters and was soon seen in more ports than the old full-rigged ship or brig.

Wood casks and barrels were used in tremendous quantities, for flour, salt fish, sugar, molasses, rum, tar, turpentine, and other goods. Many farmers, millers, weavers, and other tradesmen made barrels in their homes during the periods of the year when they could not work the fields or were not needed at their usual places of business. They also produced hand-hewn shingles, clapboards, and staves, which brought in rich returns when shipped to the islands or Europe.

Self-reliance was the hallmark of the colonist. He tilled the fields for his food, did a little trapping for furs, and often made barrels and shingles in the winter to bring in extra cash. Early in the colonial era the women became adept at spinning and weaving wool, and by the end of the seventeenth century most people were wearing clothing made in their own homes.

Milling was something else. The waterpower needed to turn the big millstones required a major investment, so a practice developed of having one gristmill in each community. New York was the first province to turn to flour milling as a major source of revenue, and long before the Dutch lost control of the colony more income was derived from flour than from furs. Pennsylvania also produced large quantities of flour, and shipped tremendous amounts of it to Europe.

It did not take long for the early colonists to find outcroppings of iron ore. Pennsylvania was one of the leading producers, and before the eighteenth century was very far along, smelters and furnaces existed throughout the colony in such abundance that England, trying to protect its home industry, passed an act forbidding the establishment of any more smelters. Nevertheless, the colonists became more and more self-reliant, and by 1722 merchants in London were complaining that they were selling no axes to the colonists.

One might think that the Puritan leaders in New England would have prevented one of the main industries in that area, rum distilling. But, as one Englishman put it, a New Englander could find more ways of escaping taxes, salving his conscience, and not noticing what he didn't want to notice than any other person in world trade. The church saw rum as a means of wealth and power and did nothing to halt its production.

All along the northern coast there were factories for making rum from molasses. Just before the French and Indian War ended, Newport, Rhode Island, boasted of twenty-two distilleries. "Long Wharf," wrote one resident, "was alive with molasses coming in and rum going out." Rum was used as a means of foreign exchange. It was used to buy slaves for the plantations in the West Indies and the South. It was a medium of exchange within the colonies because everyone liked it and would trade their own woolens, flour, pig iron, tobacco, or lumber for a few kegs.

New England held the lead in shipping, because its shipwrights were imaginative in designing fast ships and because the Yankee instinct for trade was so highly developed. The typical New England trader-merchant-shipper in the middle 1700s was a true cosmopolite. He was at home on the docks along the Thames, in the harbors of

Barbados, St. Eustatius, and Jamaica, and along the coast of Guinea.

Many a Yankee shipowner was a pirate and smuggler, and his conscience was not in the least bothered by his double life. He made trick barrels that held a little flour at both ends and tobacco in the center. He knew what lonely stretches of coast along Maine, Cape Cod, and Long Island would provide him with a safe place to transfer cargo out of sight of the royal collectors. He could alter a bill of sale to make it appear that sugar or silks bought in Curaçao had been picked up in one of the British islands.

The colonists devised many schemes to outwit England and avoid paying duties and taxes. There was an important side effect to their success at trading with forbidden nations, cheating on customs, and making scapegoats of the royal collectors and surveyors: it bred contempt for the English government. When the time came for independence, the colonists were already old hands at gulling the mother country and scoffing at the royal proclamations.

As people in the colonies prospered, they were no longer content to eat from pewter plates with wooden utensils, or to read by guttering tallow candles and smoky lanthorns. They wanted education for their children. They wanted glass at the windows instead of oiled paper or silk. They demanded better transportation between their towns.

For many of the better-off colonists life had become as genteel as any their forefathers had known in England. There were quite a few institutions of higher education. Harvard had led the way, but William and Mary in Williamsburg, Yale at New Haven, King's College—which became Columbia University—in New York, and the Philadelphia Academy—which was founded by Franklin, and which became the University of Pennsylvania—all prospered, and the early practice of sending sons to Cambridge and Oxford died out.

Yet with all the prosperity evident in the larger communities, life in the rural villages remained austere. Merchants and plantation owners might dance the minuet in silks and satins, and imported crystal chandeliers might sparkle in fine homes in Boston and Charleston, but there was no lack of frivolity along the Mohawk and Susquehanna or in the backwoods areas of New England, the Piedmont, and the Appalachian wilderness. The common man too had his pleasures. A house-raising, a quilting bee, a corn-husking, or a trip into the woods to "sugar off" the maples became an excuse for jollity and communal amusement. While a few Virginians raced thoroughbred horses or rode hell-for-leather after foxes, most colonists made do with wrestling matches, tests of strength lifting logs or heavy sacks of flour, or shooting at nails driven into posts.

Aside from the differences caused by economic levels, social barriers were already to be noticed in colonial life. Although the northern provinces had their strong social differences, the poor man in Connecticut, New York, or Pennsylvania never felt too keenly his position down the ladder from the wealthier residents of his community. But in the South the gap between rich and poor was much more marked. The poor white farmer had to grub for his food. If he went into the labor market, he had to compete at depressed wages set for black slaves. Indentured white servants were hardly better off than Negroes; the townspeople refused them social equality.

Generally speaking, life was better in the country than in the city. By the time of the French and Indian War the larger cities had their seamy sides, with noisome slums, bad housing, crime and prostitution, unsanitary sewerage systems, poorly heated living quarters, and jails where hunger and brutality were commonplace. Poorhouses and orphanages were managed as if the inmates were criminals instead of unfortunates, and the mentally ill suffered from hideous mistreatment. In some communities insane persons were tied to the tail of a cart and whipped before being banished from town, and illegitimate children were punished for their parents' misconduct, made to work for almost nothing, and denied decent care.

The church was extremely rigid in its thinking and exerted little influence for alleviating social distress. Religious leaders showed little sympathy for those crushed by poverty and misfortune. They preached that a person had only himself to thank for his misery: any distress he suffered was God's way of punishing him for his shortcomings.

The tavern was one of the most important institutions in colonial America. It was here that news was disseminated, gossip passed, and politics discussed. Many town meetings were held in taverns or alehouses. Legal notices, stock sales, and announcements of auctions, stage services, and land sales were nailed up for the customers to read, and notices of runaway slaves or indentured servants were posted with offers of reward for their return to the owners.

Taverns were the way stations for the stagecoaches that were beginning to link the colonies together. There were no hotels, so the upstairs rooms of the grogshop served for the traveler who had to stay overnight to await the next stage. Food was usually horrible, the beds were hard or broken down, and it was seldom that a traveler could have a room, or even a bed, to himself. Servants, peddlers, tinkers, itinerant tanners, cobblers, and pewter-smiths were lucky if they found clean hay to sleep in above the stables. It was no wonder that passengers on the early stage routes consumed large quantities of beer or rum toddies to ease their way to sleep.

Women stayed at home. Few were seen in the taverns, except for the bar wenches, and far fewer did any traveling. The old German belief that women should concern themselves only with *Kinder, Küche, Kirche*—"children, kitchen, and church"—prevailed in most homes. On the frontier, women worked in the fields, helped build the cabins, and often fought off the Indians with their husbands. In the more built-up communities their recreation was limited to church and occasional meetings where sewing and quilting was done. They ran the home, and it was no easy task. In most rural houses the cooking was done at a large fireplace. Utensils and equipment were crude. Meat was roasted on a spit, which had to be turned by hand, or stewed in a pot over the wood fire. Bread was baked in a beehive oven built in the back or side of the hearth, always at an awkward angle, and only after the oven had been preheated by shoveling hot coals into the cavity. The floor was either hard-packed earth or rough pine boards that had to be scoured with water and sand. Furniture was hand-hewn and inadequate. Water was drawn from a well or a nearby stream, and the woman usually carried the buckets.

Many women knew the bitter loneliness of isolation, the eerie sounds of wild animals outside their log walls, and some had heard the chilling war whoops of Indians. The housewife welcomed the coming of spring because it meant surcease from howling winds and bitter cold, but it also meant arduous work. She had to aid her husband in the fields, playing the role of hired man; sowing and tilling the soil, harvesting, threshing the grain, winnowing it, and helping lift the sacks of wheat and corn onto a wagon so it could be taken to the gristmill. She had to pick berries, cure herbs, pare and dry apples on strings in the sun, grow pumpkins, which were

an excellent food requiring little care to keep, and bake hard bis-
cuit. There was meat to be smoked over the hearth or on a fire
outside, and in between she made aprons for her husband out of
deerskin, spun and wove and washed and ironed and churned and
made cheese.

In most communities there were no physicians. When they were
to be had they were often little better than apprentices. They knew
few cures and bled their patients when they could think of nothing
else to do. So the housewife was usually her own doctor. She ground
the bark of white cedar and mixed it with hog's grease to fashion
a poultice for rheumatism. She dried holly leaves, cooked them in
beer, and hoped the broth would cure pleurisy, and made mullein
leaves into a tea she prayed would end her baby's dysentery.
Crushed tulip tree leaves applied to the forehead was a common
treatment for migraine headaches. Sassafras bark, made into a
hot tea, was used by everyone for almost every malady.

When bones were broken they were set with no anesthesia except copious draughts of brandy or whisky. Dentistry was almost
unknown. When a tooth hurt, it was pulled out. Strive as she might,
the rural housewife could not cope with the vitamin deficiency that
came with winter. The basic foods were meat and cereals. There
were few fruits and vegetables that wintered well, and when the
cow went dry, the children had to drink cider, beer, or home-
made drinks which were odd mixtures of cereal, beer or wine, malt,
vinegar, and spices.

Life was rigorous for all the colonial women, but the Massachusetts Bay woman was probably the unhappiest of all. The old illus-
trations show her happily going to meeting with her husband and
children or performing the housewifely chores necessary to maintain a contented family. But it is an illusory picture. The Puritan
woman was forbidden to discuss religious matters lest she influence
men through her emotionalism. She was reprimanded for wearing
a veil, for curling her hair, and for gossiping. The General Court
issued an edict banning "short sleeves, whereby the nakedness of
the arms may be discovered," and she was forbidden to wear rib-
bons, ruffles, or cuffs.

Anne Hutchinson was hated and criticized by the church leaders more because she was a woman uttering blasphemy than because she honestly differed with the ruling powers in the church.
In the eyes of men like Cotton Mather, women were inherently

sinful and dangerous, weak in spirit and morals, and ready dupes for the machinations of the Devil.

The Puritan woman was aware that her husband could be punished cruelly at the whipping post for daring to ride off in search of a midwife if she went into labor on the Sabbath. Surely she must have suffered through many sermons that preached of hell's fire and torment and ignored the beautiful teachings of love, understanding, and forgiveness in the words of Jesus.

Quaker women also tended to be meek, but women attending the Dutch Reformed Church in New York or the Catholic or Anglican church in the southern colonies were not so repressed. As a matter of fact, in Virginia, according to that prolific diarist, William Byrd, both men and women who belonged to the established church thought membership a cloak "to sanctifie very loose and profligate morals."

Education for women was considered a waste of time and money. More than half the women who signed legal documents prior to the mid-1700s had to "make their mark" with a cross because they had never learned to write. Society, at least male society, saw little purpose in sending a girl to school when all she was expected to do was to bear children, keep house, and go to church on Sunday. The few who did attend "dame's schools" learned knitting, sewing, embroidery, enough arithmetic to keep the food accounts, and, less often, how to write.

There were exceptions, of course. The wives of some plantation owners received formal educations, and some Quaker women attended church schools. The first wife of Frederick Philipse, the Dutch immigrant who started life as Peter Stuyvesant's carpenter and ended up as probably the richest man in all New York, was one of the most striking exceptions that only proved the rule. She too was Dutch, named Margaret Hardenbroeck, and she refused to stay in the kitchen. Before she was in her thirties she was a trader with business on both sides of the Atlantic, a fleet of ships to carry her cargoes, and agents in many foreign ports. She could read, write, handle accounts, keep books, and run her business without any man's help. She was shrewd and daring in business affairs and carried her independence into her personal life, being involved in several extramarital affairs.

In the South, girls whose parents could afford it went to school or had tutors to teach them such social graces as dancing, playing a musical instrument, drawing and painting, and needlework. Some studied English, and a few learned conversational French.

As the larger cities became more cosmopolitan life for both men and women changed considerably. By the early 1700s Philadelphia was a fashionable place surpassed only by New York. Affluent families knew the luxury of state dinners, concerts, and dances. An early writer, St. John de Crèvecoeur, who was a sort of gossip columnist, described the fashion scene in New York in these words: "You will find here the English fashions. In the dress of the women you will see the most brilliant silks, gauzes, hats and borrowed hair. . . . If there is a town on the American continent where English luxury displayed its follies it was in New York." Many wives and daughters were outfitted in velvets, bombazine, satin, and other imported stuff, carried white kid gloves made in Paris, wore boots fashioned in London, and employed dozens of lotions and unguents to beautify their complexions.

On the farms and in the country food was plentiful, if limited in variety, but in the cities the upper strata of society never spared the local chefs when entertaining governors, traveling dignitaries, or military heroes. Some of the dishes served sound bizarre today, but it would have been a strange man indeed who could not have found something to his liking in the menus of the day. Terrapin soup laced with sherry was commonplace, as were venison, mallard and canvasback duck, wild turkey, and grouse. "Tripe and cowheel," "fools and trifles," "flummeries," and "sillabubs" were served with sirloins of steak, joints of mutton, smoked hams, custards, tarts, and floating islands, and washed down with great quantities of cider, beer, ale, porter, Madeira, port, and rum. That men could get up from the table after a meal with seventeen or eighteen courses is a marvel today, but they did, and they built a new country in the intervals between such feasts.

XX

"The American Is a New Man"

THE MELTING POT was steaming away, making French Huguenots, Scots-Irish, Swiss, Germans, Dutch, and other nationalities into good American provincials. In New England the strain was largely English, but from New York to Georgia blood streams were mixing without let or hindrance.

Between the last war with the French and the war for independence the population of the thirteen colonies passed the two-million mark. Nowhere in Europe could such a heterogeneous mixture be found. There were more than twenty ethnic strains present, aristocrats from England, cottagers from Scotland, tradesmen from Holland and Switzerland, Quakers from several lands, and religious refugees, debtors, jailbirds, adventurers, and itinerant teachers and preachers from everywhere. All had fused into a number of colonies differing from one another in some ways and resembling one another in others. One thing was sure, however: the colonists had come to rely upon themselves. England could hardly realize just how self-sufficient they had become. The authorities in London saw that the popular assemblies were taking the bit of government in their mouths, but as a practical matter they failed to realize that times had changed in America.

The new king, George III, was a stubborn, arrogant, and not-too-bright young man who was totally unaware of how the winds of change had blown across his dominions in North America. The long and bitter struggle with the French had been enormously expensive, and George found his treasury nearly empty. He asked Parliament to pass laws taxing his subjects at home and abroad, so as to replenish it. Colonies that had taxed themselves to the hilt during the war resented the idea of having new taxes levied from across the ocean. Worse yet, they resented paying the salaries of royal officers named by the king and sent to the colonies by him. Had the assemblies been able to fix those salaries there would have been little friction, but the idea of home rule was spreading everywhere from Canada to Florida.

The Americans were no fools. They knew that most of the men in Parliament were corrupt and venal, not truly representative of the people at all. And they sensed that, with the exception of a few outstanding men like Pitt and Burke, they could not expect any support from that body. Such was the feeling that existed when the king decided to put teeth into the old Navigation Acts. These restrictive laws had been allowed to fall into general disuse, and the economy of the colonies, particularly in the coastal cities, had improved in direct proportion to their nonenforcement. In an effort to enforce the acts, the home government authorized the use of the writs of assistance mentioned earlier and which James Otis was instrumental in knocking down. The king and his ministers were willing to turn to force and oppression in a vain effort to set back the clock, the significance of which was not lost on the colonists. Even if the older communities had found a means of getting along with the mother country, their independent-minded relatives and friends in the uplands and interior valleys would not have stood for such a détente. Life at the edge of civilization bred a strong spirit of democracy. Social standing meant nothing; the man who could handle his gun best was the most valuable member of the community. As the frontiersmen made their way farther and farther out into the Ohio country and along the Cumberland and Tennessee rivers they objected to the idea of taxation without representation, whether imposed by king or colonial assembly.

If England had hoped that disunity based upon racial antagonisms would play into its hands, it was soon made to see the light. There were many Germans in Pennsylvania, but those in the counties immediately back of the coast were strongly conservative while those on the Susquehanna, Juniata, and upper reaches of the Potomac were just as strongly liberal. The Scots-Irish who remained in the cities had less in common with their countrymen in the hills than with their Huguenot, English, and Dutch neighbors.

Many Europeans still saw the colonial world as a raw society, generally lacking in culture, education, and spiritual values. This was faulty thinking born of a failure to keep up with the times. Such a generalization might have been made in the first half-century after

Jamestown and Plymouth Rock, but it was no longer valid. American colleges were turning out educated men—educated as well as they would have been anywhere on earth with the possible exception of a few institutions like Oxford, Uppsala, and Bologna. Franklin's Academy in Philadelphia boasted of a curriculum that combined the purely academic with a new scientific emphasis.

Andrew Burnaby, a Scot, traveled in the colonies in the 1760s and went home to write that they could never be a united nation, citing the differences in agricultural pursuits, religion, and social standards, and the great vastness of the continent most of all. He failed to sense that the bigness itself might be a force for unity. Many decades before he visited the New World a proposal had been made to join eastern New York and the Great Lakes by a canal across the province of New York. And he failed to note the interreliance of the colonies. For example, the middle colonies were shipping hundreds of thousands of pounds of flour to New England, where the rocky farms could not meet the needs of the growing populations on the coast. New England vessels were carrying Maryland and Virginia tobacco and Carolina cotton and rice to the far ends of the earth.

Men of intellect and great stature were beginning to arise in the colonies, men with only nominal or sentimental ties to the Old World. Jonathan Edwards, a pastor in a small village in western Massachusetts, preached of man's innate need for heavenly guidance while Franklin was writing of his success in experiments with electricity. Both men had great influence on the minds of the colonists. Andrew Hamilton, who defended Peter Zenger, was a power in the judicial halls of Pennsylvania.

If King George had had the wisdom to consider what sort of people he was trying to oppress, he would have seen that the colonies had produced men of strong character and considerable means. Because their wealth was in the New World, their loyalties tended to be there too, although there were a few notable exceptions. The colonies were peopled, not only by millions of ordinary citizens, but by families of influence like the Calverts, Penns, Fairfaxes, Washingtons, Byrds, Wentworths, Carrolls, Van Rensselaers, Schuylers, Bowdoins, Mathers, and Pinckneys. In addition to these men of wealth and power there were men of brains and character, like Patrick Henry, James Otis, John Hancock, John Adams, Benjamin Franklin, and Thomas Jefferson.

It has been said that never before in history had there been such a rich source of great men as the era when the Revolutionary War broke out. These men did not appear on the scene, phoenix-like, on a certain day in 1776. They had been in the colonies for years, and their influence had been all-pervasive. The house of burgesses in Virginia, the general court in Massachusetts, the assemblies in Pennsylvania and New York and Connecticut—all had been practical workshops for the men who would one day sit in the Continental Congress and later in the Congress of the United States.

If the victory over the French gave the colonists a feeling of power and self-reliance, it also had its darker side. Factories that had been manufacturing clothing, ammunition, and guns for the armies closed their doors. Shipyards finished the craft then on the ways and dismissed their workers. Joblessness reached dangerous levels. Boston, for example, disbursed £1,881 for the relief of the poor out of a total expenditure of £7,841 in 1763. Already the urbanization of the New World was producing serious problems. Rural residents, even when buffeted by drought, freezes, insect plagues, or other natural phenomena, could usually get by from one harvest to the next. Everyone in the family had to work hard—children were taught how to sew, knit, and weave before they were ten so that they might help in making their own clothing—but at least there was the opportunity for improving one's position. With the concentration of thousands in the cities, opportunities were fewer.

City officials wrestled with unemployment and poverty in varying ways. The most common solution was expulsion. In large cities like Philadelphia, Charleston, and Boston any person who could not support himself stood a better than even chance of being shipped back to whatever country of origin the local judges thought applicable. When it could be proved that the jobless man had been in the colonies for a long period, or his family for several generations, the authorities placed him in the workhouse. It wasn't a good solution, as it was abused by conscienceless overseers, but the holders of entrenched power thought it would protect them from an element that already was being referred to occasionally as "the Mob."

The people in the cities were faced with a broad spectrum of problems in the years immediately preceding the war for independence. First of all, food prices started climbing, due in part to the high profits obtained by shipping flour, grain, and meat to Europe. There just wasn't enough to go around. Artificial shortages were created by greedy middlemen, and actual hunger was avoided only by the establishment of city markets. But already the problem was a hard one to solve, especially with slow transportation from farm to city. A shortage of leather in the northern colonies resulted from restrictions laid down in Charleston to protect home industry.

One of the strangest shortages came in a commodity that once existed everywhere but that was already beginning to disappear around the cities: wood for fuel. All homes were heated with firewood. In the early decades a man had only to go out into the woodlot behind the house to get all the wood he needed. Franklin had invented the Franklin stove, which burned either wood or coal, but coal was used only in the mining areas of Pennsylvania and Maryland. As New York City grew apace, the question of where to get firewood became a major source of concern. For years Staten Island had been a prime supply area, but the cordwood had to be shipped across the bay by boat. Prices went up and up until finally New Yorkers found it cheaper to buy their fuel from Connecticut, much farther away.

The Treaty of Paris, which tied up the loose ends of the French and Indian War, did the colonies in North America little good. Self-interest directed the efforts of the English negotiators, and they gave back to France the islands of Guadeloupe and Martinique and swapped Cuba, which had been taken from the Spanish when they foolishly entered the conflict, for Florida.

The colonies had been doing a thriving business based on cheap sugar from the French Caribbean islands, and the treaty brought an end to this trade. The sugar market in Europe slumped, and many American firms faced bankruptcy. But the English government wanted its pound of flesh. It disliked the idea of New England making rum and selling it in competition with home distilleries; it disliked the idea that England should be bypassed in any commercial venture at all. The Molasses Act of the early 1700s had been evaded successfully by the colonists, so this time the king's ministers drafted a new regulation, the Sugar Act, and Parliament passed it in 1764. It outlawed foreign-made rum, added various tariffs to protect sugar, indigo, and coffee originating in British islands, and imposed other trade restrictions.

Ben Franklin, always one to use graphic figures of speech or fables to make his point, told English officials that "what you get from us in taxes you must lose in trade. The cat can yield but her skin." The colonial assemblies warned that unemployment, business failures, and a general depression would follow enforcement of the Sugar Act, but England was adamant. The law stayed on the books.

The colonies stood together on commercial matters, but they disagreed on many other points. While the Treaty of Paris was being fashioned, an example of the disunity came to the fore in northern New England. New Hampshire, most exposed of the colonies in the northeast, had suffered from eighty years of Indian strife. When the war ended, the people went back from the coast to the hamlets and farms that had been burned and ravished by the French and the Indians. Some crossed the Connecticut River into the Green Mountains and down on the far side to the shores of Lake Champlain, where they established new villages. Free land was given in this generally uninhabited territory to the men of Roger's Rangers and other soldiers who had fought so valiantly for the colonies. Governor John Wentworth of New Hampshire, believing that the royal grant gave him the power to do so, set up 150 townships, and at once settlers from New Hampshire, Massachusetts, Connecticut, and New York trekked into the wilderness to build new homes. It was a time of jubilation for the New Englanders, who were already beginning to feel hemmed in by their larger neighbors to the west.

To the consternation of every pioneer, in 1763 the lieutenant governor of New York proclaimed his jurisdiction over all land west of the Connecticut River and north of Massachusetts. Governor Wentworth sent a plea to Lord Halifax in London, asking for support of his claim. His message included these angry words: "A number of armed men, attended by the patroon and High Sheriff of Albany, seized upon and carried off from Pownall a justice of the peace, a captain of the militia, a deputy-sheriff who was executing a legal process; with one other principal inhabitant."

The Privy Council decided in favor of New York—a decision that was not final and would ultimately be upset. In less than fifteen years the two colonies would be fighting shoulder to shoulder against England, but now they glowered at one another across the disputed border, raided one another's herds, initiated lawsuits, and petitioned their provincial assemblies for support.

New Englanders, freed of worry about Indians and apparently willing to take their chances with the "Yorkmen," moved into what is now northern New Hampshire and Vermont in a sudden, if small, migration. Connecticut residents, including a considerable number of soldiers who had fought in the area and found the countryside fertile and attractive, drove their farm animals through western Massachusetts and into the Green Mountains, naming their settlements after their old homes. The influence of Connecticut people in Vermont was to last for many decades. Seven years later a group of Congregational ministers rounded up enough support to establish Dartmouth College on the New Hampshire bank of the Connecticut River. Civilization of a rude sort reached into the north country as frontiersmen found new passes over the White Mountains. The English flag waved from forts and town meeting-houses within a hundred miles of the St. Lawrence River.

Connecticut, second most populous colony in New England, had played a notable role in the French and Indian War. While the conflict never entered the colony, protected as it was by New York and Massachusetts, it carried its full share of the burden in supplying soldiers and supplies. Taxes were raised sky-high, and the residents paid them gladly. Droves of cattle were gathered together and sent, on the hoof, to depots for feeding the English and colonial troops. But Connecticut's biggest contribution was in men. Throughout the war there were never less than one thousand Connecticut men under arms, and at times the figure rose to more than five thousand, three times more in proportion to total population than any other colony. The "nutmeggers" were good fighters, as Washington was to find out later.

Even with a heavy out-migration of its younger citizens, Connecticut swiftly paid off its war debts and returned to a profitable peacetime footing, only to find that England was moving to restrict the colonies' overseas commerce.

If Connecticut had shone as a loyal province, its neighbor Rhode Island showed its loyalty in other ways. More of its sons had been at sea as privateers, making life miserable for any French ship in the Atlantic, than were under arms on land. Nevertheless, this smallest of all the colonies was as truculent toward England as it was toward its parent colony, Massachusetts. Its ships were everywhere, it seemed, engaging in trade that shifted from simple commerce to out-and-out smuggling and freebooting. During the war the superiority of the Rhode Islanders' seamanship was a thorn in the side of the French merchant marine. The Gulf Stream kept

Narragansett Bay open to shipping even when ice clogged the
harbors of New York and Boston, and the Rhode Islanders took
advantage of it. Newport, one report noted, was

> a central point in the long coast-line of the colonies, not only as a
> refuge for the small vessels of the lively American trade, but where
> "lawful privateers in time of war could . . . easily refit . . . run in
> with their prizes, or land their plunder. More than once during
> those years, when a Frenchman was seen in the offing, a well-
> manned ship hurried out of Newport harbour in pursuit, and after
> a gallant fight sailed back again with a prize in tow."

The independent spirit that caused so many headaches for the
English also caused trouble at home. Roger Williams would have
been sorely wounded in spirit had he lived to see the changes. The
Church of England was established in the larger cities, and
straightaway the Quakers, Anabaptists, and other dissident sects
that had flourished in the early years fell on evil days. The general
assembly had forgotten the early teachings of the founder so completely that it could order the founders of the Seventh-Day Baptists at Westerly to observe the Sabbath on the first day of the
week. The pure democracy fostered by Roger Williams was further
diluted: The colony passed laws restricting the vote to those owning a freehold worth £100 or with an annual income from real
estate amounting to £2.

Back in the days of early exploration along the North American coast Adriaen Block, a Dutch captain, had discovered the island to which he gave his name, just southwest of Narragansett
Bay. There is some difference of opinion as to whether he tried to
establish a settlement there or if he just put a few men ashore to
catch fish to supply his ship, but regardless of its inauspicious beginnings, Block Island had grown into a very important point of
rendezvous for Rhode Island skippers in the years before the war
for independence. The island was a no man's land where shipmas-
ters swapped cargoes, recruited seamen from other ships, or re-
fitted while on privateering ventures. What seemed legal in war-
time went on hardly unchanged in time of peace, and the English
customs collectors fretted over the way the colonials were outwitting them. It was a foretaste of what the patriot sea-rovers would
do once war was declared.

At this time in colonial history the Bahamas were totally under
the power of pirates. Some idea of the character of Rhode Is-

land's seafarers can be gained from the angry words of a Massachusetts official loyal to the Crown: "These practices [the piracy at Block Island] will never be put an end to till Rhode Island is reduced to the subjection of the British Empire, of which at present it is no more a part than the Bahama Islands when they were inhabited by the buccaneers."

It all depended on the point of view. England wanted all revenue for itself. Rhode Island saw trade and shipping as its only way to survive because it had almost nothing to sell. At the time Parliament invoked the Sugar Act, this smallest of the colonies could boast of 184 ships doing business with Europe, the West Indies, and Africa and another 352 vessels in coastal trade, plying from Newfoundland's Grand Banks to Georgia's fast-growing port of Savannah.

The Rhode Island assembly put its fears on the record in a remonstrance sent to London, saying the Sugar Act would paralyze all this trade "in a colony under a debt of 70,000 pounds for the expenses of the recent war alone." This call for kindness based upon the colony's loyalty fell on deaf ears, and the Rhode Islanders, from governor to lowliest seaman, determined to go it alone.

Ships moved in and out of the bay under cover of night or foul weather, easily eluding the English men-of-war sent to support the king's collectors. The resistance grew worse. Small boats of the English fleet were burned at the docks, warehouses were set afire, and a colonial vessel seized by the English and impounded at Providence was recaptured by a party of sailors who blackened their faces with burnt cork to escape identification.

What did all this mean? The quick answer is that people will do anything to make a profit. But there was more to it than that, much more. The colonists were no longer what they had been in the early days—frightened subjects of a king three thousand miles away. They had matured. They had fought for their survival and won against the Indians and the French. They had driven the Dutch out of New York, scotched the hopes of the Swedes for a new home of their own, held the Spaniards in Florida at arm's length, and reduced the strength of the Indian tribes. They had shown by capturing Louisburg that colonials could wage modern warfare. Then, under Washington, they had made it clear that they were masters of frontier war, avoiding the mechanical gyrations and the heavy bloodshed of large armies meeting on flat terrain.

And they had laughed at attempts to keep them off the high seas; they sailed where they wanted to and did business where they wished.

These were group manifestations. Individually, too, the colonials had advanced. In Connecticut and Massachusetts the common man had won the right to vote whether he held land or not. He had defied the power of the church hierarchy, taking temporal affairs out of the hands of Puritan churchmen. Women no longer walked two paces behind their husbands like well-trained setters. Marriage was still a stable and admired form of social life, but the day had passed when a woman who had erred had to wear a red A on her bosom. Girls were marrying whom they wished. General Philip Schuyler had four attractive daughters, only one of whom married the man approved by her father. Another climbed down a rope ladder from her bedroom into the arms of a lover, and the remaining two eloped, although in a less melodramatic manner.

Women of Dutch descent in New York were living a very cosmopolitan life, almost on equal terms with their husbands legally, and entirely so socially. There was even some hint of laxness in the colonies when it came to such things as marriage mores. The Quakers, all of whom led rather circumspect lives, took no steps to halt the marriage of Ben Franklin to a woman whose husband had deserted her and for whom there was no document proving a divorce had been obtained.

The Dutch had an interesting custom designed to ensure a high degree of marital success. Children were influenced early to play with limited groups of companions, usually children of good friends. It was thought that by growing up in close proximity they would learn of one another's tastes and idiosyncrasies and thus avoid marrying someone who would not be congenial.

In New England the practice of bundling was still prevalent, especially in the rural districts. This was an odd arrangement born of simple necessity. Young men and women were allowed to go to bed together, provided they followed two rules. They had to leave their clothes on, and had to sleep on opposite sides of a board placed down the middle of the bed. Many justifications were voiced in defense of the custom. First, most homes were little more than cabins, and there was a shortage of beds. The winter nights were cold, and two persons in one bed could use the same quilts and blankets. Finally, the custom was common among engaged couples. In the colonial philosophy, engagement was almost as sacred as marriage, and parents saw little evil in the betrothed couple spending the night together in bed. After all, there were not too many places where young lovers could go a-courting in winter without getting chilblains.

There were those who called the custom scandalous. Others sought to excuse it as a practice introduced from some other place. Connecticut people accused Cape Codders or New York Dutchmen with having promoted the custom, while the Dutch blamed the Yankees. Regardless of its origin, the bundling went on well into the years after independence, and although, as might be expected, it led to the birth of many "premature" babies, society as a whole was rather lenient about it. Surely it was a more civilized attitude than that which existed sixty or seventy years earlier when a woman who had been caught in adultery was often stripped to the waist in front of the townspeople, tied to the tail of a cart, and whipped unmercifully. The old Puritanism, which had been so opposed to sin, was losing its hold in the eighteenth century.

Morality in the southern colonies was less rigid than in those above Chesapeake Bay. In some degree, this was due to the wider use of indentured servants. The double standard existed both in the cities and on the plantations: A girl was criticized for adulterous affairs with her master, but the master went free of public censure. Society frowned even more on affairs between blacks and whites, establishing laws forbidding it and calling for the banishment of any woman having relations with a slave. But here too, there was less tendency to scold a white owner if he had intercourse with a black girl. White wives often had to suffer silently because of the immorality of their husbands, as divorces were not easy to obtain without full disclosures being made in open court —and few women wanted this.

All things considered, life had improved during the period when the frontier wars claimed prime attention. It seems a historical truth that wars bring few benefits in their train, but one of these is surely a tendency to forgive the little peccadilloes that seem important in peacetime.

In New England the Puritan church was losing much of its influence and this was a good thing. Some people even repented that their grandparents had been so ruthless in interpreting the Bible. The Anglican Church, the state church of England, had been established in most of the colonies, but with a difference. It had to get along without a colonial episcopate, as the democratic atmosphere was not a salubrious one for hierarchies of any sort.

Another factor in the generally improved situation was the waning of the practice of bringing in indentured servants from Europe. This was due not only to the widespread slavery in the South, but also to the growth in population in the middle and New England colonies. Labor shortages were disappearing and there was even some unemployment, so pressures were brought to end the importation of bonded servants.

Conditions were no better for the blacks, but for the white inhabitants life was much easier. They had escaped the penury and hopelessness of Europe. In all but a few cases they had improved their status, and the beginnings of democracy, despite its flaws, were apparent to everyone. De Crèvecoeur, witnessing the changes that had come in the New World, especially in New York, where he had turned to farming at the close of the Seven Years War, was astounded at the onward march of democracy among the common people. These are some of his words, too lyrical perhaps, but based on sound observation:

> The American is a new man, who acts upon new principles; he must therefore entertain new ideas, and form new opinions. From involuntary idleness, servile dependence, penury and useless labor, he has passed to toils of a very different nature, rewarded by ample subsistence.
> This is an American.

XXI

"Nothing Will Save Us But Acting Together"

MORE THAN A century and a half had passed since the first English colonists had erected their weak outpost at Jamestown. Thirteen colonies had come into being, most of them had prospered, and all showed great promise. Reliance upon the mother country had altered into a partnership of sorts during the wars, but that unity born of necessity had now deteriorated into open conflict.

It was almost as if a feeling of inevitability existed on both sides. No one in America was in any mood to accept the thesis laid down by George III that the colonies existed solely for England's benefit and that they should not be allowed to injure British commerce.

More and more customs officers were sent out from Britain to plug the loopholes that colonial traders had cut into the trade restrictions. When this did not do the trick, every captain in the royal navy was given a special commission authorizing him to stop any merchantman under the British flag and search it for contraband. Being a tricky fellow, and well aware of human weakness, King George provided fat rewards for any captain seizing a ship in "unlawful" trade.

Overnight the sea lanes off the North American coast were crowded with men-of-war blockading the main ports. The customs men searched ships, inspected cargo, and decided questionable cases in the king's, and their, favor. Colonial trade with foreign nations dried up, and imports became scarce and expensive.

Responding to this situation, the colonies tried to do more manu-

facturing themselves. But it wasn't easy for the colonists to boycott English goods because so few of them could be duplicated. Un-
expectedly, certain British merchants extended credit and sent over
technicians to aid the colonists in producing iron products, alkalis,
dyes, raw silk, hemp, undressed flax, and lumber. These items were
largely noncompetitive with English products, so the help given by
the English manufacturers was hardly altruistic.

The restrictions on colonial trade with other nations worked
great economic hardship on the colonists, but didn't antagonize them
nearly as much as George's next move. The king decided in 1764
that a standing army ought to be maintained in the American colonies, with twenty battalions housed there and supported by the
colonists. He tried to soften the blow by saying he would pay the
initial costs and would reduce the land tax, but the idea of having
"lobsterbacks" quartered in colonial homes was repugnant to every
patriot.

This "Quartering Act" required the colonists not only to supply
lodging for the redcoats, but to provide them with bedding, firewood, soap, candles, and whatever they wanted to drink. Extreme
loyalists saw nothing evil in this, but the majority of the colonists,
who had fought with English soldiers in the wars on the frontier,
had little respect for them and considered the edict an insult to
their own status as English citizens. Massachusetts men were the
angriest, but in Pennsylvania feelings ran high because of the large
number of Germans in that colony. Many were members of religious sects that opposed war, and none of them had much love
for the English.

Then another blow fell upon the colonies. George Grenville, the
king's financial minister, proposed that a new tax be laid upon the
residents of the thirteen colonies as a way of getting funds to pay
for the costs of the last war. Falsifying the facts without shame,
Grenville said the colonists had never paid their share of any of the
wars to "protect" them from the French. Grenville's proposed tax,
called the Stamp Act, was to be collected by the sale of special
stamps to be used in the drawing up of all wills, deeds, bills, re-
ceipts, drafts, and letters of credit. No one could prepare such a
document—many of which were in everyday use by businessmen—
without affixing the necessary stamps. The crusher in the proposal
was inserted when Grenville called for all violators of the act to
be tried without a jury in the admiralty courts, notorious for
their subservience to the Crown.

The Stamp Act, passed in 1765, more than any other single law imposed by the home government, polarized sentiment among the colonists. Those who stood by the king became known as Tories, and those who opposed the act were called Whigs, or more often as the years passed, Patriots.

One colonial assembly after another petitioned the Crown not to support Grenville's tax. The press exploded with editorials denouncing the proposal, and it became the main topic of conversation in taverns and alehouses. In Virginia opposition reached its peak during a meeting of the house of burgesses at Williamsburg. Members busied themselves in committee drafting remonstrances, but it was that fiery lawyer, Patrick Henry, who finally carried the day. Many thought his argument too strong. Henry cited the many occasions on which English kings had stated that Englishmen overseas were entitled to all the rights and liberties of their brothers at home. His version of the message to be sent to London included these words:

> . . . his Majesty's liege people of this, his most ancient and loyal colony, have, without interruption, enjoyed the inestimable right of being governed by such laws respecting their internal policy and taxation, as are derived from their own consent, with the approbation of their sovereign or his substitute; and that the same hath never been forfeited or yielded up, but hath been constantly recognized by the kings and people of Great Britain.

The scene in the legislative chamber was one of excited opposition, but Patrick Henry had a way of winning converts. The burgesses voted to send the version Henry had penned; relations between the colonies and mother country would never again be the same. The governor dissolved the Virginia assembly, but the members doffed their robes and powdered wigs and went into session at the Raleigh Tavern to figure out ways of contravening the Stamp Act. The task was made easier, of course, by the imbibing of copious amounts of ale and claret.

Massachusetts and the other northern colonies resisted the Stamp Act as valiantly as did Virginia, sending petitions to the king and voting to disregard the tax, but Virginia, that first and "most loyal" of all the king's provinces, as Patrick Henry called it, had protested most dramatically, touching off a fire that would not be extinguished.

The act was supposed to go into effect in November 1765, and it did, legally, but nowhere in the American colonies was one stamp purchased. Benjamin Franklin led a group of men from several colonies to London to seek repeal of the odious law, knowing that back home in Pennsylvania his provincial government had voted against using the stamps and had closed down all public offices that might have sold them. (The Quakers, Mennonites, and other pacifist groups, though absolutely opposed to using the stamps, permitted no violence or destruction of property. Everyone behaved so circumspectly that even George III commended the Pennsylvanians.)

When a call came from the northern colonies for a congress to discuss the tax, the governor denied Georgia's assembly the right to meet in session, but the people outside the legislative hall decided to fight both the tax and the Quartering Act. Later the Georgians had to eat humble pie, as the threat of Negro uprisings and Indian raids forced them to allow the hated lobsterbacks to dwell in their midst.

Rebellion swept across Massachusetts. Forming themselves into a body called the Sons of Liberty, hundreds of men rioted in Boston and tore down the building where the stamps were to be sold. James Otis inveighed against taxation without representation, and the officials empowered to sell stamps became so panic-stricken that they fled to English men-of-war in the harbor.

Everywhere in the colonies the pamphleteers were in their glory. Handbills appeared overnight defending the colonists' rights to set their own taxes, attacking Grenville, and chastising the king for mistreating his own people. The Adamses, Samuel and John, sent word throughout the colonies inviting delegates to gather in New York to discuss the unfair taxation. Nine colonies sent representatives to the congress, at which it was declared that taxation without representation was evil. The delegates made it clear that there was no objection to the paying of taxes, but that the right to levy such taxes rested in the hands of the colonists' own elected representatives.

As for the man in the street, he wanted more than rhetoric out of the congressional delegates. He got it by mob violence. Marylanders chased a stamp official out of the colony. In New York crowds of men stoned the building in which stamps were kept and burned the home of the mayor, who had been unwise enough to say he would stuff the stamps down the people's throats and make them like it. After burning the governor's carriage—the governor was elsewhere—the mob rushed off to the red-light district, invaded the houses of prostitution, and ended the night drinking and carousing with the ladies of easy virtue.

England had not foreseen the effect of the Stamp Act on that section of the population that was best able to protest. It was the lawyers, editors, pamphleteers, and booksellers who would have been hardest hit by the act, and these were the most articulate men in the colonies. An avalanche of protest poured from the printing presses in every city. The printed word showed beyond any doubt that well-to-do, conservative businessmen, landowners, and professional men stood shoulder to shoulder with tenants, workers, and other men without fortunes in staunch opposition to the tax.

In England the revolt created pandemonium. In Parliament friends of the colonies read the petitions from overseas and fought for revocation of the Stamp Act. There were more men opposed to the tax than anyone had suspected, and when a bill for its withdrawal was introduced it was passed, largely due to the support given by Pitt, who led the forces of repeal from his sickbed. Finally, in March 1766, George III signed the repeal against his will, convinced that his American subjects were the most ungrateful on earth.

South Carolina, one of the weaker colonies, had not hesitated to defy the Stamp Act. It was, as a matter of fact, the first colony to answer the call from Massachusetts to attend the congress. Christopher Gadsden and John Rutledge were among the leaders "answering the trumpet" from the north. Even before much thought had been given to combined resistance to England, young Rutledge voiced a thesis that in a few years was to become a rallying cry. "Nothing will save us," he said, "but acting together; the province that endeavors to act separately must fall with the rest and be branded besides with everlasting infamy."

In retrospect, it is not easy to determine just why the Stamp Act had such an effect when earlier levies and repressive laws had not roused the colonists. It might have been simply the straw that broke the camel's back. Some evidence of this can be seen in the behavior of the Pennsylvanians.

In the decades before the passage of the hated law the people of

Pennsylvania had been entirely concerned with internal problems, paying little attention to foreign affairs. John Penn, the founder's grandson, was proprietor and governor. His predecessor had taken advantage of the Indians in a dozen ways, forgetting the wise tenets of William Penn, and this had led to many troubles. When his father, Richard, and his uncle Thomas Penn had the audacity to propose that taxes on their estates be set at the level of the least valuable land in the colony, the people rebelled and sent Franklin to England with a petition to abolish the proprietary form of government. If Philadelphia was still a city of brotherly love, there was little evidence of it to be found there, or elsewhere in Pennsylvania.

But then George III imposed the Stamp Act. Whatever dissension existed in the colony disappeared in a trice. Local feuds were patched up, and everyone rallied against the detested impost. When it was finally repealed, the celebrations in Pennsylvania were anything but Quaker-like in their rowdiness.

Repeal of the Stamp Act was a psychological victory for the colonists, but it did little to improve the economic slump into which America had fallen after the Treaty of Paris. In Philadelphia the loss of a market for wheat was a serious blow. New Englanders had invested heavily in facilities for distilling and trading in rum and in sizable fleets for fishing off the Grand Banks. Where were the rum and salt cod to go if the English navy kept the trade with foreign lands to a trickle?

Panic hit the countinghouses and large mercantile firms. Several were unable to meet their debts and went bankrupt. As if to aggravate the condition, Parliament passed a new law levying a tax of about 30 percent on the wholesale price of molasses, which nearly wrecked the rum trade. A short time later new duties were imposed on imported goods from England—goods the colonists needed badly, or thought they needed. These included tea, paper, glass, and paint.

Realizing that the patriots would do everything possible to escape paying these new duties, England sent agents to the seaport cities in America, hopeful that they could be protected by the guns of English men-of-war lying at anchor in the harbors. General Thomas Gage, who had followed Jeffrey Amherst as commander in chief of British forces in North America but had gone home to retire, was sent back to Boston in 1768 as governor of Massachusetts and took over his old military command. Four regiments of

British soldiers accompanied him—a not-too-oblique reminder that the English government meant business.

For many years New Yorkers had thought of themselves as different, perhaps a little better, than Virginians, and the planters of Carolina had often quarreled with traders from Massachusetts or Pennsylvania. This was now changing. Young Christopher Gadsden, of Charleston, said there should no longer be New Englanders or New Yorkers, but all should be called Americans. Patrick Henry was to put it even more succinctly: "The distinctions between Virginians, Pennsylvanians, New Yorkers, and New Englanders, are no more. I am not a Virginian, but an American." Loyalty to the Crown was fading; a sense of unity was growing stronger day by day.

All across the land, from Boston Common to the Mohawk Valley, from the Chesapeake Bay to the mountains of South Carolina, patriots erected liberty poles, symbols of the rising spirit of independence. Their origin is in doubt; some thought they were suggestive of the gibbet and therefore a warning to the English, while others thought they resembled the ancient trees of the Teutonic forests where Germanic tribes had met in fateful assemblies.

One of the poles was erected on Golden Hill, a small eminence in downtown Manhattan, near today's Wall Street. On January 18, 1770, English soldiers were sent to cut it down. Scuffling between soldiers and patriots broke out where the pole had stood. Suddenly shots rang out, and a sailor fell wounded, dying later without knowing that he was the first man to die in the colonial rebellion against the mother country. The Sons of Liberty put up another liberty pole, which stood until the British occupied New York after the outbreak of actual war.

Less than three months later there was more bloodshed as the feelings of colonists and soldiers polarized even further. An English soldier, all accoutered in scarlet tunic, musket, powder horn, knapsack, and bayonet, was on sentry duty in front of a public building near Boston Common. Young men started to harass him, calling him "lobsterback," and others joined in the game. The soldier called for help and a squad of soldiers came on the run, firing when they reached his side. Three men were killed, one of them a mulatto slave named Crispus Attucks, who became the first black man to die for his country. The incident has become known, exaggeratedly, as the "Boston Massacre."

James Otis, the patriot lawyer, proved his highly ethical standards by defending the redcoats and saved them from murder charges. Two were found guilty of manslaughter, however, and were publicly branded for the crime.

Feelings were running so high that thoughtful leaders of the resistance feared events would get out of hand. In these troubled times tempers were short on both sides. England insisted it had the right to patrol offshore in search of illicit cargo, and Rhode Island's chief justice answered that if any English ship operated in that colony's waters without first getting a commission from the governor it would be guilty of trespassing, if not of actual piracy.

This set the stage for a test of strength. A British cruiser, the *Gaspée,* had been operating for some weeks in Narragansett Bay. Her commander was a young lieutenant who, feeling his oats, insulted the residents of the colony, fired at any ship that did not heed his orders immediately, and plundered farms for whatever he needed to feed his crew. When Rhode Islanders protested, an admiralty judge in Boston ruled against them and thundered that any persons trying to rescue seized vessels would be hanged as pirates.

This was strong language, and was resented by every patriot in the province. As if the fates were playing into the colonists' hands, a storm came up in the bay and the *Gaspée* ran aground off Namquit. The Newport-to-Providence packet, sailing by, saw the hated cruiser's plight and reported it to the townspeople in the capital city. Then, under cover of a particularly dark night, a party of the leading merchants in Providence, together with an assortment of lawyers, editors, and a few professional sailors, rowed down to where the *Gaspée* was stranded by low tide and seized the ship. The uppity young lieutenant was hurt in a scuffle, but the other sailors were permitted to go ashore. Then the *Gaspée* was burned to the waterline.

After this act of rebellion in Rhode Island, the scene of revolt shifted to North Carolina. There the atmosphere was already tense because of the activities of the royal governor, William Tryon. Tryon had been in North Carolina for more than six years, during which he had antagonized everyone except a small coterie of loyalists in the lowlands. He had picked New Bern as his capital city and forced the inhabitants to finance the building of an elaborate mansion.

The outraged patriots formed an organization called the Regulators and spent several hours a week drilling under arms. Most of the members were Scots-Irish settlers who, in truth, had as little love for the colonists who lived on the tidewater as they had for Tryon and his lackeys. They didn't want to be taxed by England, and they didn't want to be taxed by the colonial assembly if they could not have more to say about it themselves.

Finally the threat implicit in the Regulators' training became too much for Tryon to ignore. He gathered a force of English regulars, who were joined by a small party of Tory sympathizers, and marched inland to teach the patriots a lesson. He had cavalry, infantry, and a few field guns manned by sailors from the British fleet. On May 15, 1771, he reached Alamance, in the sand hills of north-central North Carolina, where he surprised a party of Regulators. There was a brisk, intense fight, but the odds against the patriots were too great. The cannon were bad enough, but the shortage of ammunition was worse, and the English finally won the field. Losses on both sides were about equal, but fifteen of the Regulators were captured and seven of them subsequently executed by the ruthless Tryon. The governor moved swiftly to stamp out the resistance movement, barbarously seizing and hanging anyone thought to be a leader.

There is a historic footnote that needs telling about this particular royal governor. King George thought so highly of the way Tryon had repressed rebellion in North Carolina that he moved him to New York, where the resistance movement was even more deeply rooted. But Tryon did not take any action until after he had made sure of personal gain. He set up a county, called Tryon after himself, in the Mohawk Valley and engaged in lively land speculation. Only after he had ensured himself of a handsome profit did he move against the patriots, but with none of the success he had had in Carolina.

The mistreatment of the Regulators rankled in the heart of every patriot. Many a colonist, unwilling to pay tribute to the king, had crossed the Appalachians and settled small towns on the Tennessee and Cumberland rivers. Among these men, who were motivated by a twin impulse to get out of Tryon's reach and to settle the lush wilderness beyond the mountains, were such men as Daniel Boone, John Sevier, and James Robertson. Boone turned northward into Kentucky territory, and Sevier and Robertson started a hamlet on Watauga Creek, one of the streams that form the Tennessee. Their geography was not too accurate, and they believed that the area lay within the confines of Virginia.

When it was made clear that they were in that vast territory given to the first proprietors of North Carolina, the pioneers decided they had had enough of English rule. So, early in 1772 the hardy frontiersmen, dressed in homespun or deerskin and carrying their long rifles with them, gathered on the banks of the Watauga and adopted a constitution of their own—the first drafted by men who called themselves Americans rather than Englishmen. It was said that this action, far off in the backwoods, "set to the people of America the example of erecting themselves into a state independent of the authority of the English King."

It was a small but significant example of the growing independence of the colonists. The enclave, which was neither colony, state, nor county, existed for years, probably because the Scots-Irish residents of western North Carolina were themselves so opposed to domination by the Crown and saw no reason to annoy others who felt the same way.

Elsewhere tempers were not so well under control. There was no unanimity within the patriot ranks. Even some of the leaders of the resistance to England were becoming frightened at the militancy shown by extremists. John Hancock wanted to go slowly, but Samuel Adams couldn't move fast enough toward revolt. Men who were willing to risk standing up to the English officials recoiled from the mob psychology evidenced during the so-called Boston Massacre and at meetings harangued by James Otis. Otis was a ringleader and fiery orator who may have acted as he did because of a head injury received some years earlier in a scuffle with a British collector. Later, well before war broke out, the injury drove Otis mad and he spent his later years in an asylum.

The more radical elements among the patriots, especially in Massachusetts, stoked the fires. There were dinners with long orations against the king and Parliament. Public meetings were frequent. The repeal of the Stamp Act was celebrated on its anniversary, and hardly a week went by without verbal attacks being launched against the redcoats quartered in Boston.

There is little solid evidence to indicate that the British soldiers behaved any worse than soldiers everywhere. Certainly their colorful uniforms may have attracted a few maidenly glances, and that would have upset any good patriot. The noisier of the anti-British colonists found it easy to arouse their audiences against the soldiers with speeches about "our beauteous virgins, exposed to all the insolence of unbridled passion."

Massachusetts and Virginia took the lead in urging unity, but no colony lacked the determination to resist unfair taxation and interference with trade. Even the youngest colony, Georgia, with barely more than five thousand white inhabitants, stood up to the Crown. There was a deep division between wealthy planters and those who formed a convention to cooperate with the other colonies, but a company of militia was formed as an earnest of Georgia's good intentions.

Pennsylvania was no longer the colony William Penn had founded, united in Christian amity and hatred of war. Sheer fright had had something to do with the change. When Braddock had been defeated, years before, Indian scalping parties had raided to within thirty miles of Philadelphia. The old live-and-let-live theories had died out, and money was appropriated to raise a militia. Now Pennsylvania was in the forefront of the opposition to England's taxes and restrictions on trade.

John Dickinson, writing articles called "Letters from a Farmer," marshaled sensible yet eloquent arguments on the rights of colonists which were published in papers all along the seaboard. Other periodicals excoriated the king and his ministers, pleading with the colonists to work together in their mutual behalf. The word "tyranny" appeared with more and more frequency as the editors helped shape the opinions of the people by telling them how their fellow patriots in other colonies were reacting to English oppression.

The *Maryland Gazette*, aware of the deepening rift, opened its columns to letters from its readers for a free and open discussion of the Stamp Act. Maryland had had more than its share of internal troubles, including a boundary dispute with Pennsylvania, and an evil proprietor, the dissolute sixth Lord Baltimore. He rigged taxes to grow rich, played favorites with appointments, raised his own salary annually, and behaved scandalously. Only the fact that by happenstance his governors on the scene in Maryland were both fair-minded men saved the colony from worse debt and travail.

The ancient dispute over Maryland's northern boundary with Pennsylvania had been settled in the years after the French and Indian War was concluded. Two English mathematicians and surveyors, Charles Mason and Jeremiah Dixon, after many difficulties born of the imprecise royal grants given Calvert and Penn, finally ran a line from Delaware into the far Appalachians. It left Maryland with far less land than its early governors had claimed, but neither colony ever again disputed the border.

None of these troubles stopped Marylanders from standing firmly with Massachusetts when that colony called for unified opposition to the Stamp Act, the Navigation Acts, the imposts on tea and sugar, the Molasses Act, and the Quartering Act.

Delaware was even more militant. It had formed militia companies and set them to drilling even before the Boston Massacre and the redcoat victory at Alamance.

From the pine forests of Maine to the rice and indigo plantations of Georgia, from the sea to the Alleghenies, men and women were moving unconsciously toward war—and independence. In every colony committees had been set up to work with one another and keep the population abreast of the resistance movement in other parts of the land.

Englishman and German, Huguenot and Dutchman, Swiss and Scots-Irish, Protestant, Catholic, and Jew—all were standing together, except for a handful of Tories. They had overcome famine and fear, established tiny settlements and seen them grow into thriving ports, and had fought the Indians and the French and the Spaniards. They had quarreled with one another, as individuals and as colonies, but it had been a sort of sibling rivalry. Now they were seeing eye to eye, aware of the greatest danger yet to confront them. Formal unity was still a few years off, but all were in it together.

This was how it was when an East Indiaman, loaded with chests of China tea, reefed her sails and tied up at a Boston wharf.

XXII

"If They Mean War,
Let It Begin Here"

ENGLAND HAD REMOVED her imposts on all the products previously taxed, with the exception of tea. This tax was left in force, not in any particular hope of reaping rich benefits, but to show the colonies that the mother country still claimed the right to tax and restrict trade.

There may even have been a little skulduggery in maintaining the duty on tea, and if there was, it wasn't the first time that business interests have turned to government to get their chestnuts off a hot stove. It was a known fact that the venerable but decadent East India Company, having fallen upon evil days because of competition abroad, was on the edge of bankruptcy. The glorious old days, when it had ruled the trade with the Spice Islands and China with the support of the royal navy, had faded, sped by inept management and the avarice of its stockholders. Parliament answered the company's appeal and granted it the privilege of selling tea in America without paying the usual English import duties. But George refused to go further and kill the tax the colonists had to pay when they purchased tea.

Tea was a far more important drink in the colonies than coffee, but there is no way to explain why the tea tax created such turmoil. Other taxes had been more onerous, and the Navigation Acts had been far more harmful to American trade and business.

Perhaps the explanation is a simple one. Every time a colonist brewed a pot of tea, every time he sipped his beverage at home or in a tavern, he could visualize the collectors rummaging in the holds of merchantmen, counting the chests, and imposing the hated duty before permitting the cargo to be put on the docks. Merchants and shipowners, naturally, feared the tax was an attempt to establish a monopoly for the benefit of the East India Company, but the man in the street would hardly have been concerned with such a theory.

Whatever the basic reasons, colonists everywhere saw the continuation of the tea duty as another sign of England's perfidy. Spontaneously, citizens' committees in the big port cities prepared for action. When tea ships arrived from Amoy and Canton, they were not allowed to unload their cargo. In New York, Philadelphia, and Wilmington, North Carolina, the ships were ordered to sea, and the glint of polished musket barrels convinced skippers they had best obey.

The tea ship *Peggy Stewart* docked in a Maryland port, but when her owner saw how adamant the patriots were about refusing to handle the cargo, he moved the vessel out into the bay and set fire to her himself. Elsewhere ships turned around of their own free will. If the tea was unloaded, it lay in the damp warehouses until it spoiled.

In Boston the patriots simply refused to allow any tea to be removed from the ships or handled in any way. In other ports the royal officers had given vessels clearance to leave the port, but Governor Thomas Hutchinson—strange grandson of that strange woman, Anne Hutchinson—refused clearance, knowing that under the regulations his own employees could unload the ships at the end of a twenty-day grace period.

The Sons of Liberty held meetings and agitated against the governor's duplicity. The Minutemen, another group of men fast growing in influence, joined in the opposition. No other topic was heard in the alehouses. No other subject was as popular at the dinner table. All over Boston there was a restlessness that boded ill for England. On the evening of December 16, 1773, a town meeting was convened for the purpose of discussing the situation. For hours speakers debated ways and means of showing Parliament how firmly opposed the people of Boston were to paying any tax on tea. The audience left the meeting with the words of John Adams ringing in their ears: "This meeting can do nothing more to save the country!"

The sixteenth was the day before the end of the period of waiting before English officials could unload the tea. On the morrow, if nothing was done, the unwanted tea would be unloaded and stowed in warehouses. In more ways than one, it was the eleventh hour.

Late that night scores of men, painted and garbed in the regalia of Mohawk Indians, poured onto the wharves where the East India ships were moored, forced the crews to pry open the hatches, and hurled the tea chests over the side into Boston Harbor. In later years the event became known as the "Boston Tea Party," but at the time it was hardly a frolic. Without question it was the most arrant affront to royal dignity and power yet offered by the colonists.

Lord North, who had come to power as prime minister in 1770, was no man to take this rebellious action lying down. Hurrying to the halls of Parliament, he demanded that the port of Boston be closed to all shipping until restitution had been made for the jettisoned tea. Parliament supinely adopted the Boston Port Bill and ordered the royal navy to see that no ships passed in or out of the harbor.

If the English thought repression would curb the spirit of independence in the American colonies, they didn't understand the feelings of the people overseas. They were ignoring past events completely—the setting up of liberty poles, the refusal to quarter soldiers, the failure to use stamps, the evasion of the molasses tax and Navigation Acts, the formation of the Sons of Liberty and the Regulators, and dozens of other actions clearly aimed at disobedience to the Crown.

Better intelligence would have warned the home government of the political atmosphere in the colonies. The year before, in 1773, the town of Mendon, that Massachusetts village that had suffered so much from the savagery of King Philip and his braves, had initiated a step toward independence. In what was nothing less than a resolution asking for separation from England, the village had voted that "all just and lawful government must originate in the free consent of the people." That was three long years before the drafting of the Declaration of Independence.

Promptly King George shifted the headquarters of his armed forces in North America from Halifax, Nova Scotia, to Boston, hoping to intimidate the Bay Colony's residents, but it had the opposite effect. When he closed off all shipping in Boston he foolishly expected that other seaports would leap at the chance to absorb that city's business. Instead, Salem, Marblehead, and other ports stood solidly beside the Boston shipping men and traders, offering them free use of their warehouses, wharves, and other waterfront facilities.

It was the same in the other colonies. Harm done Boston was done to all of them, the patriots realized. Four months after the Boston Tea Party the first tea ship to reach New York, the *Nancy,* sailed into the harbor, but before it could dock citizens dressed much like the "Mohawks" who had dumped the tea in Massachusetts Bay went on board and convinced the *Nancy's* skipper to head for London posthaste. Pleading need to take on fresh water and supplies, the captain went ashore. While in port he saw the same "Mohawks" rush on board the tea ship *London,* already tied up, and dump her cargo into the bay. And that wasn't all. He witnessed crowds parading to martial music, flags run up on several liberty poles and on colonial ships in the harbor, and the bells of the town's churches pealing out in loud defiance.

Finally a committee of New Yorkers called upon the *Nancy's* captain, escorted him politely from Custom House to pilot boat, and told him to tell the directors of the East India Company exactly what he had seen with his own eyes. The committee adjured him to impress upon the company that New York had no use for laws that infringed upon individual freedoms.

Up and down the Atlantic seaboard support for Boston was almost unanimous, with only a few Tories trying vainly to stem the tide of popular revolt. In Virginia the house of burgesses set aside June 1 as a day of prayer and asked for divine help to stave off "the heavy calamity which threatens the civil rights of America." The Virginians turned to rhetoric and proud words, but didn't stop there. They sent food and money to ease the burdens of Bostonians who were suffering from the embargo.

Every colony called a special session of its assembly and adopted such virulent condemnations of Parliament that the royal governors felt constrained to dissolve them—with one exception. This was sturdy little Connecticut, the stronghold of a people's charter, whose governor, Jonathan Trumbull, stood steadfastly beside the people in opposing the king. South Carolina called a session of the "Committee of Ninety-three," whose members promptly named delegates to a convention at which steps were taken to support Boston.

Quakers, Mennonites, Moravians, and all the other people of Pennsylvania agreed not to import any goods from England until restitution had been made to Boston. More than eight thousand persons rallied at a great mass meeting in Philadelphia to vote aid for the New England port.

There was a sticky situation for a time in New York, as Tories had gained control of that colony's assembly. But now there was no stopping the patriots. Eleven of the members withdrew from the assembly hall, and after a huge gathering in the open fields north of the city, urged the General Court of Massachusetts to call a colonial congress.

So many colonial assemblies or "vigilance committees" called on Massachusetts to initiate a congress that it is not clear which one first thought of the need for a meeting of all the colonies. The point is an academic one, though, as patriotic Americans from Georgia to Maine all sensed the urgency of the situation and the need for unified steps to defy Britain. No matter what the origin, the patriots of Massachusetts issued a clear call for a Continental Congress to meet in Philadelphia, a central point in the colonies.

Without exception, the assemblies in the other twelve colonies held special sessions or, when these bodies had been dissolved by royal governors, convened meetings in the open or in taverns to select delegates to the congress. The process was uniformly democratic in most instances. For example, in New York the tax-paying freemen of New York City, Albany, and other sizable communities selected the delegation to represent that colony. No provision was made to poll that portion of the electorate that lived in rural areas or on the frontier, but this was not because of any desire to exclude them, but simply because time was short.

Rhode Island took time out from choosing its delegates to perform other chores of singular importance. Parties of disguised men swooped down on Fort George in Newport Harbor and rifled the royal arsenal. Guns, ammunition, and other stores were removed and sequestered in hiding places.

General Gage in Boston saw what was brewing and tried to thwart it, even breaking up a session of the General Court, but he did not move fast enough. Before his redcoats appeared in the chamber, the members had issued the formal call to the congress and had appointed their own delegates, including John and Samuel Adams and John Hancock.

The oldest colony of all, Virginia, held its nominating convention at the provincial capital, Williamsburg. Thomas Jefferson, who was very young and a true firebrand, spoke defiantly of England's ingratitude and oppression and detailed many of the rights he said belonged to British America. The words were nothing if not revolutionary. But it was George Washington who voiced the sentiments of the colonists most accurately: "We have proved the inefficiency of addresses to the throne and remonstrances to Parliament. I am ready to raise one thousand men, subsist them at my own expense, and march at their head to the relief of Boston."

On September 5, 1774, the delegates from the various colonies met in Carpenter's Hall in Philadelphia in the first Continental Congress, so called because it would serve as a general legislature for all the colonies. It was an illustrious assemblage of men who gathered in that attractive chamber. There were John and Samuel Adams and John Hancock, of Massachusetts; Peyton Randolph, Richard Henry Lee, and Patrick Henry, of Virginia; John Jay and Philip Livingston, of New York; Benjamin Franklin, of Pennsylvania; and Christopher Gadsden and John and Edward Rutledge, of South Carolina. Georgia was the only colony missing. There was so much trouble at home that the convention had been unable to pick a delegate, but this was corrected the next time around.

Richard Henry Lee of Virginia drew up an important document called the Articles of Association, which called upon all the people of all the colonies not to buy or sell any British goods until the hated acts passed by Parliament were rescinded, to push forward agricultural development in order to become self-sustaining, and to form committees to enforce these proposals, by coercion if necessary: any person who attempted to evade the boycott by continuing to trade with Britain or deal in British goods faced imprisonment or banishment.

Delegates to this Continental Congress then commended Massachusetts for its heroic resistance to the British restrictions and promised that if force were used against one of the colonies, all would rally to its support. Agreeing to meet in another congress the following May, the delegates went home to gird for the struggle all sensed was very close.

The New England colonies assumed that whatever reprisals England took would be aimed at them, so they hastily organized interim assemblies to govern themselves without supervision by royal governors. The southern provinces moved almost as swiftly, training militia and gathering stores of war. Local militia were organized in many colonies under an arrangement whereby the men would not leave home or don uniforms but would continue to work on the farms or in the cities, ready at a signal to spring to arms. Because of this instant reaction to a call to duty, they took the name "Minutemen."

It was not all smooth sailing for the patriots. New York and Pennsylvania had many conservatives who had to be won over. Virginia's Governor Dunmore threw sand into the bearings at every opportunity, and, though there is little hard evidence to support it, there was a rumor widely held that he negotiated with Indian tribes in the Tennessee country to threaten the frontier and cause dissension among the patriots. When Virginia's interim congress next went into session, the meeting was held on a grassy hillside outside Richmond because of fear that Dunmore and his supporters in Williamsburg would disrupt the assembly. It was at this meeting that Patrick Henry, using his most colorful oratory, dragooned the delegates into voting for raising a sizable force of militia. And it was here too that he is supposed to have said: "War is inevitable, and let it come. . . . As for me, give me liberty or give me death."

Busily the patriots went about the work of secreting powder and balls, guns and tents, food supplies and what few cannon they could lay hands upon against the day when they might need them. In Massachusetts twelve thousand militiamen, nearly half of them Minutemen, oiled their guns and waited for England's next move. General Gage, aware of the gathering menace, tried to fortify Boston and sent patrols into the countryside to seize arms caches.

In London shock and disbelief existed in palace and Parliament. A majority of those in government considered the colonists in a state of rebellion. A proposal was made that taxes be ended provided that the Continental Congress agree to make a payment of a sum of money to be used at the pleasure of Parliament. This sum was to equal the amount that taxes would normally bring in, but the congress would have the power to allocate how much each colony would pay. The proposal was never acted upon.

Edmund Burke, who had argued for understanding and fair treatment of the colonies, submitted an alternative proposal, which was voted down. He was even prevented from reading grievances from the petitions sent to Parliament from the colonies.

Lord North punished New York, North Carolina, and Georgia by excluding them from the fishing grounds off Nova Scotia and Newfoundland, acting out of sheer spite because of the activities of those who had signed the Articles of Association.

Seemingly powerless to arbitrate the differences between Crown and colonists, Parliament decided to try the iron fist. It passed the Restraining Act in early 1775, prohibiting all trade in New England. The king's men-of-war sailed to blockade every port of any size from New Haven to Maine, and the colonists, seeing how intransigent the home government was, hurried to prepare for armed conflict. Militia drilled on scores of town commons, cannon were moved to the outskirts of Boston, and powder was gathered in secret magazines near the city.

Irresistibly, the colonies and the mother country drifted toward war. The Massachusetts area, always the focus of unrest, attracted the most attention from the English authorities. For the time being, it seemed, the other colonies were forgotten. In the eyes of the king, the patriots of New England were the hard core of the rebellion. This was where the Pilgrims, meek and deeply religious, had landed on the inhospitable, rocky shore of the northern coast. This was where the Puritans, prejudiced, self-righteous, and arbitrary though they were, had encouraged ideals that would be invaluable in time of war. They had fostered a lasting sense of the dignity of man and had struck down institutions that had held men in thrall for centuries.

These were the people General Gage faced during the early spring of 1775. He knew the patriots were gathering arms and ammunition and, aware of Tryon's temporary success in North Carolina, decided to execute a similar swift raid into the interior to seize colonial war stores.

Quartered in a town where every resident was a potential enemy, the English forces could not move without being observed. When, eight hundred strong, they started for Concord on the evening of April 18, 1775, a signal was flashed from Boston's Old North Church to a rider waiting in Charlestown, across the river.

He was no Puritan, this Paul Revere, who had volunteered to make what became a historic midnight ride to alert the patriots. He was the descendant of one of the many Huguenot families whose blood enriched the stock of every one of the thirteen colonies. He was a printer, engraver, silversmith, and a liberal. Revere wanted no more truck with the forces of oppression; he had been a leader in the Boston Tea Party and was still Britain's sworn enemy.

Hour after hour he rode through the dark countryside north of the Charles, through Lexington and on to Concord, crying the alarm as he went. The next morning, at just about break of day, enough Minutemen had gathered on the green in the first village to form a pitiful company of eighty half-armed men. As the column of redcoats approached, Captain John Parker lined his men up and spoke to them in simple words, never dreaming they would be repeated in a thousand books, graven on stone, and etched in bronze: "Stand your ground; don't fire unless fired upon, but if they mean war, let it begin here."

British soldiers lifted their muskets and fired, killing seven or eight Minutemen. A ragged volley from patriot guns wounded several redcoats, but none was killed. The dead men sprawled upon the village green had given their lives in a cause now sacred to every American.

Later that day, after seizing the hidden stores at Concord, spilling the powder on the ground, and tossing cannon balls into deep wells, the British column started back to Boston. At a bridge over the river they came under galling fire from at least five hundred Minutemen who had rallied at word of the slaughter in Lexington. One of those Minutemen, his identity lost in the smoke of battle, must have pulled the trigger an instant before his comrades-in-arms, and thus "fired the shot heard 'round the world."

At that instant he was no longer a colonist. He and his fellow Minutemen were Americans. As Americans they aimed and fired their rifles together, and as Americans they would fight on together for years, suffer the bitter cold of winter and the gnawing pain of hunger together, and in the end, by their fortitude, create a new nation.

Selected Bibliography

Original Sources

A Colonial Courting: Extracts from Judge Samuel Sewall's Dairy, 1720, Sept.-Dec. Haddon Heights, N.J.: W. L. Washburn, 1940.

Colonial Records of Pennsylvania. A collection of early documents printed by T. Fenn & Co., Harrisburg, Penna., 1838–53.

Colonial Records of South Carolina. Documents in the State Archives, Columbia, S. C.

Colonial Records of the State of Georgia. Documents compiled and published by Allen D. Candler and printed by Franklin Printing & Publishing Co., Atlanta, 1904.

Journal of Major George Washington, 1753–54. Original documents now in archives of Colonial Williamsburg, Williamsburg, Va.

The Philipsburg Story, by Carol Elliott. Unpublished manuscript prepared for Sleepy Hollow Restorations and now in library of that organization in Irvington, N. Y.

Private Journal of Sarah Kemble Knight, Being the Record of a Journey from Boston to New York in the Year 1704. Privately printed in Norwich, Conn., 1901.

Periodicals

Arnett, Frank S. "The Evolution of Manhattan," *Munsey's Magazine,* Vol. 28, 1902.

"The Dutch Physician in New Amsterdam," *Medical Library and Historical Magazine,* Brooklyn, N. Y., 1906.

Porter, Marjorie L. "Frontier Towns and Frontier Life," *North Country Life,* Vol. 7, No. 3.

Schoolcraft, Henry L. "The Capture of New Amsterdam," *English Historical Review,* Vol. 22 (1907), London.

Van der Mandere, C. Ch. G. J. "The True Story of the Founding of New York City," *Current History,* Vol. 25 (1926).

Books

Adams, James Truslow. *The Epic of America.* New York: Blue Ribbon Books, 1931.

———. *The Founding of New England.* Boston: Little, Brown, 1921.

Andrews, Charles M. *Colonial Background of the American Revolution.* New Haven, Conn.: Yale University Press, 1931.

———. *Colonial Folkways, a Chronicle of American Life in the Reign of the Georges.* New Haven, Conn.: Yale University Press, 1919.

Aptheker, Herbert. *The Colonial Era.* New York: International Publishers Co., 1959.

Ayres, Harral. *The Great Trail of New England*. Boston: Meador Publishing Co., 1940.

Bell, Margaret. *Women of the Wilderness*. New York: Dutton, 1938.

Bliss, William Root. *Colonial Times on Buzzard's Bay*. Boston: Houghton Mifflin, 1900.

Boorstin, Daniel J. *The Americans: The Colonial Experience*. New York: Random House, 1958.

Booth, Mary Louise. *History of the City of New York*. New York: W. R. C. Clarke & Co., 1859.

Brady, Cyrus Townsend. *Colonial Fights and Fighters*. New York: McClure, Phillips & Co., 1901.

Bridenbaugh, Carl, ed. *Gentleman's Progress. The Itinerarium of Dr. Alexander Hamilton. 1774*. Chapel Hill, N. C.: University of North Carolina Press, 1948.

————. *Seat of Empire*. Williamsburg, Va.: Colonial Williamsburg, Inc., 1950.

Buranelli, Vincent, ed. *The Trial of Peter Zenger*. New York: New York University Press, 1957.

Calder, Isabel M., ed. *Colonial Captivities, Marches and Journeys*. New York: Macmillan, 1935.

Coffin, Charles Carleton. *Old Times in the Colonies*. New York: Harper & Bros., 1880.

Colton, Julia M. *Annals of Old Manhattan*. New York: Brentano's, 1901.

Crane, Verner W. *The Southern Frontier, 1670–1732*. Durham, N. C.: Duke University Press, 1928.

Davis, Asahel. *History of New Amsterdam*. New York: R. T. Young, 1854.

Dexter, Elizabeth Anthony. *Colonial Women of Affairs*. Boston: Houghton, Mifflin, 1931.

Earle, Alice Morse. *Colonial Dames and Goodwives*. New York: Macmillan, 1924.

Farish, Hunter Dickinson, ed. *Journal and Letters of Philip Vickers Fithian, 1773–1774*. Williamsburg, Va.: Colonial Williamsburg, Inc., 1943.

Field, Edward. *The Colonial Tavern*. Providence, R. I.: Preston & Rounds, 1897.

Goodwin, Maud Wilder. *The Colonial Cavalier*. New York: Lovell, Coryell & Co., 1894.

Greene, Evarts Boutell. *Provincial America*. New York: Frederick Ungar, 1905.

Griffis, William Elliot. *The Romance of American Colonization*. Boston and Chicago: W. A. Wilde & Co., 1898.

Gutman, Judith Mara. *The Colonial Venture*. New York: Basic Books, 1966.

Harper, Lawrence A. *The English Navigation Laws: A Seventeenth Century Experiment in Social Engineering*. New York: Columbia University Press, 1939.

Harper, Lillie Dupuy, ed. *Colonial Men and Times*. Philadelphia: Innes & Sons, 1916.

Holliday, Carl. *Woman's Life in Colonial Days*. Boston: Cornhill Publishing Co., 1922.

Horsmanden, Daniel. *The Negro Conspiracy in the City of New York*. New York: G. W. Schott, 1851.

Innis, Harold. *The Cod Fisheries*. New Haven, Conn.: Yale University Press, 1940.

Jefferey, Reginald W. *The History of the Thirteen Colonies of North America*. London: Methuen & Co., 1908.

Jernegan, Marcus Wilson. *The American Colonies, 1492–1750*. New York: Frederick Ungar, 1929.

Kemmerer, D. L. *Path to Freedom: The Struggle for Self-Government in Colonial New Jersey, 1703–1776*. Princeton, N. J.: Princeton University Press, 1940.

Kessler, Henry H., and Eugene Rachlis. *Peter Stuyvesant and His New York*. New York: Random House, 1959.

Kittredge, George L. *Witchcraft in Old and New England*. Cambridge, Mass.: Harvard University Press, 1929.

Konwiser, Harry M. *Colonial and Revolutionary Posts*. Richmond, Va.: Dietz Printing Co., 1931.

Lathrop, Elise. *Early American Inns and Taverns*. New York: McBride & Co., 1926.

Lossing, Benson J. *History of New York City*. New York: G. E. Perine, c. 1884.

Middleton, Arthur P. *Tobacco Coast: A Maritime History of Chesapeake Bay in the Colonial Era*. Newport News, Va.: Mariner's Museum, 1953.

Morison, Samuel E. *Builders of the Bay Colony*. Boston: Houghton, Mifflin, 1930.

———. *The Maritime History of Massachusetts*. Boston: Houghton, Mifflin, 1921.

Morris, Richard B., ed. *The Era of the American Revolution*. New York: Columbia University Press, 1939.

———. *Government and Labor in Early America*. New York: Columbia University Press, 1946.

Osgood, Herbert L. *The American Colonies in the Seventeenth Century*. 2 vols. New York: Columbia University Press, 1904.

———. *The American Colonies in the Eighteenth Century*. New York: Columbia University Press, 1924.

Pares, Richard. *Colonial Blockade and Neutral Rights, 1739–1763*. New Haven, Conn.: Yale University Press, 1931.

Philipps, Mary Schuyler. *Colonial Massachusetts*. Cincinnati: Ebbert & Richardson Co., 1916.

Rutland, Robert Allen. *George Mason, Reluctant Statesman*. Williamsburg, Va.: Colonial Williamsburg, Inc., 1961.

Sachs, William S., and Ari Hoogenboom. *The Enterprising Colonials*. Chicago: Argonaut Inc., 1965.

Schlesinger, Arthur M. *The Colonial Merchants and the American Revolution*. A thesis written in 1918 for a Ph. D. degree, now in the library of Columbia University, New York.

Simms, Jeptha Root. *Trappers of New York*. Albany, N. Y.: J. Munsell, 1850.

Smith, Abbot E. *Colonists in Bondage: White Servitude and Convict Labor in America, 1607–1776*. Chapel Hill, N. C.: University of North Carolina Press, 1947.

Smith, Helen Ainslie. *The Thirteen Colonies*. 2 vols. New York: G. P. Putnam's Sons, 1901.

Smith, Samuel. *History of the Province of Pennsylvania*. Edited by William M. Mervine for the Colonial Society of Pennsylvania. Philadelphia: J. B. Lippincott, 1913.

Sweet, W. W. *Religion in Colonial America*. New York: Scribner's, 1953.

Trumbull, Benjamin. *A Compendium of the Indian Wars in New England*. Hartford, Conn.: Edwin Valentine Mitchell, 1926.

Turnbull, Archibald Douglas. *John Stevens: An American Record*. New York: Century Co., 1928.

Usher, Roland G. *The Pilgrims and Their History*. New York: Macmillan, 1918.

Wish, Harvey. *Society and Thought in Early America*. New York: Longman's, Green, 1950.

Wright, Louis B. *The Atlantic Frontier: Colonial American Civilization*. New York: Knopf, 1947.

———. *The Cultural Life of the American Colonies*. New York: Harper & Bros., 1957.

———, and Marion Tinling, eds. *The Secret Diary of William Byrd of Westover, 1709–1712*. Richmond, Va.: Dietz, 1941.

Wroth, Lawrence C. *The Colonial Printer*. New York: Grolier Club, 1931.

Index